BRIGHTEST DAY
OMNIBUS

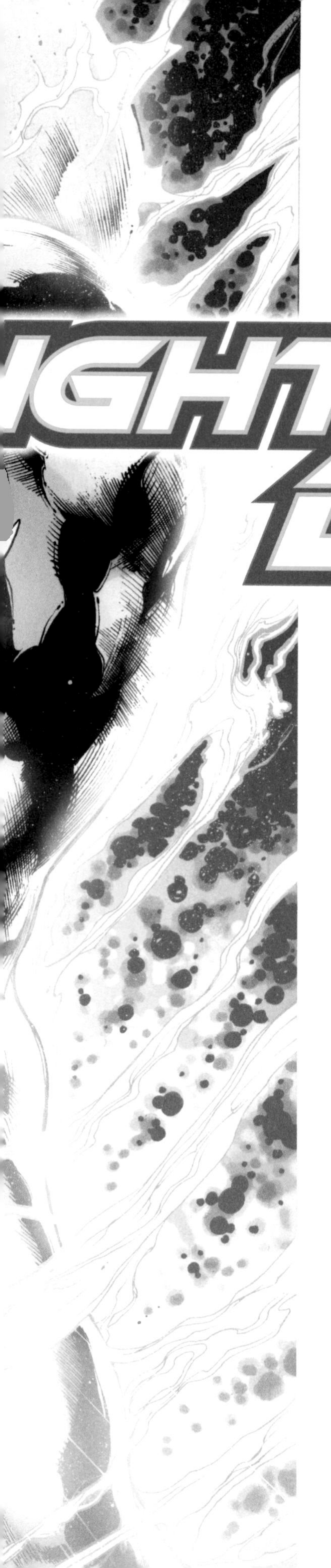

BLACKEST NIGHT
OMNIBUS

GEOFF JOHNS
& PETER J. TOMASI
WRITERS

SCOTT CLARK
FERNANDO PASARIN
IVAN REIS
PATRICK GLEASON
JOE PRADO
ARDIAN SYAF
PENCILLERS

CHRISTIAN ALAMY
MARLO ALQUIZA
REBECCA BUCHMAN
SCOTT CLARK
JOHN DELL
PATRICK GLEASON
SANDRA HOPE
MARK IRWIN
TOM NGUYEN
FERNANDO PASARIN
IVAN REIS
CAM SMITH
DEXTER VINES
OCLAIR ALBERT
DAVID BEATY
KEITH CHAMPAGNE
VICENTE CIFUENTES
JULIO FERREIRA
MICK GRAY
ROB HUNTER
NORM RAPMUND
ANDY OWENS
JOE PRADO
PRENTIS ROLLINS
ART THIBERT
INKERS

MARK BAGLEY
FABRIZIO FIORENTINO
AARON LOPRESTI
MIKE MAYHEW
ED BENES
ANDY KUBERT
FRANCIS MANAPUL
GUEST ARTISTS

ASPEN MLT'S PETER STEIGERWALD
WITH BETH SOTELO, JOHN STARR & RAY DILLON
BRIAN BUCCELLATO
COLORISTS

ROB CLARK JR.
NICK J. NAPOLITANO
KEN LOPEZ
LETTERERS

IVAN REIS & CHUCK PIRES
COVER ARTISTS

SUPERMAN created by JERRY SIEGEL & JOE SHUSTER
By special arrangement with the Jerry Siegel family

BRIGHTEST DAY OMNIBUS

DC COMICS 1700 Broadway, New York, NY 10019 A Warner Bros. Entertainment Company

Printed by RR Donnelley, Willard, OH, USA. 7/18/14. First printing.

ISBN: 978-1-4012-4597-9

SUSTAINABLE FORESTRY INITIATIVE
Certified Chain of Custody
20% Certified Forest Content, 80% Certified Sourcing
www.sfiprogram.org
SFI-01042
APPLIES TO TEXT STOCK ONLY

Library of Congress Cataloging-in-Publication Data

Johns, Geoff, 1973-
Brightest Day Omnibus / Geoff Johns, Peter J. Tomasi.
pages cm
ISBN 978-1-4012-4597-9 (hardback)
1. Graphic novels. I. Tomasi, Peter. II. Title.
PN6727.J57B84 2014
741.5'973—dc23

2014011629

BRIGHTEST DAY 0

Cover by David Finch, Scott Williams and Peter Steigerwald

CARPE DIEM

IT'S A NEW DAY.

AFTER ALL THAT'S HAPPENED, SOME ARE CALLING IT THE *BRIGHTEST*.
CHRRP CHRRCHRRP

I'M NOT SO SURE ABOUT THAT.

MY NAME'S BOSTON BRAND.
I WAS AN AERIALIST KNOWN FOR WORKING WITHOUT A NET UNTIL I WAS SHOT DURING THE HIGH WIRE ACT OF MY LIFE.
BOSTON BRAND
Forever With Us
THE BULLET SHATTERED MY STERNUM AND TORE THROUGH MY BACK, BUT IT LEFT ME ALIVE.
IT WAS THE *FALL* THAT DID ME IN.
FOR SOME REASON, ONE I'M STILL NOT EXACTLY SURE OF, MY SPIRIT STUCK AROUND, BURDENED WITH AN ETERNITY OF HELPING OTHERS.
I COULDN'T BE SEEN OR HEARD. NOT UNLESS I POSSESSED SOMEONE ELSE'S BODY AND TOOK IT FOR A SPIN.
IT WAS AN OKAY GIG FOR WHAT IT WAS. PURGATORY. HELL. HEAVEN. NAME YOUR POISON.
THEY CALLED ME ***DEADMAN.***

BUT DEADMAN'S GONE NOW.

GONE IN A FLASH OF LIGHT.

I'M BACK WITH NO HOME, NO JOB, A HUNGER IN MY BELLY AND THAT OLD ACHE IN MY LEFT KNEE.
I'M NOT SURE WHERE TO TURN OR WHO TO TURN TO.

THE TRUTH IS, I WAS A PRETTY BIG BASTARD BACK IN THE DAY.

I NEVER CARED ABOUT LIFE UNTIL I LOST IT.

DAMN.

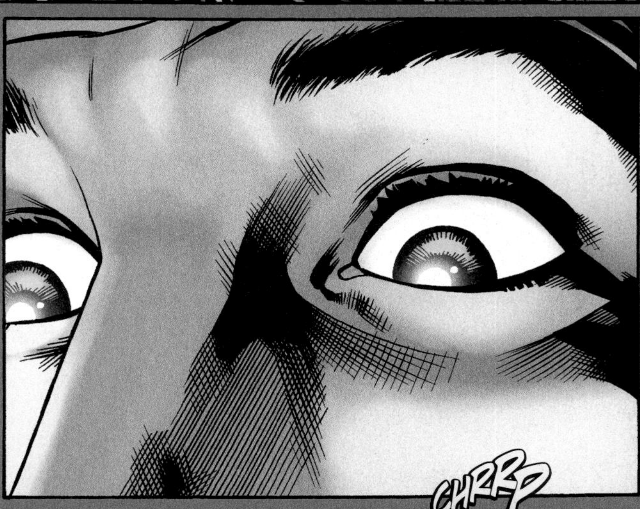

DEADMAN A.K.A. BOSTON BRAND.

AMNESTY BAY.

AQUAMAN A.K.A. ARTHUR CURRY.
Powers: Half-human/half-Atlantean heritage provides undersea adaptation, enhanced strength, and telepathic control of sea life.

ARTHUR?

WHAT ARE YOU DOING?
I DIDN'T WANT TO WAKE YOU.
I WOULD'VE LIKED IT IF YOU HAD.
I WAS GOING TO GO FOR A SWIM. I HAVEN'T BEEN IN THE WATER SINCE I...

CAME BACK FROM THE DEAD?

IT'S HARD TO EVEN SAY. AS HARD AS IT IS TO IMAGINE.
BUT WHY ME, MERA?
WHY DID I COME BACK WHEN SO MANY OTHERS DIDN'T? GARTH? TULA?

AT LEAST GARTH AND TULA ARE TOGETHER.
I SUPPOSE.
I DON'T HAVE AN ANSWER AS TO WHY, ARTHUR. AND I'M NOT SURE ANYONE WILL. BUT YOU'RE HERE NOW. WITH ME.
AND IT'S A BEAUTIFUL DAY.

IT *IS* BEAUTIFUL.

SO LET'S NOT WASTE IT.

ARE YOU COMING?

I DON'T KNOW.

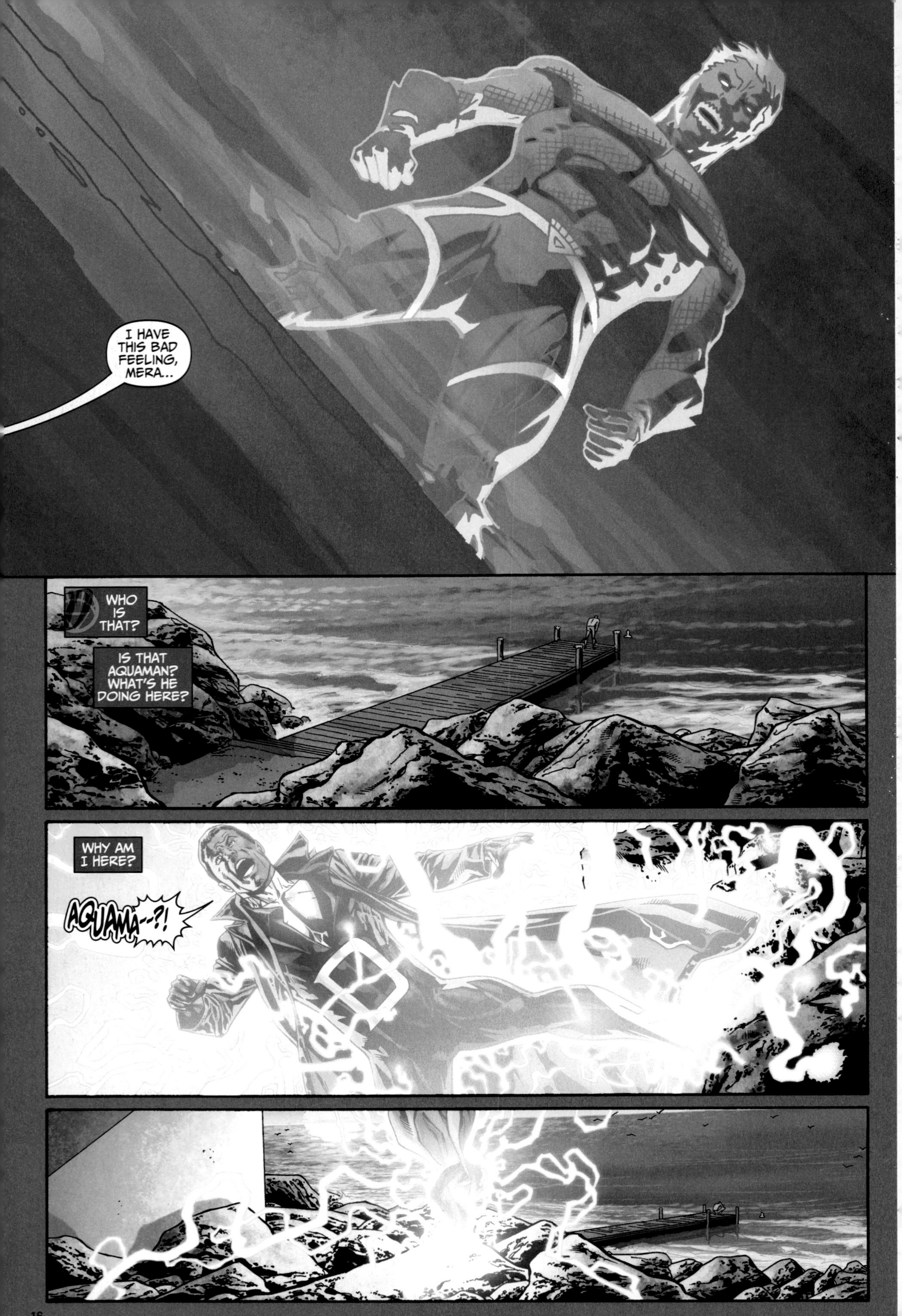

I HAVE THIS BAD FEELING, MERA...

WHO IS THAT?
IS THAT AQUAMAN? WHAT'S HE DOING HERE?

WHY AM I HERE?
AQUAMA--?!

IRON HEIGHTS PENITENTIARY.
I KNOW THIS GUY.
BAD NEWS.
THAWNE, EOBARD
THE REVERSE-FLASH
THE REVERSE-FLASH a.k.a. PROFESSOR EOBARD "ZOOM" THAWNE
Powers: Living generator of the parasitic Negative Speed Force.
WHY WOULD THE LIGHT PICK A 25TH CENTURY PSYCHO TO LIVE AGAIN?
WHOA.

OR IS IT *NIGHT*, MATE? I CAN NEVER TELL FROM DOWN HERE.

CAPTAIN BOOMERANG a.k.a. DIGGER HARKNESS.
Powers: Wields an array of deadly trick boomerangs with uncanny accuracy.

DAY, BOOMERANG. EIGHT O'CLOCK.
IN THE MORNING? WHAT THE HELL DO YOU WANT?
I'M SORRY ABOUT YOUR SON.
WELCOME TO THE FAMILY BUSINESS, EH?
OUT OF ALL THE PEOPLE THAT WERE BURIED SIX FEET UNDER, YOU GOT A SECOND CHANCE, DIGGER. YOU GET TO LIVE AGAIN.
AND I WISH I COULD SAY I THINK YOU'LL TURN OVER A NEW LEAF, BUT I KNOW YOU.
I KNOW WHAT YOU'RE GOING TO DO SO I CAME HERE TO TELL YOU NOT TO BOTHER.
BOTHER DOIN' WHAT, MATE?
HARKNESS, DIGGER
TRYING TO ESCAPE. TO PULL MORE JOBS. TO HURT MORE PEOPLE.
TO MAKE ME RUN AFTER YOU.

THERE WAS THIS FILM SOME YEARS BACK. WON ALL SORTS OF AWARDS. IT WAS ABOUT THIS BLOKE, THIS BANKER, WHO WAS CONVICTED OF KILLING HIS WIFE. TWIST IS, HE WAS INNOCENT, BUT THEY NEVER LET HIM OUT.
BLOODY GOOD FLICK. YOU SEE IT?
I'VE MISSED A FEW MOVIES.
'COURSE YOU HAVE.
AND IF YOU'RE TRYING TO PLEAD INNOCENT--
NO. IT'S NOT ABOUT THAT.
IT'S ABOUT HOW A MAN WITH NOTHING TO LOSE HAS TWO CHOICES.
YOU EITHER GET BUSY LIVIN'...OR YOU GET BUSY DYIN'.
WHY ME AND NOT MY SON OR COLD'S SISTER OR YOUR RIDICULOUS FRIEND THE ELONGATED MAN?
HELLUFIKNOW. BUT I'M NOT GOING TO SIT IN HERE LETTIN' THAT ROT MY BRAIN.
IS THAT A THREAT?
NAW, MATE.
IT'S A FLASH FACT.

ST. ROCH, LOUISIANA.
THE STONECHAT MUSEUM.
HAWKMAN A.K.A. CARTER HALL.
AND THIS ONE?
HAWKGIRL A.K.A. SHIERA HALL.
RANGDA, THE DEMON QUEEN.
RANGDA PUT US UNDER A SPELL WHEN WE WERE RULERS IN BALI BACK IN THE 12TH CENTURY. SHE MADE US TURN OUR WEAPONS ON OURSELVES.
DEFINITELY ONE OF OUR MESSIER ENDINGS, CARTER.
Powers: Harness belts made with Nth Metal, an alien alloy that defies gravity and affords them enhanced strength, vision, and a healing factor.
SOUTH AMERICA.
THE PERUVIAN ANDES MOUNTAINS.
CHANK
WHAT ABOUT THIS ONE, SHIERA?
AH, MY STRONG SILENT KNIGHT.
I WAS LADY CELIA TO YOUR DASHING BRIAN KENT.
AND 1584 WAS A DAMN COLD YEAR FOR ENGLAND.
REMEMBER HOW WE KEPT WARM?

AW JEEZ...
...DOESN'T THIS RING KNOW... WHEN IT'S *MATING* TIME AT THE BIRD GALLERY?
LOVE.
B-DEEP
B-DEEP
B-DEEP

...SHIERA...
WHAT IS IT, CARTER-- WHAT'S WRONG?
I SEE ALL OUR GHOSTS--OUR PAST LIVES--THEY'RE AROUND US--REMINDING ME THAT ALL THIS IS...FLEETING.
IS THIS THE LAST NIGHT I GET TO KISS YOU BEFORE THE CURSE PULLS US APART AGAIN, SHIERA?
IS THIS THE LAST NIGHT I GET TO LOOK INTO YOUR EYES AND SEE THAT YOU RECOGNIZE ME--THAT YOU LOVE ME--EVEN AFTER ALL THESE THOUSANDS OF YEARS?
HOW LONG DO WE GET TO HOLD EACH OTHER UNTIL WE'RE COVERED IN EACH OTHER'S BLOOD AGAIN?
WHEN WILL HATH-SET APPEAR THIS TIME TO TEAR OUR SOULS APART?

DON'T YOU SEE, DARLING, THE CURSE, IN A STRANGE WAY, IS A BLESSING--IT SHOULD BE FORCING US TO LIVE, NOT HIDE.
YES, I CAN REMEMBER EACH TIME I LOST YOU LIKE IT WAS YESTERDAY...
IT'S LIKE YOU SAID TO ME ONCE, THE PAST IS FOR US TO USE TO OUR ADVANTAGE. HISTORY CAN BE--
--AN INCREDIBLY STRONG WEAPON IF YOU KNOW HOW TO LISTEN TO IT.
I'M NOT GONNA STOP LOVING YOU BECAUSE THERE'S A CHANCE OF LOSING YOU, CARTER.
I'M TIRED OF REMEMBERING OUR DEATHS, CARTER.
IT'S TIME TO REMEMBER OUR LIFE.
YOU'RE RIGHT.
AND GOD HELP HATH-SET IF HE TRIES TO--

SHRIPP
SKASSH
WHAT'S THIS CRYSTAL SHARD?
MIRI, THE STAR SAPPHIRE, GAVE IT TO ME.
SHE SAID IT WAS A PIECE OF MY HEART FROM ZAMARON.
SO THAT WAS THE EXTENT OF THE SAPPHIRE'S EXPLANATION ABOUT THE CRYSTAL?
YES. THEN SHE FLEW OFF.
IT'S NOT COMING OFF. IT'S ATTRACTED TO THE CLAW OF HORUS LIKE A SUPER-MAGNET.

WHAT DO YOU THINK IT MEANS?

I THINK IT MEANS WE'RE GOING UP.

AND LOOKS LIKE WE'RE HEADING SOUTH.

I'D RATHER FIGHT SOMEWHERE WARM.
RRRN
SHIERA.
DID YOU JUST FEEL THAT?
KHUFU.
B-DEEP
YES.
IT'S AS IF SOMEONE JUST TOUCHED MY SOUL.
CHAY-ARA.
B-DEEP
INFORM THE CLIENT THAT WE'VE LOCATED THE BONES OF HAWKMAN AND HAWKGIRL'S FIRST BODIES.
THEY BELONG TO US NOW.

IT'S BEEN EASY.
EASY TO GET THE PLASMA.
EASY TO GET THE TRANSFUSION DEVICES.
ALL IT COST ME WAS A FEW NOSEBLEEDS TO GET READY FOR MY BIGGEST PUSH YET.
NEW YORK CITY
ABANDONED JUSTICE LEAGUE INTERNATIONAL EMABASSY.
AS THEY SAY, THIS IS FOR ALL THE MARBLES.
MAXWELL LORD.
Powers: Extreme Mind Control.

IF THIS PUSH ISN'T SUCCESSFUL I SEE ONLY TWO ENDINGS.
I'LL EITHER BE THROWN INTO SOME DARK HOLE FOREVER AND BECOME A GUINEA PIG FOR THE MILITARY...
...OR EXECUTED FOR MY ALLEGED CRIMES AGAINST THE WORLD, A WORLD I'VE ALWAYS WANTED TO PROTECT, NOT ENDANGER.

I'VE TAKEN ALL PRECAUTIONS TO AVERT BLEEDING OUT.
I'VE GOT TO DO THIS JUST RIGHT.

YAAGH!

NNRGH!

ARRGHH!
SPLAAASH
I SEE HIS LEG *TWITCH*, AND THE *LAST* THING HE PROBABLY FEELS IS A SHARP *CHILL* UP HIS BACK.
PROBLEM IS, I'M FEELING A CHILL RIGHT UP MY BACK TOO.
THIS GUY ONCE CONTROLLED *SUPERMAN'S MIND* AND WAS READY TO HAVE HIM TEAR THROUGH EVERYONE AND EVERYTHING UNTIL WONDER WOMAN STEPPED IN AND SNAPPED HIS NECK.
RAMA HELP US ALL NOW THAT HE'S SUCKING AIR AGAIN...
...'CAUSE IF THERE'S ONE THING MAX LORD'S *ALWAYS* BEEN

GUESS THIS WHITE RING'S GOT A LOT OF SURPRISES...
...LIKE MAKING SURE I CAN BREATHE AND EXIST WITHOUT MY BUZZ LIGHTYEAR SPACESUIT ON THE COLD SURFACE OF...
...MARS...
...THE HOME OF J'ONN J'ONZZ.
THE LAST SURVIVING MARTIAN.
AND IT LOOKS LIKE HE'S GOT VISITORS.
MARTIAN MANHUNTER A.K.A J'ONN J'ONZZ.
Powers: Super-strength, super- speed, flight, intangibility, telepathy, molecular manipulation, and energy vision.

ZZZRAPPPP
J'ONN, YOU AROUND?
HEY, GREEN JEANS, WHERE ARE YA?!

HAL. GUY. GREETINGS.
HOPE WE DIDN'T INTERRUPT ANYTHING.
FIGURED WE'D DROP IN UNINVITED AND BUST YOUR CHOPS FOR LEAVING EARTH SO QUICK.
IT IS A PLEASURE TO SEE FAMILIAR FACES.
BROUGHT YA *SOMETHING.*
ALWAYS BEWARE OF LANTERNS BEARING GIFTS.
TA-DA. IT'S SNACK TIME, GUY STYLE.
VERY THOUGHTFUL. I HOPE YOU BROUGHT SOME COLD MILK TO WASH THEM DOWN.
DAMN STRAIGHT I BROUGHT MILK--MAMA GARDNER DIDN'T RAISE NO FOOL.
THANK YOU, GUY.
NICE PLACE YOU HAVE HERE.
LET ME SHOW YOU THE REST OF IT.

YEARS AGO, WHEN I WALKED THESE PLAINS IN DESPERATION AFTER MY PEOPLE WERE WIPED AWAY, THESE SAND GEYSERS' LOUD STACCATO ERUPTIONS ONLY REMINDED ME OF MY DESOLATION...
...NOW THEY ARE MUSIC TO MY EARS. IT IS LIKE LISTENING TO MY PLANET BREATHE AGAIN.
I DON'T WANT TO BE A KILLJOY HERE, J'ONN, BUT HOW ARE YOU EXPECTING TO GET MARS UP AND RUNNING AGAIN?
WITH WATER.
YA GOT ONE PROBLEM, BUDDY-- THERE AIN'T ANY.
I AM HAPPY TO SAY FOR SOME REASON THERE NOW IS, GUY. I HAVE DISCOVERED A DEEP MARTIAN AQUIFER.
AND I WILL NURTURE IT.
MARS WILL LIVE AGAIN JUST AS IT DID WHEN MY ANCESTORS WALKED BESIDE RIVER VALLEYS AND 13,000 FOOT WATERFALLS.
GOT SOME GRAND VISION THERE, J'ONNY APPLESEED.
PLEASE DON'T TAKE THIS THE WRONG WAY, J'ONN, BUT I'VE NEVER HEARD SUCH PURE HOPE IN YOUR VOICE BEFORE.
IT ALWAYS SEEMED TEMPERED WITH A CERTAIN AMOUNT OF...
FATALISM.
YEAH.
THAT FATALISM IS NOW FOREVER IN THE PAST, HAL, BUT I DO HAVE TO ADMIT, I HAD BOUTS OF INTENSE ANGER...
...ANGER THAT MY WIFE AND DAUGHTER DID NOT RETURN IN THE WHITE LIGHT.

BUT WITH PROFOUND MEDITATION I'VE PUSHED AWAY THAT DESTRUCTIVE ANGER-- ESPECIALLY KNOWING THAT SOULS LIKE BARRY'S AND ARTHUR'S WERE ONCE AGAIN AMONG THE LIVING ON THE ...
BRIGHTEST DAY.
YES, BRIGHTEST DAY SEEMS AN APT CHOICE OF WORDS TO DESCRIBE IT, GUY.
HEARING BARRY AND ARTHUR'S THOUGHTS IN THE CROWD FILLED ME WITH AN INNER PEACE THAT I CARRIED BACK HERE TO MARS.
THAT NEW HUNK OF RED ROCK ON YOUR CHEST MEAN SOMETHING...
...YOU PLANNING ON STAYING UP HERE FOR GOOD?
CLINK
CLINK
NO, GUY, I AM A SON OF TWO WORLDS--MARS AND EARTH.
BOTH WILL FOREVER BE THE OBJECTS OF MY SUPREME AFFECTION AND DEDICATION.
YOU LEFT A BIG HOLE, J'ONN, AND WE CAN'T BEGIN TO TELL YOU HOW HAPPY WE ARE THAT YOU'RE BACK TO FILL IT.
DITTO WHAT HE SAID, J'ONNY. WE'RE DAMN GLAD TO HAVE OUR FAVORITE MARTIAN BACK.
I AM YOUR ONLY MARTIAN.
FOR NOW.

OA.
HOME TO THE GREEN LANTERN CORPS.
YOU DON'T GET TO SEE THIS KINDA SUNSET GROWING UP IN GOTHAM.
I WANT TO STOP.
IN A FEW MORE MINUTES, JADE.
IF NONE OF THESE GL'S CAN SEE ME, I GUESS THE INVISIBLE MAN ACT'S STILL IN PROGRESS.
I SAID I'D LIKE TO STOP NOW.
AND BY THE LOOK ON JADE'S FACE, I'M SURE SHE'D LIKE TO BE INVISIBLE TOO.
Jade a.k.a Jennifer-Lynn Hayden.
Powers: Generates and manipulates green energy due to the Starheart on her left palm. Her energy is self-renewing and enables her to fly.
IT'S IMPORTANT THAT WE FINISH THIS BATTERY OF TESTS.
WHY?
BECAUSE.
BECAUSE WHY?
BECAUSE THE STRENGTH LEVEL OF YOUR POWER ALSO INDICATES HOW WELL YOUR BODY IS RECUPERATING.
WE'VE BEEN DOING THIS FOR DAYS, NATU-- I'M SURE YOU'VE GOT ALL THE INDICATIONS YOU NEED!
I'M THE DOCTOR, SO DON'T PRESUME TO TELL ME WHAT I NEED AND DON'T--
ZZRAK
DO YOU REALLY THINK THAT MAKING ME JUMP THROUGH ALL THESE HOOPS IS KEEPING ME FROM SPENDING TIME WITH KYLE?
THAT'S NOT WHY I'M--
COME ON, I'VE BEEN AT A HUNDRED PERCENT SINCE THE DAY THAT WHITE RING HIT MY HAND AND I CRAWLED OUT FROM UNDER MOGO'S GRASS, HAVEN'T I?

YES.
YES YOU HAVE.
LOOK, IF I WANTED TO BE WITH KYLE, I WOULD BE WITH KYLE.
WHAT'S STOPPING YOU?
HIS EYES.
WHAT ARE YOU TALKING ABOUT?
THE WAY HE LOOKS AT ME...IT'S NOT THE SAME ANYMORE...
...BUT THE WAY HE LOOKS AT YOU...
KYLE CAN BE AN OPEN BOOK WHEN HE LETS HIS GUARD DOWN...
YOU BOTH HAVE SOMETHING SPECIAL, AND I'M NOT GETTING IN THE WAY OF THAT.
KYLE AND I HAD OUR TIME... OUR CHANCE...IT JUST WASN'T MEANT TO BE AND THAT'S OKAY BUT...
I DON'T KNOW HOW I'M GOING TO FIT INTO EVERYONE'S LIVES ANYMORE--I'VE BEEN GONE TOO LONG.
NO YOU HAVEN'T, JEN.

YOU'VE ALWAYS BEEN IN OUR HEARTS, WHICH MEANS YOU NEVER LEFT.
ALL YOU'VE GOT TO DO IS OPEN SOME DOORS, JEN, BECAUSE BEHIND THEM'S A HELLUVA LOT OF PEOPLE WHO'VE MISSED YOU AND CAN'T WAIT TO LET THEMSELVES BACK INTO YOUR LIFE AGAIN.
ESPECIALLY YOUR FATHER.
ALAN'S BEEN GRIEVING SINCE THE DAY HE LOST YOU IN BATTLE. NO PARENT WANTS TO OUTLIVE THEIR CHILD.
BUT WHY AM I STILL ALIVE, KYLE?
WHY DID THE WHITE RING PICK ME--WHY AM I SO SPECIAL?
WHEN I WAS A BLACK LANTERN, I KILLED GREEN LANTERNS--I MURDERED THEM--BLASTED THEM APART WITH THAT BLACK RING.
YOU DIDN'T MURDER ANYBODY, JEN.
I TRIED TO KILL YOU, KYLE--I TRIED TO KILL NATU.
LOOK, YOU NEED TO GET YOUR HEAD AROUND THIS. YOU WERE USED BY NEKRON LIKE ALL THE OTHER POOR SOULS.
NOT AS A WEAPON OF RAGE OR FEAR...
..BUT AS A WEAPON OF LOVE, JEN.
BECAUSE OF WHO YOU WERE AND WHAT YOU MEANT TO PEOPLE.
NOW YOU'RE BACK, AND IT'S ALL ABOUT FORGETTING THE PAST AND EMBRACING THE PRESENT.
WH-WHAT WAS THAT?

NEW YORK CITY.
LOVE LIVES FOREVER

WHERE'S RONNIE, PROFESSOR STEIN?
I LEFT HIM ANOTHER MESSAGE ON THE WAY HERE, RAY.
HE MISSED THE FUNERAL.
I KNOW HE DID.
JASON'S A WRECK.

SO IS **RONNIE.** HE'S BARELY SAID A WORD TO ME.
HE DOESN'T REMEMBER **ANYTHING** BETWEEN DYING AT THE HANDS OF THE SHADOW THIEF AND COMING BACK IN COAST CITY ALONG WITH EVERYONE ELSE.
HE'S ADJUSTING TO THE FACT THAT JASON HAS CONTROL OVER THE FIRESTORM MATRIX AND, **WORSE,** THAT HIS BODY WAS USED BY ONE OF THOSE BLACK RINGS TO MURDER JASON'S GIRLFRIEND.

HE MISSED HIS APPOINTMENT WITH THE LEAGUE YESTERDAY TO FIGURE OUT HIS PAPERWORK AND GET HIM OFFICIALLY BACK TO THE LAND OF THE LIVING--
ATOM?

IT'S YOU, ISN'T IT? PROFESSOR PALMER?

RONNIE? YOU MADE IT.

YEAH, I'M SORRY I WASN'T AT THE FUNERAL BUT...*LATE NIGHT.*

I WAS, Y'KNOW, TRYING TO...

...RECONNECT WITH FRIENDS AND FAMILY.

WELCOME BACK RONNIE!

TALK TO JASON, RONALD.

I DON'T EVEN KNOW HIM, PROFESSOR. WHAT AM I SUPPOSED TO SAY?

WHATEVER'S ON YOUR MIND.

UH... JASON?

YOU'RE SORRY SHE DIED? MY GIRLFRIEND DIDN'T JUST DIE. SHE WAS TORTURED. AND WE DID THAT TOGETHER.
YOU PICKED THROUGH MY BRAIN AND WE TRANSMUTED HER INTO TABLE SALT FROM THE OUTSIDE IN.

YOU MADE ME AN ACCOMPLICE IN HER MURDER.

HEY, I'M NOT THE BAD GUY, JACE.
THAT BLACK LANTERN FIRESTORM WAS THE THING THAT REALLY KILLED YOUR GIRL, JASON.
DON'T CALL ME JACE. IT'S JASON.
YOU DON'T EVEN REMEMBER HER NAME, DO YOU?

SAY IT.
TELL ME HER NAME!

TELL ME HER NAME!

WHAT THE HELL DID YOU DO?
I DIDN'T DO ANYTHING!
FZZAMM
FIRESTORM A.K.A. RONNIE RAYMOND AND JASON RUSCH.
Powers: Able to transmute inorganic atomic and molecular matter, flight, create blasts of nuclear energy and intangibility.
RONNIE? JASON?
HEY, YOU HIT ME!
NO, I'M NOT TRYING TO STEAL ANYTHING!
YOU LET GO!
SO THIS IS FIRESTORM NOW? AT LEAST UNTIL THEY KILL EACH OTHER.
ALL OF US THAT CAME BACK...SOME ARE WRENCHES THROWN INTO OTHER PEOPLE'S LIVES.
SOME ARE MURDERERS AND THIEVES.

SOME ARE MEN WHO WERE BETTER OFF DEAD.
KAHNDAQ.
‹I AM HOME AT LAST, MY FELLOW COUNTRYMEN.›
I AM NO LAWRENCE OF ARABIA. I FORGOT HOW MUCH I HATE THIS DAMN HEAT.
‹BY THE GRACE OF *RA* I AM SOMEHOW ABLE TO *WALK* OUT OF THE DARKNESS ONCE AGAIN...›
‹...UNCORRUPTED BY THE SINISTER POWER RING THAT RECENTLY TOOK POSSESSION OF MY BODY AND SOUL HERE IN OUR BELOVED CITY.›
‹I CAN SMELL OUR DESERT FLOWERS IN BLOOM. I CAN HEAR YOUR PRAYERS OF JOY.›
‹AND MOST IMPORTANT, I CAN SEE THAT IT'S TIME TO PUT AWAY ALL MY YOUTHFUL FEAR AND MISGIVINGS AND REVEL IN ALL THESE SIMPLE THINGS I HAVE TAKEN FOR GRANTED.›
‹I AM AMON TOMAZ.›
‹AND YOU, MY FAITHFUL ONES, HAVE BEEN WAITING FOR *MY FAMILY* TO RETURN.›

BLACK ADAM!
KRAKOOOOM

‹MY DEAR SISTER, ISIS AND HER HUSBAND, MY MENTOR, TETH-ADAM...›
‹...HIS LAND WAS SUPPOSED TO BE A PLACE OF BEAUTY...›
‹...OF NEW BEGINNINGS...›
‹...OF HOPE...›

‹...INSTEAD IT'S STILL A WASTELAND OF DESOLATION AND ANGUISH.›
‹BUT NOT FOR LONG.›
‹MY FELLOW CITIZENS, YOU WAIT FOR ME TO SAVE YOU...›
‹...RESTORE YOU!›

OSIRIS A.K.A. AMON TOMAZ.
Powers: Superior strength, speed, flight, and physical and magical invulnerability.
‹AND THIS I WILL DO.›
‹WITH THE HELP OF MY FAMILY BURIED BENEATH THIS COLD STONE.›
‹I WILL BE BACK!›
‹AND WITH ME A GOLDEN AGE OF PROSPERITY AND POWER!›

ARLINGTON, VIRGINIA.
WE WERE SUPPOSED TO BE ON THIS OPERATION TOGETHER.
WHERE ARE YOU, HAWK?
WHERE I'M SUPPOSED TO BE, DOVE.
ON THE FRONT LINES.
HAWK A.K.A. HANK HALL.
Avatar of War.
Powers: Enhanced vision, agility, strength, body density and healing factor.
YOU CAN'T JUST RUSH IN AND START ATTACKING THEM WITHOUT--
THEY'RE ARMS DEALERS.
SELLING WEAPONS TO ENEMY COMBATANTS WHO ARE GONNA USE THOSE WEAPONS TO EITHER ATTACK OUR COUNTRY OR OUR TROOPS--WHICH TO ME IS ONE AND THE SAME.
THERE'S A RULE OF LAW, HANK, THAT WE HAVE TO ABIDE BY--
RULES? C'MON, THAT'S THE BEST YOU GOT?
THERE'S GOOD AND THERE'S BAD, DAWN, AND WE KNOW IT WHEN WE SEE IT.
WE EITHER LET IT FESTER OR WE ADDRESS IT.
AND JUST HOW ARE YOU PLANNING ON ADDRESSING IT, HANK?
SINCE YOU'RE NOT HERE TO SLAP MY KNUCKLES, I WAS FIGURING SOME-THING SIMPLE LIKE THIS...

HELLO, BAD GUYS!

SKAASSH

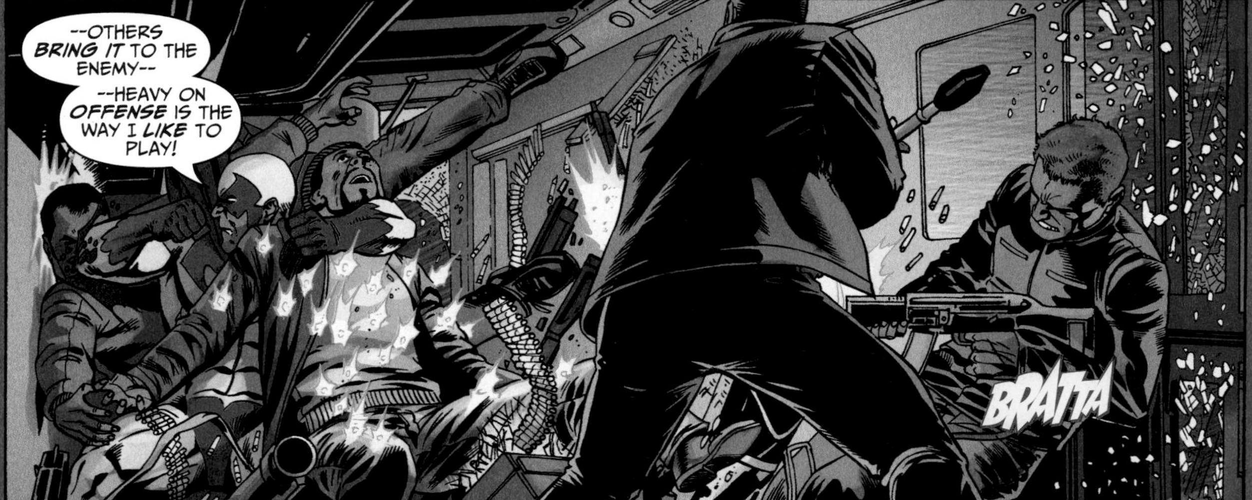

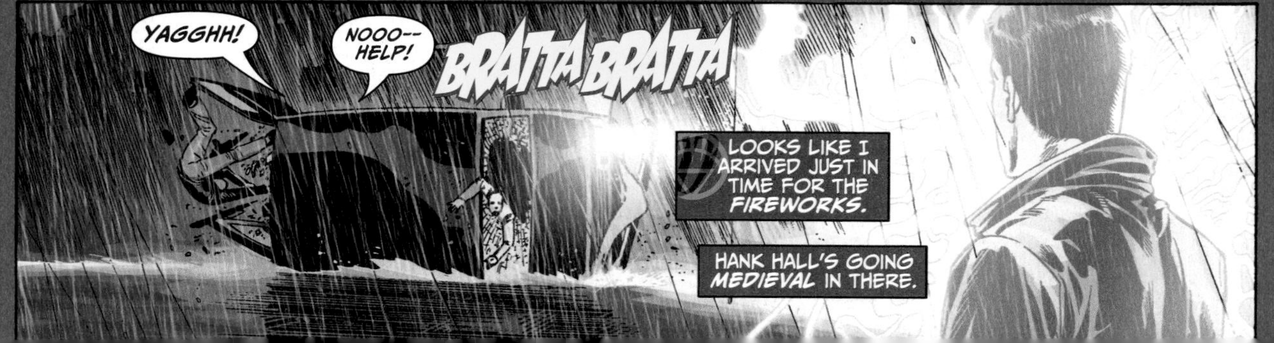

ARGHH!
BRATTA BRATTA
AAIIEEE!
"PEACE IN OUR TIME," DOVE?
SOME OLD POLITICIAN DUDE SAID THAT BEFORE ANOTHER GREAT WAR ONE TO END ALL GREAT WARS GOT GOING AGAIN.
YOU'VE BEEN GONE A LONG TIME, HANK, THE WORLD'S GOTTEN SMALLER SINCE YOU DIED--THERE'S A DIFFERENT APPROACH TO CONFRONTING--
KRAKK
FOOOM
THERE'S ONLY THREE RULES YOU SHOULD FOLLOW WHEN IT COMES TO WAR: GO IN HARD, GO IN FAST, AND GO IN TO WIN.
I'M ASSUMING THAT EXPLOSION I HEARD MEANS YOU JUST ACCOMPLISHED ALL THREE?
YEP. WE DO HAVE HISTORY FINALS TOMORROW MORNING. NO TIME TO WASTE.
YOU BASTARDS TRAFFICKING THIS STUFF IN THE SHADOW OF THIS MEMORIAL MAKES ME SICK.
YOU'RE LUCKY I DIDN'T LET YOUR ASSES BURN IN THE VAN WITH THE WEAPONS.
SKKRAK
AAGH!
WE WERE GRANTED OUR POWERS BY A MYSTERIOUS VOICE SO WE COULD FIGHT TOGETHER, HAWK.
BUT THIS WHITE LIGHT I'M NOW CONNECTED TO--
WE'RE EXACT OPPOSITES, DOVE. I DON'T SEE THE DAMN POINT PULLING IN DIFFERENT DIRECTIONS IN THE MIDDLE OF A FIGHT.
MIGHT MAKES RIGHT IS THE ONLY THING THESE EVIL BASTARDS UNDERSTAND.
CONSIDER THIS THE FIRST OF MY PREEMPTIVE STRIKES.

ANOTHER MAGIC LEAP. WHERE AM I NOW?
LOOKS LIKE A BOMB WENT OFF...
...BECAUSE ONE DID.
I RECOGNIZE THE WRECKAGE FROM THE PICTURES ON TV.
THOUSANDS OF PEOPLE DIED HERE WHEN ONE OF THE JUSTICE LEAGUE'S ENEMIES DETONATED A BOMB SMACK IN THE CENTER OF GREEN ARROW'S HOME TOWN.
IT INCINERATED OVER FOUR SQUARE MILES, LEAVING AN EMPTY COURTYARD OF DEATH SURROUNDED BY THE MOST CORRUPT CITY IN AMERICA.
DEATH.
IT DIDN'T REALLY SEEM SO BAD WHEN I WAS ONE OF THE DEARLY DEPARTED.
BUT BREATHING IN THE AIR AGAIN, COUGHING ON THE DECAY ATOMIZED IN IT...
...EVEN AFTER ALL THESE WEEKS THE SMELL IS INESCAPABLE.
ASHES TO ASHES. DUST TO--
BOSTON BRAND OF EARTH.
HELP ME.

AAARRRGHHH!
HELP THEM.

NNNNNG!
KKTCCH
KKTCCH
KKTCCH
KKTCCH
KRNKK
KKRAAANNNKK

STAR CITY.

WHAT THE HELL?
WHAT ARE YOU? WHO'S TALKING TO ME?
WHAT DO YOU WANT?
THE WHITE LIGHT CHOSE TWELVE OF US TO RETURN FROM THE DEAD.
WHY US?
I LOOKED AT EVERYONE CLOSE. BEYOND TAKING THIS TRIP, I'M DIFFERENT THAN THEY ARE. OUT OF THE TWELVE--
--I'M THE ONLY ONE STILL WEARING A WHITE RING.
YOU DON'T WANT TO SPILL, FINE. GET OFF OF ME.
BOSTON BRAND OF EARTH.
WHAT?
WHAT WERE WE BROUGHT BACK TO DO?!
HELP ME LIVE.

EPILOGUE
SILVER CITY, NEW MEXICO.
WHERE'D IT COME FROM?
HELL IF I KNOW, RUSSELL.
IT CAME DOWN FROM THE SKY!
IT LOOKED LIKE AN ANGEL. IT HAD WINGS AND A HALO!
BLASPHEMY! THAT AIN'T NO ANGEL!
ARE ANGELS REAL, GRANDMA?
WHAT THE HECK?!

AH. THERE YOU ARE.
Once dead, twelve heroes and villains were resurrected by a white light expelled deep from within the center of the Earth. Deemed a miracle by many and a sign of the apocalypse by others, the reasons behind their rebirths remain a mystery. But it will not be a mystery for long. This is the BRIGHTEST DAY

BRIGHTEST DAY 1
Cover by David Finch, Scott Williams and Peter Steigerwald

SECOND CHANCES

SILVER CITY.
NEW MEXICO.

IT'S *HOT* OUT HERE. THINK IT'S THE SUN OR *THIS* GLOWIN' DOOHICKEY?

HELL IF I KNOW, RUSSELL. MAYBE *BOTH.*

NOW BUCK UP, SON, AND LET'S TRY THIS AGAIN.
HOPE I DON'T PULL MY *BACK* OUT.
ONE...
TWO...
THREE!

UHN!
MMF!

DARN *THING* WON'T *BUDGE,* JERRY.

LITTLE HELP, GUYS!

THINK YER ABOUT TO GET IT, SHERIFF.

STAR SAPPHIRE A.K.A. CAROL FERRIS.
Power: Love.
SINESTRO.
Power: Fear.
GREEN LANTERN A.K.A. HAL JORDAN.
Power: Will.

SINESTRO'S BACK!
DON'T MOVE!

YOUR LAW OFFICERS CONTINUE TO AMUSE ME.

SINESTRO. STOP IT.

I'M SIMPLY DEFENDING MYSELF FROM YOUR LOCAL POLICE FORCE, GREEN LANTERN. AS UNTHREATENING AS THEY ARE.

IF THEY ***PAID*** ATTENTION, THEY WOULD'VE NOTICED I HELPED ***SAVE*** YOUR WORLD. ***WARTS*** AND ***ALL***.

WE MAY HAVE CALLED A TEMPORARY ***TRUCE***, BUT THAT DOESN'T MEAN YOU'RE WELCOME HERE, SINESTRO.

I WOULD'VE LEFT ALONG WITH MY CORPS, ***SAPPHIRE***--

--BUT IT'S STILL ON EARTH.

WHAT ***IS*** THAT?

THAT IS THE ENTITY THAT WAS UNEARTHED FROM THE CENTER OF YOUR WORLD. THE WHITE LIGHT THAT SPARKED THE VERY CREATION OF LIFE THROUGHOUT THE UNIVERSE.
THIS IS THE WHITE LIGHT THAT RESURRECTED AQUAMAN AND THE OTHERS?
AFTER IT BROUGHT THEM BACK, IT DISSIPATED INTO THE SKY...BUT IT COALESCED BACK TOGETHER...
AND TRANSFORMED INTO A POWER BATTERY?
IT'S EVOLVED INTO A WHITE LANTERN.
IT FELL BACK TO EARTH.
YOU DIDN'T BRING ME HERE BECAUSE YOU WANTED TO, SINESTRO.
YOU COULDN'T LIFT THE WHITE LANTERN.
CAN YOU?

RRRRGH!

NO.
SO IT'S THE SWORD IN THE STONE?
WHAT IN THE GUARDIANS' UNSPOKEN NAMES IS THE SWORD IN THE STONE?

A SWORD THAT COULD ONLY BE LIFTED BY THE TRUE KING OF THE LAND.

SO IF THIS WHITE LANTERN IS THE SWORD--

"--WHERE'S KING ARTHUR?"
I USED TO BE DEAD.
NNNN.

THEN A WHITE LIGHT CREATED TWELVE WHITE RINGS TO RESURRECT TWELVE PEOPLE. GOOD AND BAD.
WHERE'D YOU BRING ME NOW, LITTLE WHITE RING? AND WHAT DO YOU WANT WITH ME?
MOST PEOPLE WOULD'VE CALLED ME GOOD, I GUESS.
NOT SURE THAT'S ENTIRELY ACCURATE.

I DIE AND I'M FORCED TO FLOAT ACROSS THE EARTH AS A GHOST, I LIVE AND I'M FORCED TO FLOAT ACROSS THE EARTH AS WHAT? THE INVISIBLE MAN?
I MIGHT AS WELL STILL BE A GHOST!

NONE OF THE OTHER RETURNEES GOT STUCK WITH A WHITE RING YANKIN' THEM FROM PLACE TO PLACE EXCEPT ME.
‹ NO! NOT THAT ONE! ›
I WANT TO KNOW WHY. WHY ME?
WHY US?

<THAT ONE STAYS WITH ME. I WANT TO SPEND SOME TIME WITH HER BEFORE WE SELL THEM.>

<COME, CHILD.>
PLEASE! I WANT TO GO BACK TO MY MOM!

MOMMY ISN'T HERE, MY BEAUTY.
BUT *DADDY* IS.

HEY! LEAVE THE KID *ALONE!*

ARRGHHH!
WHAT ARE YOU *DOING,* RING? LET ME *MOVE!*
PLEASE.

DAMMIT, WHY WON'T YOU LET ME *HELP* HER?

MERA.
Powers: Mysterious origins provide undersea adaptation, enhanced strength and control over water.

WHOA.
‹SHOOT THEM!›
KTANG
KTANG
KTANG
KTANG
KTANG
KTANG
KTING
KTANG
KTANG
KTANG

YAAAA!!
ANYONE WHO HURTS CHILDREN--
KTANG
--WILL FEEL MY RAGE!

HOW MANY DID THE NAVY SAY THEY TOOK FROM THAT CIVILIAN SHIP, MERA?
FIFTEEN. ARE THEY ALL--?
GET DOWN!
LOOKS LIKE THESE SCAVENGERS HAVE FRIENDS.
SO DO WE.
VUU VUU VUU VUU VUU
ARTHUR?
WHAT DID YOU SUMMON?

IT'S A GIANT SQUID. I COULD HEAR IT DEEP BELOW THE SURFACE, BUT IT'S...
IT'S DEAD.

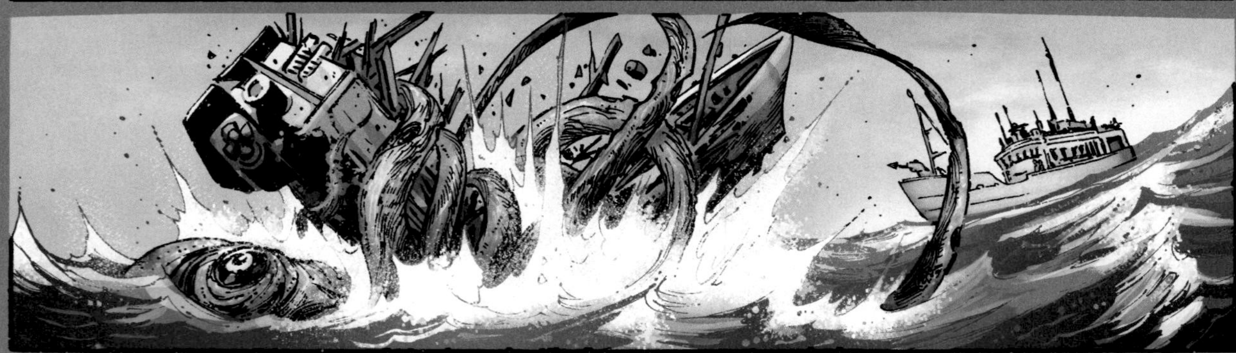

IT'S KILLING EVERYONE. ARTHUR, TELL IT TO STOP!
I'M TRYING!

‹WE RULE THESE SEAS, NOT YOU--›

AAAAHH--
HE'S COMMANDING DEAD SEALIFE LIKE HE DID WHEN HE WAS A BLACK LANTERN.
ARTHUR...?
SOMETHING'S VERY WRONG.
SO WHAT AM I SUPPOSED TO DO ABOUT IT, WHITE RING? AM I SUPPOSED TO STOP AQUAMAN--

WESTPORT.
MASSACHUSETTS.
--OR IS SOMEONE ELSE?
...REPORTS COMING NOW AT ARE SURE TO LIEVE ALL THOSE PARENTS OUT THERE.
OUR OWN LOCAL HEROES, AQUAMAN AND HIS WIFE MERA, HAVE RESCUED FIFTEEN CHILDREN WHO WERE KIDNAPPED EARLIER THIS MORNING FROM A EUROPEAN CRUISE SHIP OFF THE COAST OF SOMALI.
GBS NEWS
AQUAMAN IS ONE OF MANY RUMORED TO AVE BEEN "RESURRECTED" IN THE ERMATH OF THE RECENT ATTACK OF UNDEAD. THE CATHOLIC CHURCH HAS T TO RESPOND TO HIS CLAIM, BUT AGGERATION OR NOT, WE'RE HAPPY THE KING OF THE SEAS HAS RETURNED.
AMAZING, ISN'T IT?
AQUAMAN'S BACK.

GG-GG
-GG.
PLEASE--
HELP!
HEL--!
--TRULY A DAY
OF CELEBRATION. AND
NOW THE WEATHER.
MARGARET?
SKIES ARE
LOOKING CLOUDY
OUT THERE,
JAMES--

"--THUNDERSTORMS WILL BE ROLLING OUR WAY BY MIDNIGHT..."
PITTSBURGH UNIVERSITY.
PROFESSOR STEIN?!?
WHERE IS HE?
I USED TO BE ABLE TO TELL. I COULDN'T READ HIS MIND WHEN WE WEREN'T FUSED TOGETHER AS FIRESTORM, BUT I COULD SUMMON HIM--
YOU COULD SUMMON HIM? IT'S ALWAYS ABOUT YOU, ISN'T IT, RONNIE?
WHAT ARE YOU TALKING ABOUT?
I'M TALKING ABOUT FIRESTORM. YOU DIED, BUT THE MATRIX FELL FROM THE SKY AND HIT ME.
YOU THINK I STILL WANT TO BE FIRESTORM, JASON? ESPECIALLY IF I'M STUCK WITH SOMEONE LIKE YOU INSIDE MY HEAD?
"WHEN THAT EXPLOSION IN PROFESSOR STEIN'S LAB WENT OFF AND HE AND I WERE STUCK TOGETHER...IT WAS WEIRD, BUT IT WAS COOL.
"I COULD FLY AND TRANSMUTE ELEMENTS...AS LONG AS THE PROFESSOR TOLD ME HOW TO...
"...BUT IT ALL WENT TO HELL PRETTY QUICK..."
...YOU CAN HAVE THE FIRESTORM MATRIX. FIND A NEW PARTNER. I DON'T CARE.
ALL I WANT TO DO IS GET OUT OF HERE AND GO HANG OUT WITH MY FRIENDS.
AND ALL I WANT TO DO IS HANG OUT WITH MY GIRLFRIEND.

WE CAN'T BRING HER BACK, JASON.
YOU CAME BACK. MARTIAN MANHUNTER AND HAWK AND CAPTAIN BOOMERANG. WHY NOT GEN?
BECAUSE WE CAN'T. ONCE I... JUST TRUST ME, OKAY?
LOOK, LET'S TRY TO SEPARATE AGAIN. YOU THINK RIGHT AND I'LL THINK LEFT.
HAT'S OUR BIG PLAN?
JUST DO IT, ALL RIGHT?
AAARGHHHH!!
DAMMIT... THAT...
...HURT.
RONALD?
PROFESSOR! ALL RIIIGHT!!
PLEASE DON'T SHOUT IN MY EARS.
SO WHAT'S THE DEAL, PROF?! TELL US HOW TO SPLIT UP!
I'M AFRAID I CAN'T DO THAT, RONALD.
THE PROFESSOR AND I HAVE SOME BAD NEWS.
HE ATOM A.K.A. RAY PALMER.
owers: Self-designed t provides the ability to ink, including traveling

THE NORTHERN POLAR CAP OF MARS.

RRRGH

SKRAKRAK

FWHAKOOOOM

ZZRRAAKK
HMM?
SO IT BEGINS.
WHAT WAS HERE ONCE...
...CAN SOON BE AGAIHHH!

...ERDEL...
MY HANDS AT PROFESSOR ERDEL'S THROAT.
THAT NEVER HAPPENED.
AND THAT WOMAN ON THE FLOOR...
ERDEL WAS ALONE WHEN HE MISTAKENLY TRANSPORTED ME FROM MARS.
FOR THAT PSYCHIC FLASH TO BREACH MY MIND FROM EARTH IT HAD TO BE DIRECTED SOLELY AT ME...
...WITH A CONVICTION AND SINGULARITY OF PURPOSE.
THE GIRL IN THIS VISION...
...I MUST FIND HER.

GH ABOVE THE PERUVIAN ANDES.
I'VE HAD THE CLAW OF HORUS ON MY HAND BEFORE, HIERA, BUT NEVER FELT THE POWER COURSING THROUGH IT AS INTENSELY AS THIS--
--AND WITH THE PIECE OF ZAMARON CRYSTAL NOW EMBEDDED ON IT, IT SEEMS TO HAVE A MIND ALL ITS OWN.
WE'VE GOT A MIND OF OUR OWN TOO, CARTER.
WE CAN'T LET EVERYTHING CONNECTED TO THE CURSE LEAD US AROUND BY THE NOSE FOREVER.
AREN'T YOU INTERESTED IN FINDING OUT IF--
THE ONLY THING I'M INTERESTED IN IS MAKING NEW MEMORIES TOGETHER AND LEAVING THE OLD ONES I'VE FINALLY REMEMBERED BEHIND.
BUT THIS CLAW WAS CAST FROM THE NTH METAL FOUND INSIDE THE THANAGARIAN SHIP--THE SAME NTH METAL THAT GIVES US OUR POWERS.
WHATEVER THE CLAW'S HOMING IN ON, IT MUST HAVE SOMETHING TO DO WITH THANAGAR, OR MAYBE EVEN OUR TIME IN ANCIENT EGYPT.
RADIOACTIVE ISOTOPE TRACE FLUID APPLIED.
IF WE LOSE POSSESSION OF THE PACKAGE WE'LL BE ABLE TO FIND IT.
AERIAL RENDEZVOUS REQUESTED.
UPLOADING COORDINATES NOW.

DOWN TO **TEN MINUTES** OF JET-PACK FUEL LEFT.
HOW **FAR** OUT ARE YOU?

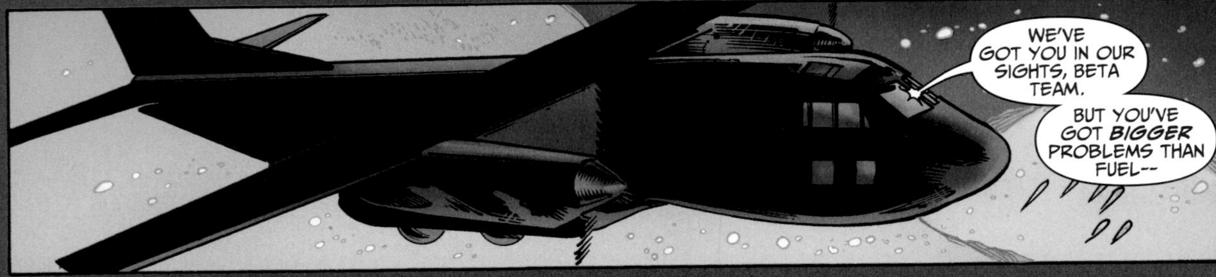
WE'VE GOT YOU IN OUR SIGHTS, BETA TEAM.
BUT YOU'VE GOT **BIGGER** PROBLEMS THAN FUEL--

--TO WORRY ABOUT.
WHAT'S IN **THE BAG**, GENTLEMEN?
CRAP--

EVASIVE MANEUVERS!

GET US OUT OF HERE NOW!

SHRANK
WE TRIED ASKING YOU POLITELY...

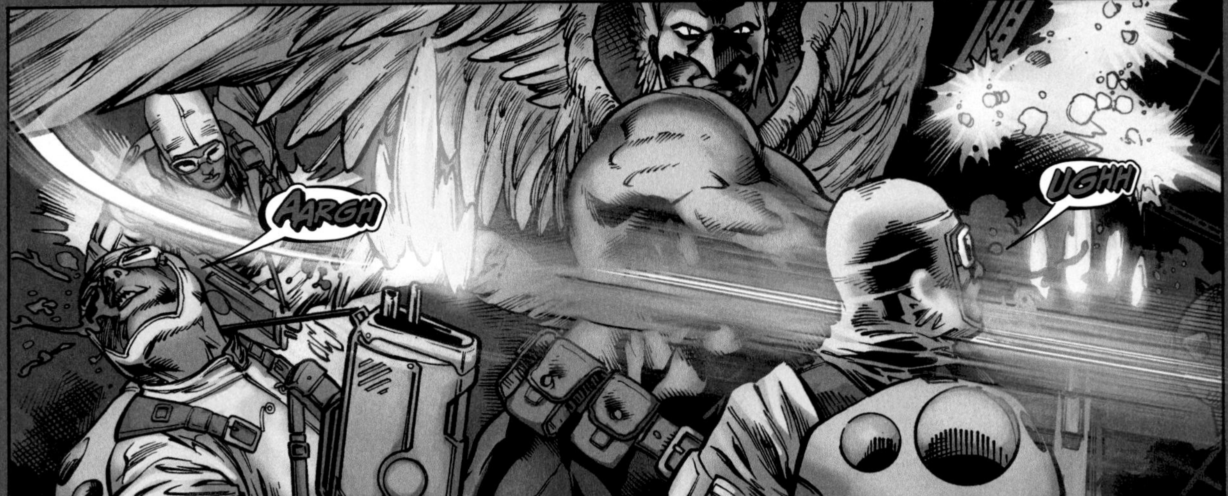
AARGH
UGHH

UFFF

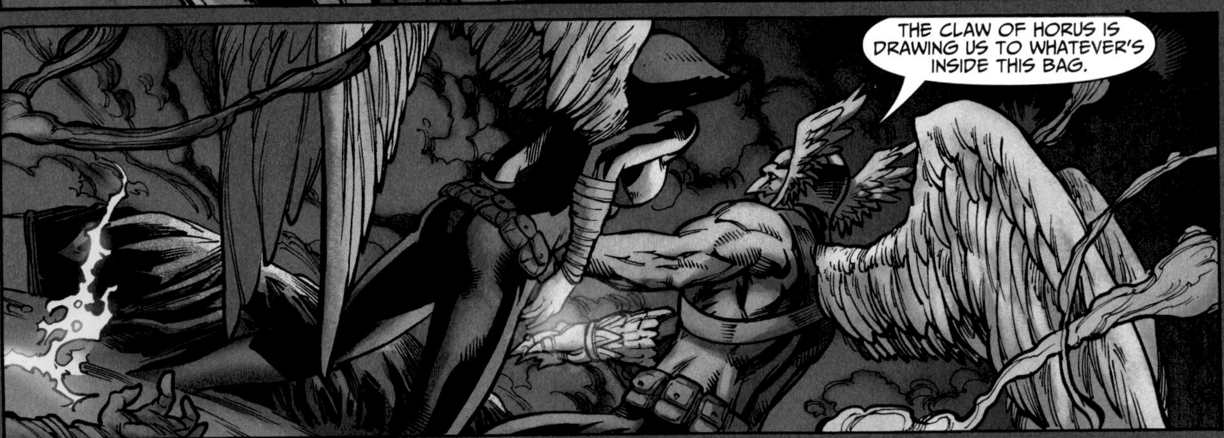
THE CLAW OF HORUS IS DRAWING US TO WHATEVER'S INSIDE THIS BAG.

OUR SOULS' FIRST HOME.
PRINCE KHUFU AND PRINCESS CHAY-ARA.
WHAT ARE THEY DOING HERE-- I THOUGHT THESE REMAINS WERE DESTROYED ALONG WITH THE REST OF THE BLACK LANTERNS.
PLING
CARTER-- LOOK OUT!
ARRGHH
UNNN

RNNN
SHIERA... NO...
...I'M...I'M ALL RIGHT...
...YOU'RE NOT GETTING RID OF ME...THAT EASY...NOT THIS TIME.
BETA ONE TO BASE! BETA ONE TO BASE!
YAAGGHH
VIP VIP VIP VIP
PLAN A'S BEEN COMPROMISED! REPEAT, PLAN A'S BEEN COMPROMISED! ALL EXPENDABLES HAVE BEEN EXPENDED.
LOCK ON ISOTOPE BEACON!

DAMN IT! THE BONES--WHERE ARE THEY--THE CLAW'S LIGHT'S GROWING DIMMER--
FORGET IT, CARTER, WE HAVE TO GET OUT OF HERE NOW!
THE GUY WHO ROLLED THE CONCUSSION GRENADE MUST'VE TAKEN THEM AND JUMPED OUT!
GRAB THE OTHER IDIOTS! THIS PLANE'S ABOUT TO--
SOMEONE WENT TO A LOT OF TROUBLE AND EXPENSE TO FIND OUR BONES...
"--AND WE'RE GOING TO FIND OUT WHO THAT SOMEONE IS."
SOUTH AMERICA.
DEEP IN THE PERUVIAN AMAZON.
HATH-SET.
Powers: Continuous reincarnation through the possession of his descendants.

BLIP

AQUAMAN.
BLACK MANTA
A.K.A. UNKNOWN.
Powers: Lethal high-tech suit provides undersea adaptation and arsenal of weapons.

BRIGHTEST DAY 2
Cover by David Finch, Scott Williams
and Peter Steigerwald

NUCLEAR OPTIONS

PITTSBURGH UNIVERSITY.
BAD NEWS? WHAT BAD NEWS?
PROFESSOR?!
IF HE DOESN'T ANSWER I'M TRANSMUTING THIS VAULT DOOR INTO JELL-O SHOTS AND GETTING THE HELL OUT OF HERE.
WHAT'S YOUR FAVORITE FLAVOR, JASON?
I'M NOT GIVING UP ANY MOLECULAR INTEL UNTIL PROFESSOR STEIN GIVES US THE ALL-CLEAR, RONNIE!
I CAN TRANSMUTE THIS DOOR INTO WATER. I KNOW WATER. OR WE CAN PHASE RIGHT THROUGH IT. YOU KNEW FIRESTORM COULD DO THAT, RIGHT?
DON'T USE YOUR POWERS. PLEASE STAY PUT.
BUT PROFESSOR, I--
I'M SENDING IN HELP, RONALD.

HEY, GUYS.
LOOKS LIKE WE'VE GOT SOME WORK TO DO.

WHAT'S THE ATOM WEARING?
I DON'T KNOW. IT'S PROBABLY JUST A NEW UNIFORM.
ACTUALLY, RONNIE, WHERE I'M GOING I NEED SOMETHING A LITTLE LESS FLAMMABLE THAN SPANDEX.
UH, OH. LET ME GUESS.
I'VE GOT TO DISARM THE FIRESTORM MATRIX BONDING YOU AND JASON.
DISARM IT? "DISARM" ISN'T A GOOD WORD, IS IT?
ASK HIM WHY WE'RE STUCK TOGETHER.
HHH. WHY ARE WE STUCK TOGETHER, ATOM?
THE PROFESSOR AND I STILL HAVE TO RUN SOME MORE TESTS.

ASK HIM IF THERE'S ANYTHING WE CAN DO TO HELP HIM?
WILL YOU STOP BACKSEAT DRIVING?
WITH MARTIAN MANHUNTER NOT AROUND, NO ONE ELSE CAN HEAR ME BUT YOU!
LUCKY ME!
HEY, ONE OF US HAS GOT TO TAKE THIS SERIOUSLY!
GUYS, DON'T.
DON'T WHAT?
DON'T ARGUE.
IT'S ONLY GOING TO MAKE THIS MORE DANGEROUS.
DANGEROUS?
BOTH OF YOU JUST KEEP QUIET. I GOT THIS.

YOU WERE RIGHT, PROFESSOR STEIN.
THE FIRE'S NOT JUST FOR SHOW ANYMORE.
TEMPERATURE'S ALREADY APPROACHING ONE THOUSAND DEGREES.
AS LONG AS THE CAMERA IN YOUR HELMET DOESN'T MELT I SHOULD BE ABLE TO WALK YOU THROUGH THIS, RAY.
JUST TAKE CARE OF THESE BOYS. THEY DIDN'T ASK FOR THIS.
THIS SHOULD BE MY PROBLEM.
PROFESSOR...

...I'M RIGHT HERE IN FRONT OF THE *FIRESTORM* MATRIX.
HEY.

WHAT?
WHAT? I DIDN'T SAY ANYTHING.
YOU JUST SAID, "HEY."
THE ATOM SAID NOT TO TALK.
HE SAID NOT TO ARGUE.
HE SAID TO STAY QUIET.
THEN WHY'D YOU SAY SOMETHING?
I DIDN'T SAY ANYTHING.
I'M GOING TO HAVE TO GET BETWEEN THE SUBATOMIC PARTICLES IN THE NUCLEUS AND LITERALLY PUSH THEM APART.
IF WE'RE RIGHT, IT SHOULD TRIGGER A CHAIN REACTION THAT WILL UNRAVEL THE FIRESTORM MATRIX AND FREE RONNIE AND JASON.
SHUT UP, WHITE BOY.
WHAT THE HELL DID YOU JUST SAY?
NOTHING. WHAT ARE YOU YELLING ABOUT?
I HEARD YOU.
SOMETHING'S HAPPENING.
AHH!
RONNIE?!

OUR FACE!
ATOM! IT'S FIGHTING YOU! IT DOESN'T WANT TO LET THEM GO!
GET OUT OF THERE. NOW!
NO, I SEE SOMETHING. I SEE--
KZZZZZZZ
PROFESSORRRRRRR!

PEARL RIVER, NEW YORK.

...THERE HAVE BEEN MANY QUESTIONS SURROUNDING THE RECENT EVENTS IN COAST CITY THAT STILL HAVE NOT BEEN ANSWERED...
GBS
RESURRECTED?
HRRRM...

D-DINNER'S R-READY!
FSSS
FSSS
BE RIGHT THERE, MOM!

AND I WON'T BACK DOWN!
DON'T SCREW UP HERE, OLIVIA!
DON'T WORRY ABOUT ME, TOMMY--WORRY ABOUT YOUR LOUSY DRUM PLAYING!

IT'S TIME.
WOOF WOOF
IN A MINUTE--SONG'S ALMOST OVER!

EHRRR
A-ALIVE... HE'S ALIVE...

MOM! I CAN'T SEE THE SCREEN!
WE'RE GONNA FAIL THE SONG, MOM!
YOU MAKE A BETTER WINDOW THAN A DOOR, HONEY.
AND YOU'D BE BETTER OFF IF YOU STOP TALKING ALL THE TIME, STEVEN.
AACKK...
ZZRRR
MOM-- NO!
SKASH BASH SMASH
J'ONZZZZZZZ...

DENVER, COLORADO.
I'M HAPPY TO SEE YOUR FINAL RESTING PLACE WASN'T DISTURBED, OLD FRIEND.
SAUL ERDEL
TEACHER AND EXPLORER
IT'S THE WOMAN FROM THE VISION I HAD ON MARS...
...THE ONE ON THE FLOOR...
...ERDEL HAD A DAUGHTER.
Me and Dad at the

THE PERUVIAN JUNGLE.
THANKS FOR THE DIRECTIONS TO YOUR COMMAND POST.
HAPPY LANDINGS!

SOMEONE'S BEEN *METICULOUS* ABOUT KEEPING TABS ON US.
AND NOT ONLY PHOTOS OF US IN ACTION, BUT AS CIVILIANS TOO.

OH MY GOD, ARE THOSE--?
HATH-SET.
THAT BASTARD...

HE TOOK THE TIME AFTER MURDERING US TO MAKE *DEATH MASKS* OF OUR FACES LIKE SOME DAMN PRIZE!
THE THOUGHT OF HATH-SET SMILING AND STANDING OVER OUR BODIES WHILE WE BLED OUT--RUNNING HIS FINGERS OVER MY FACE AS HE SET THE PLASTER MOLDS-- MAKES MY STOMACH TURN...

THIS ANCIENT CURSE HATH-SET PLACED ON US IS LIKE THE SWORD OF DAMOCLES OVER OUR HEADS, SHIERA...

...INSTEAD OF LETTING IT SWING DOWN AND KILL US HE KEEPS DANGLING IT--TOYING WITH US--LETTING US KNOW HE'S IN CONTROL OF US--OF *OUR* DESTINY--

WELL NO MORE!
HE'S BEEN SKATING THROUGH THE AGES ON OUR BLOOD--RIDING THROUGH IMMORTALITY ON OUR BACKS-- ON OUR DEATHS--
--HUNTING US DOWN--KILLING US AND ANYONE ELSE IN HIS WAY!
FROM HERE ON OUT WE'RE TAKING CONTROL OF OUR OWN DESTINY, SHIERA!
WE'RE GOING TO MAKE OUR OWN FATE!
IT'S TIME WE HUNT HATH-SET DOWN AND KILL HIM.

DENVER, COLORADO.
MOUNT HOPE SENIOR HOME.
NOW DON'T GO TO BED LATE, MELISSA.
IT'S NOT GOOD FOR YOU TO KEEP STARING AT THE STARS EVERY NIGHT.
HEY THERE, SWEETHEART...
...HOW'S MY LITTLE GIRL?
I'M DREAMING, AREN'T I, DAD?
WHAT MAKES YOU SAY THAT?
I REMEMBER SOMETHING BAD HAPPENING TO YOU--TO ME--BUT I...SOMETIMES FORGET THINGS--IMPORTANT THINGS...
YOU REMEMBERED ME.
I DID, DIDN'T I?
THE RAIN'S STOPPED. WOULD YOU LIKE TO GO OUTSIDE?
YES, VERY MUCH.
CAN WE TALK?
OF COURSE, DAD, WHAT ABOUT?
THE NIGHT...
THE NIGHT WE BROUGHT THE MARTIAN HERE.

I'VE BEEN THINKING ABOUT HIM THE LAST FEW DAYS, DAD...
...HE'S BACK... SEEN HIM ON THE TV...BUT I CAN'T REMEMBER ANYTHING ELSE BUT HIM STANDING THERE IN THE LAB...SURROUNDED BY SMOKE... IT JUST KEEPS SLIPPING AWAY...
...PLEASE DON'T BE MAD--DON'T MAKE ME WAKE UP--I LIKE SPENDING TIME WITH YOU LIKE THIS...
MAD? I CAN NEVER BE MAD AT YOU. AND DON'T WORRY, YOU DO REMEMBER THAT NIGHT.
IT'S ALL IN HERE.
IT IS?
YES, WE CAN GO BACK TO THAT NIGHT TOGETHER, YOU AND I, BUT THERE'RE PAINFUL MEMORIES LINGERING THERE. ARE YOU SURE YOU WANT--
YES, DAD, I'M SURE.
I REMEMBER WHEN YOU FIRST SHOWED ME THE PIECE OF THE STONE TABLET YOU FOUND IN THE CIENT RUINS OF THAT AZTEC TEMPLE WHEN YOU WERE A BOY... I CAN STILL HEAR THE WONDER IN YOUR VOICE WHEN YOU TOLD ME THE SAME DTIME STORY EVERY NIGHT OF HOW PACE TRAVELERS FROM THE RED STAR ONCE VISITED OUR PLANET AND HELPED AN ANCIENT PEOPLE SURVIVE AND THRIVE.
ONCE YOU HAD IT TRANSLATED IT BECAME YOUR LIFE--OUR LIFE--AND I WAS GLAD MOM LEFT--SHE NEVER UNDERSTOOD WHAT WE WERE TRYING TO DO--
ALL SHE SAW WAS AN OBSESSION--
--AND ALL WE SAW WAS THE FUTURE...

...BUT THE FUTURE WAS PAIN...
...AND HORROR.
WE SHOULD HAVE RUN, DAD.
WE SHOULD HAVE RUN AS FAST AS WE COULD.
BUT WE DIDN'T.
BECAUSE INTERTWINED IN ALL OUR FEAR WAS *HOPE*...
...HOPE THAT SOMEHOW PEACE AND UNDERSTANDING WOULD WIN THAT TERRIBLE NIGHT.
BUT IT DIDN'T.
ALL OUR DREAMS OF REACHING OUT TO A NEW WORLD...
...ONLY PUT OURS IN JEOPARDY.

SO YOU HAD A NEW MISSION, DAD.
A NEW *OBSESSION.*
AND I HATED YOU FOR MAKING ME HIDE IN THE SHADOWS AND NOT ALLOWING ME TO BE PART OF IT.
I REMEMBER WHEN I ASKED YOU WHY IN THE WORLD YOU WOULD TRY SOMETHING LIKE THIS AGAIN AFTER EVERYTHING THAT HAPPENED.
A SAD SMILE CROSSED YOUR LIPS, DAD, AND ALL YOU SAID WAS: I'M A SCIENTIST, MELISSA, AND SCIENCE IS BUILT ON THE FOUNDATION OF FAILURE. HOW COULD I NOT TRY TO RIGHT A WRONG?
AND THEN ONE NIGHT, THERE *HE* WAS.
STANDING BEFORE YOU-- BEFORE US-- THE *SAME* TYPE OF BEING WE SAW ETCHED INTO THE ANCIENT STONE TABLET.
THE ONE I WOULD LEARN YEARS LATER IS CALLED J'ONN J'ONZZ, THE MARTIAN MANHUNTER.
HE WAS GOING TO BE OUR SAVIOR--DELIVER US FROM THE EVIL WE HAD UNLEASHED.
I DIDN'T SEE THE CYCLONIC POWER GENERATOR ARCING FROM BEHIND THE DOOR...
...BUT YOU DID.
I STILL HEAR YOUR SCREAM EVERY NIGHT, DAD, JUST AS I CAN SEE THE FLASH OF THE EXPLOSION THAT BLINDED ME FOR WEEKS...
...ALONG WITH A PIECE OF THE TRANSPORTER CONSOLE THAT LEFT ITS MARK ON ME FOREVER.

I COULD HAVE HEARD YOUR LAST WORDS TO HIM, DAD.
HAVE HELD YOUR HAND AND TOLD YOU EVERYTHING WOULD BE ALL RIGHT NOW...
...FORGIVE ME...FOR TAKING YOU FROM...YOUR HOME...
...NEEDED SOMEONE...TO SAVE US...
...SAVE US FROM MY ARROGANCE...
...MY *RECKLESSNESS...*
...THAT YOU DID BRING TO EARTH A HERO...
...A HERO WHO WOULD SAVE THIS PLANET A HUNDRED TIMES OVER IN THE YEARS THAT FOLLOWED.
BUT I COULDN'T...
...BECAUSE YOUR WISH TO KEEP ME AWAY FROM YOUR NEW EXPERIMENTS SAVED MY LIFE THAT NIGHT.
...BUT I'M SO TIRED NOW.
I KNOW YOU ARE.
'NIGHT, DAD.
GOODNIGHT, MELISSA, WE'LL SEE EACH OTHER AGAIN SOON.
YOU PROMISE, DAD?
I PROMISE.

DUBAI.
HEY, WAIT! AQUAMAN! MERA!
C'MON, RING. I KNOW YOU'RE NOT LETTIN' ANYONE SEE ME, BUT LET 'EM AT LEAST HEAR ME.
WAIT DAMMIT!
WHOA.
WHAT DID THAT BLACK RING DO TO AQUAMAN?
AND WHY DO I HAVE THIS FEELING IT'S NOT ONLY HIM AND ME THAT'RE HAVING PROBLEMS?
NO. STOP JERKING ME AROUND AND--
HELP THEM LIVE.

--TALK?!
OH, CRAP!

C'MON. FLY! THAT'S WHAT THE RINGS CAN DO, RIGHT?
SO DO IT.
FLY!

FLY--

--NNFF!
FIGHT.
WHAT?

FIGHT?
FIGHT.
FIGHT WHAT? FIGHT WHO?
OH...

THE ANTIMATTER UNIVERSE.
THE PLANET QWARD.
ANTI-MONITOR.
Powers: Universe Destroyer.

YOU GOTTA BE JOKING.

BRIGHTEST DAY 3
Cover by David Finch, Scott Williams
and Peter Steigerwald

REVELATIONS

DO YOU WANT ME TO DIE AGAIN?

THE ANTIMATTER UNIVERSE.
THE PLANET QWARD.
BECAUSE 'PORTING ME IN FRONT OF THE ANTI-MONITOR IS PROBABLY THE FASTEST WAY TO DO IT.
FIGHT.
YOU THINK I CAN GO TOE-TO-TOE WITH A UNIVERSE EATER? THIS GUY CONSUMES PLANETS. MY CLAIM TO FAME WAS PERFORMING AERIAL ACTS WITHOUT A NET AND THAT DIDN'T WORK OUT SO WELL, WHICH YOU PROBABLY KNOW.
WELL, AT LEAST HE CAN'T SEE--

WHO ARE YOU?
NOW YOU TURN THE INVISIBILITY OFF. THANKS.

FIGHT.
WHAT ARE YOU--?

FIGHT.
AANNGGGGGAAHHH!

FIGHT FOR YOUR LIFE, BOSTON BRAND OF EARTH.

RAARGH!
IS THIS...ARE YOU TRYING TO TELL ME SOMETHING?
ARE ALL OF US...THE ONES THAT YOU BROUGHT BACK...ARE WE BACK TO STOP THE ANTI-MONITOR?
NO.
THOOOMM

BACK OFF, BIG BOY!
UNLESS YOU WANT ANOTHER BLAST OF--
HEY. FIRE!
COME ON!
YAAAAH!
ZRAAAAK

WHAT THE HELL DID YOU BRING ME *HERE* FOR?
I'M NOT USED TO TRYING TO STAY ALIVE.
OR IS *THAT* THE POINT?
IF IT *IS*, YOU *MADE* IT, OKAY? I'LL BE *CAREFUL!*
NEXT TIME I LEAP INTO THE AIR I'LL USE A SAFETY NET, OKAY?
OKAY.

PITTSBURGH.
RONALD?
PROFESSOR? AH...GOT A HELLUVA HEADACHE.
WHERE AM I?
THE UNIVERSITY'S MEDICAL CENTER.
WHAT HAPPENED?
THE ATOM MANAGED TO SEPARATE YOU AND JASON FROM THE FIRESTORM MATRIX, BUT IT CAUSED A UNIQUE EXPLOSION.
THE RESULTANT DETONATION TRANSMUTED EVERYTHING INSIDE THE VAULT INTO TABLE SALT.
AND... WHAT ABOUT THE ATOM?
HE'S CLEANING UP THE LAB. FORTUNATELY, FIRESTORM'S POWERS ARE STILL APPARENTLY UNABLE TO AFFECT ORGANIC MATTER--
--UNLIKE WHAT THE BLACK LANTERN WAS ABLE TO--
WHERE'S JASON?
IN THE NEXT ROOM WITH HIS FATHER.
"IT'S IMPERATIVE WE KEEP YOU AND JASON SEPARATED."
THEY'RE GOING TO DISCHARGE YOU IN A FEW MINUTES, JASON, THEN I'LL GET YOU HOME.
HOME?
BACK TO DETROIT.

NO, DAD. I HAVE A PHYSICS TEST TOMORROW. I HAVE TO GET BACK TO MY DORM ROOM AND STUDY.
YOU NEED MORE TIME BEFORE YOU JUMP BACK INTO EVERYTHING.
I WANT TO LEARN MORE FROM PROFESSOR STEIN ABOUT MY POWERS. THAT'S WHY I TRANSFERRED HERE.
JASON, PROFESSOR STEIN MADE IT CLEAR THAT YOU CAN'T FUSE FIRESTORM TOGETHER ANYMORE. THE EXPLOSION COULD'VE--
I'M NOT GIVING UP. I'M GOING TO STAY HERE AND I'M GOING TO STUDY.
YOU'RE COMING HOME. TODAY.
I DIDN'T TELL YOU WHAT TO DO WHEN MOM DIED, DID I?
HAVE IT YOUR WAY.
"JASON SAID YOU HEARD A VOICE BEFORE THE DETONATION."
HUH? I DON'T KNOW WHAT HE'S TALKING ABOUT. I DIDN'T HEAR ANYTHING. WHERE ARE MY SHOES?
RONALD, WHAT'S THE HURRY--?
ALL YOU'RE TELLING ME IS JASON AND I CAN'T BE FIRESTORM ANYMORE, BUT YOU WON'T SAY WHY. YOU'RE JUST TELLING ME IT'S DANGEROUS.
YOU HAVE TO TRUST ME. WE DON'T WANT ANY MORE... EXPLOSIONS.
BUT THERE'S SOMETHING YOU'RE NOT TELLING ME OR JASON. WHATEVER.

ALL JASON'S DOING IS BLAMING ME FOR WHAT THE BLACK LANTERN FIRESTORM DID.
BUT I DON'T EVEN REMEMBER DOING IT BECAUSE IT WASN'T ME! HE'S GOTTA GET IT THROUGH THAT THICK HEAD OF HIS.
RONALD, CALM DOWN.
THIS IS MY LIFE, PROFESSOR! I GOT ANOTHER CHANCE!
AND I'M NOT GOING TO WASTE ONE MORE MINUTE OF IT FEELING GUILTY BECAUSE SOMEONE ELSE DIDN'T--
I...
I'M GONE.

RONNIE, MAN...
...YOU SHOULD'VE TOLD THEM...
NO! DON'T DO THIS. PLEASE, RONNIE!
NO! NO, PLEASE!!
YOU'RE SCARED, BUT HOW SCARED ARE YOU?
SHOW ME!
IT HURTS!
HEY, YOU! RAYMOND!
YOU STAY AWAY FROM MY SON, YOU HEAR ME?
STAY THE HELL AWAY.

SOMEWHERE IN THE NORTH ATLANTIC.
VUU
VUU
VUU
VUU
VUU

ARTHUR!
SPLOOSH

I DON'T KNOW WHY... OR HOW I'M SUMMONING DEAD SEA LIFE, BUT I'VE GOT TO FIX THIS.
THE JUSTICE LEAGUE HASN'T BEEN ABLE TO LOCATE J'ONN.
MAYBE THE SCIENTISTS IN ATLANTIS--
NO.
I'M NOT GOING BACK TO ATLANTIS.
THEY'VE ONLY HELPED ME WHEN THEY NEEDED SOMETHING.
MY MOTHER GAVE HER LIFE TO SAVE ME FROM THEM. THEY HUNTED ME FOR YEARS...
...UNTIL THEY NEEDED A LEADER. THEN THEY CAST ME OUT AGAIN. THE CYCLE BECAME TOO FAMILIAR.
THEY NEVER TRULY STOOD BY ME.
NEITHER DID I.

I MAY NOT BE FROM ATLANTIS, BUT I WAS EXACTLY LIKE THEM. I DESERTED YOU WHEN YOU NEEDED ME.
BUT I PROMISE NOW. HERE. I WILL BE BY YOUR SIDE ALWAYS, ARTHUR.

MERA, MAYBE YOUR PEOPLE--

MY PEOPLE CANNOT HELP. AND EVEN IF THEY COULD, THE UNDERWATER DIMENSION THEY INHABIT IS SEALED OFF FROM OURS.
THEN THERE'S NO GOING HOME FOR YOU EITHER?

I AM HOME.

PEARL RIVER, NEW YORK.
ROCKLAND COUNTY MORGUE.
SOMEONE IS MAKING THIS PERSONAL.
THE PSYCHIC FLASH THAT HIT ME ON MARS ALONG WITH READING MELISSA ERDEL'S THOUGHTS HAVE MADE IT CLEAR I WAS NOT THE ONLY ONE BROUGHT TO EARTH BY HER FATHER'S TRANSPORTER...
...AND NOW MY INVESTIGATION LEADS ME HERE...
...TO THE COLD BODIES OF THIS FAMILY, BUTCHERED FOR NO APPARENT REASON--
THIS...HORRENDOUS METHOD OF KILLING--FAMILIAR IN SOME STRANGE WAY...
DOG HAIR ON THEIR CLOTHES.
A FAMILY PET.
LET'S HOPE YOU SURVIVED...
ROCKLAND COUNTY ANIMAL SHELTER.
"...BECAUSE I COULD USE ALL THE HELP I CAN GET."

WOOF
WOOF
WHAT DID YOU SEE, BOY?
WERE YOU ABLE TO GET A GOOD LOOK AT WHO--
NO.
IT'S NOT POSSIBLE.
WE NEED TO GO BACK TO COLORADO AND I KNOW AN OLD WOMAN WHO WILL ENJOY YOUR COMPANY, BOY...
A SLIGHT ADJUSTMENT TO YOUR FRONTAL LOBE AND THE HORROR YOU WITNESSED WILL BE GONE...
...I JUST HOPE THE STORM OF HORROR THAT'S FORMING CAN BE BLOWN AWAY AS QUICKLY.

THE BERMUDA TRIANGLE.
...TOWER, WE'RE EXPERIENCING SOME KIND OF INTERFERENCE UP HERE. INSTRUMENTS ARE SPINNING.

SILVER CITY, NEW MEXICO.
I DON'T KNOW WHERE GREEN LANTERN WENT, BUT HE'LL BE BACK, RUSSELL, AND UNTIL HE GETS HERE WE GOTTA--
HEY, JERRY, YOU SEE THAT?!
SEE WHAT?

WE'RE FREE.
KRAKKKKL

THE WHITE LANTERN.
IT JUST STARTED BLINKING.

KABAOOOMMMM

DEEP IN THE PERUVIAN JUNGLE.
THE BATTLE GLOVE YOU DESCRIBED HIM WEARING IS THE CLAW OF HORUS.
WITH ITS HELP, IT WILL ONLY BE A MATTER OF TIME BEFORE--
AAGH!
SKRAKKK
RRARGH!
THE SCREAMS OF YOUR MEN GROW LOUDER. THE HAWKS HAVE REACHED THE PERIMETER FORCES SOONER THAN EXPECTED.
KEEP THEM AWAY FROM THIS GATE BY ANY MEANS NECESSARY UNTIL I AM THROUGH.
THWIP THWIP THWIP
UGNN!
YAAGH!
BUDDABUDDA
NOT THAT I GIVE A CRAP, BUT AREN'T YOU TAKING SUPPLIES OR OTHER WEAPONS WITH YOU?
THWIP
THWIP
THWIP
EVERYTHING I DESIRE IS WAITING FOR ME ON THE OTHER SIDE.
THWIP
AND MY MONEY FOR FINDING THE BONES?
THE FUNDS AGREED UPON HAVE BEEN WIRED TO YOUR SWISS ACCOUNT.

WE'RE OMING, ATH-SET!
WE'RE COMING TO FINALLY END THIS!
SKRAKKK
SKRAKKK
YES! THE GATE HAS *RECOGNIZED* THEIR BONES!
I ONLY WISH I COULD SEE THE HAWKS' FACES NOW THAT THEY REALIZE WHO'S BESTED THEM...
...BUT THAT WILL HAVE TO WAIT FOR ANOTHER DAY, A WORLD AWAITS MY GUIDING HAND.
YOU BETTER GET THROUGH THE GATE BECAUSE THEY'RE ALMOST--
--HERE*AAAGH!*
AND I THOUGHT THE *DEATH MASKS* HE MADE OF US WERE *TWISTED* ENOUGH...
LOOKS LIKE WE FOUND WHAT HATH-SET WAS DIGGING FOR.
YEAH...OUR BONES...

FROM EACH AND EVERY ONE OF OUR PAST LIVES.
...ALL OF THEM.

BRIGHTEST DAY 4
Cover by David Finch, Scott Williams
and Peter Steigerwald

THRESHOLDS

DEEP IN THE PERUVIAN JUNGLE.
THAT'S WHY I'VE NEVER BEEN ABLE TO FIND THE BONES OF OUR OTHER BODIES THE CURSE CLAIMED...
...HATH-SET'S BEEN GATHERING THEM ALL--USING THEM FOR THIS.
IT'S WARM, VIBRATING WITH SOME KIND OF INTERNAL ENERGY.
AND IT LOOKS LIKE EACH BONE'S BEEN ABSORBED INTO THE SURFACE, LIKE PIECES OF A PUZZLE.
LIKE A HUNDRED DIFFERENT KEYS INTO A HUNDRED DIFFERENT LOCKS.
IT'S A GATEWAY--A DOOR--BUT TO WHERE?

I DON'T KNOW, BUT THE CLAW OF HORUS SURE AS HELL WANTS IN, AND I THINK I KNOW WHY.
I'M ALL EARS.
WHAT'RE THE TWO THINGS MISSING FROM THIS GATE?
KHUFU AND CHAYARA'S BONES.
EXACTLY.
CARTER... LET'S DESTROY THIS...THING...THIS ABERRATION.
IF HATH-SET IS SOMEWHERE ON THE OTHER SIDE MAYBE WE CAN TRAP HIM THERE--LOCK IT FROM THIS END--KEEP HIM AWAY FROM US FOREVER.
WHAT ARE YOU TALKING ABOUT, SHIERA? LOOK AT HOW FAR HE'S GONE TO TRY TO DESTROY US.
WE WILL KILL HATH-SET BEFORE HE KILLS US THIS TIME, IT'S THAT SIMPLE.
SIMPLE IS US OBLITERATING THIS GATE, CARTER...
...WIPING IT ALL AWAY AND GETTING ON WITH OUR LIFE.
A LIFE SPENT LOOKING OVER MY SHOULDER IS NOT A LIFE I WANT TO LEAD, SHIERA.
I WANT US TO WALK AWAY WHILE WE HAVE THE CHANCE.
WE ARE NOT GIVING UP NOW--NOT WHEN WE'RE SO CLOSE TO FINALLY PUTTING AN END TO THIS ONCE AND FOR ALL.
IF THAT'S YOUR FINAL DECISION THEN I'LL STAND BY IT JUST AS I'VE ALWAYS STOOD BY YOU.

SO, THE CRYSTALLIZED BONE THE STAR SAPPHIRE GAVE ME THAT'S NOW ATTACHED TO THE CLAW IS--
--PROBABLY A PIECE OF OUR ORIGINAL BODIES SEEKING TO RECONNECT TO THE WHOLE.
THAT'S WHY THE CLAW DREW US HERE AND THAT'S WHY--
--IT STILL WANTS TO FOLLOW HATH-SET AND OUR FIRST BONES THROUGH THE GATE.
BUT IF HATH-SET'S HERE AND SO CLOSE, IT DOESN'T MAKE SENSE THAT HE WOULDN'T TAKE THE OPPORTUNITY TO TRY TO KILL US AND RESUME THE CURSE.
WELL, THERE'S ONLY ONE WAY TO FIND OUT.
LET'S GO ASK HIM.
IF THIS GATEWAY ALLOWS US TO STEP THROUGH.
I DON'T THINK WE HAVE TO WORRY ABOUT THAT, SHIERA.
I HAVE A FEELING WE'RE PREDESTINED FOR AN ALL ACCESS PASS...

WE'RE THROUGH TO THE OTHER SIDE. ARE YOU OKAY?
...MY GOD... THAT WAS HORRIBLE... TO FEEL ALL THAT PAIN INFLICTED ON US AGAIN AND AGAIN...
WHAT THE HELL--
GUESS WE'RE NOT IN PERU ANYMORE.
OR KANSAS FOR THAT MATTER.

GEORGETOWN.
YOU THOUGHT I WAS GRUMPY BEFORE I DIED, RING, NOW I'M ACTUALLY GETTING TIRED...
...OH, COME ON. WHAT AM I DOING IN A GIRL'S BEDROOM?
WHO IS SHE? SHE SMELLS...
SHE SMELLS LIKE LILACS.
AHHH!!
OW!
YOU CAN SEE ME?
OF COURSE I CAN SEE YOU. WHO THE HELL ARE YOU?
MY NAME'S BOSTON BRAND.
DEADMAN?
YEAH. WHO THE HELL ARE YOU?

DOVE
DOVE A.K.A. DAWN GRANGER. AVATAR OF PEACE.
Powers: Intelligent, compassionate and possessed of great strength and flight.

YOU... USED TO BE AN INVISIBLE SPIRIT WHO POSSESSED PEOPLE TO INTERACT WITH THE LIVING.
SURE, THAT WAS MY OLD M.O. NEW ONE TO BE DETERMINED.
UH... WHY ARE YOU STARING AT ME?
DOCTOR FATE DESCRIBED YOU ONCE AS A PALE, WRINKLED CORPSE, BUT NO ONE REALLY KNEW WHAT YOU LOOKED LIKE.
I WOULD'VE GOTTEN A GLIMPSE IN COAST CITY WHEN EVERYONE CAME BACK, BUT I WAS TOO BUSY TRYING TO CALM DOWN HAWK.
SEEMS LIKE A FULL-TIME JOB. AFTER HIS PREVIOUS LIFE JOURNEY, I WAS SURPRISED A RED RING DIDN'T GO FOR HANK HALL INSTEAD OF--
A WHITE RING? YOU'RE STILL WEARING ONE?
ME AND NO ONE ELSE APPARENTLY. AND UNTIL IT BROUGHT ME TO YOU, I WAS AS INVISIBLE ALIVE AS I WAS DEAD.
THE JUSTICE LEAGUE HAVE BEEN LOOKING FOR YOU. THEY WANTED TO OFFER YOU THE SAME THING THEY DID HAWK.
WHICH WAS WHAT?
DOCUMENTATION SO YOU CAN OFFICIALLY BE BACK AMONG THE LIVING.
WHAT IF I DON'T WANT TO BE?

HAWK

I FELT YOU CHANGE, DOVE. I KNEW YOU WERE IN TROUBLE SO I CAME TO GIVE TROUBLE--
I'M NOT IN TROUBLE. THAT'S DEADMAN!
THIS--
--IS DEADMAN?
WHAT THE HELL'S HE DOING IN YOUR BEDROOM AT THREE IN THE MORNING?

TIME DOESN'T MEAN MUCH TO ME. HASN'T SINCE I DIED, REALLY. OR EVEN WHEN I CAME BACK.
WHAT ARE YOU *TALKING* ABOUT? MAKE *SENSE.*
I'LL TRY IF YOU DON'T THROW ME INTO ANY MORE WALLS.

"DAYS AFTER YOU AND I CAME BACK WITH THE OTHERS, I PICKED UP A DEAD BABY BIRD.
"AND THIS *WHITE RING* STARTED GLOWING.
"IT BROUGHT THE BIRD BACK TO LIFE THEN IT JERKED ME ACROSS THE UNIVERSE ON A FIELD TRIP TO VISIT THE RECENTLY RESURRECTED.
"IT EVEN BROUGHT ME TO STAR CITY WHERE I PLAYED LIKE SOME KIND OF SUPER-JOHNNY APPLE-SEED."

THAT *FOREST* THAT GREW OVERNIGHT... THAT WAS *YOU?*
THAT WAS ME. OR I GUESS THE WHITE RING.
WHY? I MEAN, *ALL* OF IT. WHAT'S IT MEAN?
I THINK IT HAS TO DO WITH THE *REASON* WE'VE BEEN BROUGHT *BACK.* THE WHITE RING SAID IT A FEW TIMES...
"...HELP ME LIVE."
HELP *WHO* LIVE?

WHO *CARES?*
LET'S STOP LOOKING AT THE FOREST AND START LOOKING AT THE TREES.
WHAT'S *THAT* MEAN?

IT MEANS I GOT SOMETHING FOR YOU AND THAT WHITE RING TO DO.

SILVER CITY, NEW MEXICO.
C'MON, JACKSON! EVERYONE'S GOING TO LOOK AT IT.
I STILL DON'T GET WHY THE WHOLE TOWN CARES ABOUT A WHITE LANTERN.
BECAUSE NO ONE CAN LIFT IT UP! AND NO ONE KNOWS WHERE IT CAME FROM OR WHAT IT'S HERE FOR! PEOPLE THINK THAT'S WHY IT'S BEEN GETTING SO HOT LATELY.
AND IF IT GETS ANY HOTTER TONIGHT, I'M GOING TO MELT.
YOU KNOW I DON'T SWIM, MARIA.

WHO SAID THAT'S ALL WE WERE GOING TO DO?

I DON'T KNOW HOW TO.
I'LL TEACH YOU.

I'M A GOOD TEACHER
WHOAAAA!

AAAA--

I GOT YOU!

WHAT HAPPENED? I WAS HERE YESTERDAY.
YOU WERE *HERE?* WITH *WHO?*
THERE WAS *WATER.* THERE WAS A *LOT* OF WATER.

WHERE'D IT ALL GO, JACKSON?

THE BERMUDA TRIANGLE.

WHAT THE HELL HAPPENED?

TOWER LOST CONTACT EARLY TONIGHT, CAPTAIN.

LOOKS LIKE THE PLANE WAS TORN APART.

I SEE SOMEONE!

WHAT'S WRONG WITH THEM?

THEY'RE BADLY DEHYDRATED.

KRAKKKL
CAPTAIN, SOMETHING'S IN THE WATER!

KILL THEM!
KILL THEM ALL.

"AND MAKE SURE THEY SUFFER."
PITTSBURGH UNIVERSITY.
ATO
HEY, WHERE'S RAYMOND?
GUESS HE'S HAD ENOUGH BEER PONG?
HEY.
RONNIE.
WAKE UP.
I NEED TO ASK YOU SOMETHING.
HUH? WHAT?

DO YOU REMEMBER MY NAME YET?
AAAHHH!
SAY IT!
LET GO!

GEHENNA.
HEY, RAYMOND?
KEG'S CALLING YOUR NAME--
PITT U
--WHOA!
WHAT'S WITH ALL THE SALT, DUDE?
CHEMISTRY COMPOSITION

I DON'T KNOW IF THIS IS A GOOD IDEA.
DEADMAN'S RIGHT, HAWK. WE SHOULD SPEAK TO GREEN LANTERN OR SUPERMAN--
SO THEY CAN *WHAT? STOP US?*
AM I THE ONLY SUPERHERO WITH *A PAIR* ANYMORE?

I HAVE NO IDEA WHAT THIS WHITE RING CAN REALLY *DO,* HAWK.

IT CAN GROW A *FOREST* IN A DEAD ZONE AND MAKE A *DEAD BIRD* BREATHE AGAIN.
IT CAN BRING BACK *LIFE.*

SO *DO* IT, DEADMAN.

A BLACK RING COULDN'T BRING BACK MY BROTHER.
LET'S SEE IF A WHITE RING CAN.
IN MEMORIAM
DONALD HALL
R.I.P.

BRIGHTEST DAY 5
Cover by David Finch, Scott Williams and Peter Steigerwald

UNDER PRESSURE

OFF THE BERMUDA TRIANGLE.
"THEY SAID IT'D TAKE WEEKS TO FIND SOMETHING THAT COULD WITHSTAND PRESSURES AT 5,000 FEET SO THEY COULD FIX THIS LEAK."
BUT THEY DIDN'T COUNT ON US, MERA.

THE OWNERS OF THIS RIG MIGHT BE *BEGGING* SOMEONE TO CLEAN UP THEIR RECKLESS MESS, BUT THEY WON'T LIKE OUR SHUTTING DOWN *ALL* THEIR WELLS.

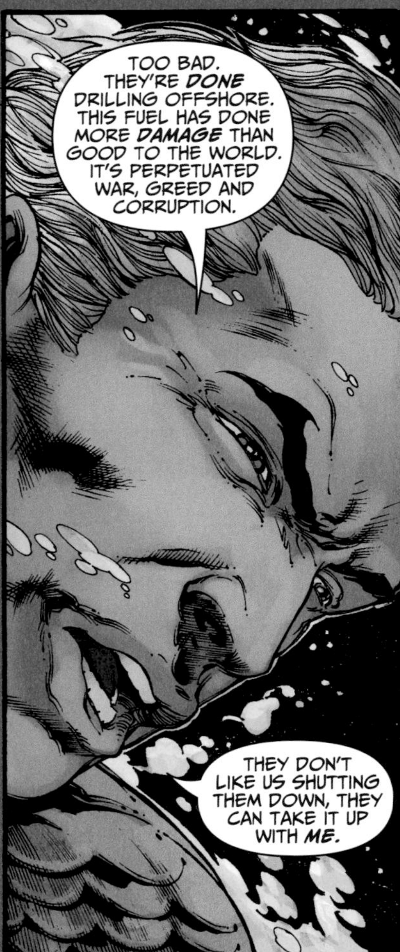
TOO BAD. THEY'RE *DONE* DRILLING OFFSHORE. THIS FUEL HAS DONE MORE *DAMAGE* THAN GOOD TO THE WORLD. IT'S PERPETUATED WAR, GREED AND CORRUPTION.
THEY DON'T LIKE US SHUTTING THEM DOWN, THEY CAN TAKE IT UP WITH *ME.*

DID YOU SEE THAT? IT LOOKED LIKE ONE OF YOUR WATER CONSTRUCTS.
FWWOOOOSH
ARTHUR, WE NEED TO LEAVE RIGHT--

--NOW!

FWAHKOOSH

KING OF ATLANTIS.

YOU WILL DIE ON YOUR KNEES.

GEORGETOWN.
THIS COULD CHANGE THINGS.
IF IT WORKS... I MEAN... I'M NOT SURE THIS IS A GOOD IDEA, DOVE.

I'VE FELT A CONNECTION TO THIS POWER, I *SPOKE* TO IT, AS SOON AS THE BLACK LANTERNS ROSE FROM THEIR GRAVES.
I'M NOT SURE *HOW* I'M CONNECTED TO IT OR *WHY*, BUT I THINK HANK'S BROTHER MIGHT BE TOO.
THE BLACK RINGS COULDN'T RESURRECT AND USE HIS BODY.

THINK OF IT *THIS* WAY, DEADMAN, THE WHITE RING BROUGHT BACK *YOU* AND *ME*, RIGHT?
YEAH.
SO BETWEEN ALL *THREE* OF US--
--WHO DESERVES A *SECOND CHANCE* MORE?

ALL RIGHT.

HERE GOES NOTHING.

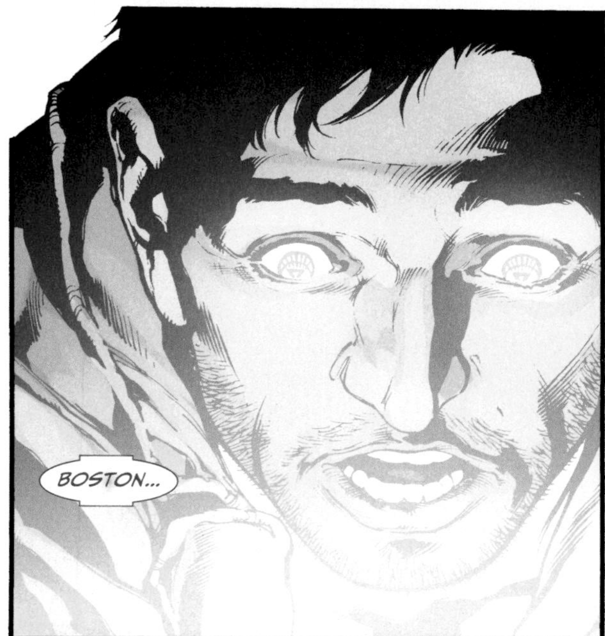
BOSTON...

"...WHAT ARE YOU DOING?"
I DON'T KNOW WHO SENT YOU TO TRY TO STOP US FROM FIXING THIS SCREW-UP--

--BUT YOU'LL TELL ME.

TALK!
ARRHHHH!!
KRAK

AAAHH
WE WEREN'T SENT HERE BY SURFACE DWELLERS, HALF-BREED.

WE ARE FINALLY FREE.
HOLD HIS NECK OUT, QUANA.

THIS KILL IS MINE AND MINE ALONE.
SIREN!

RELEASE HIM.

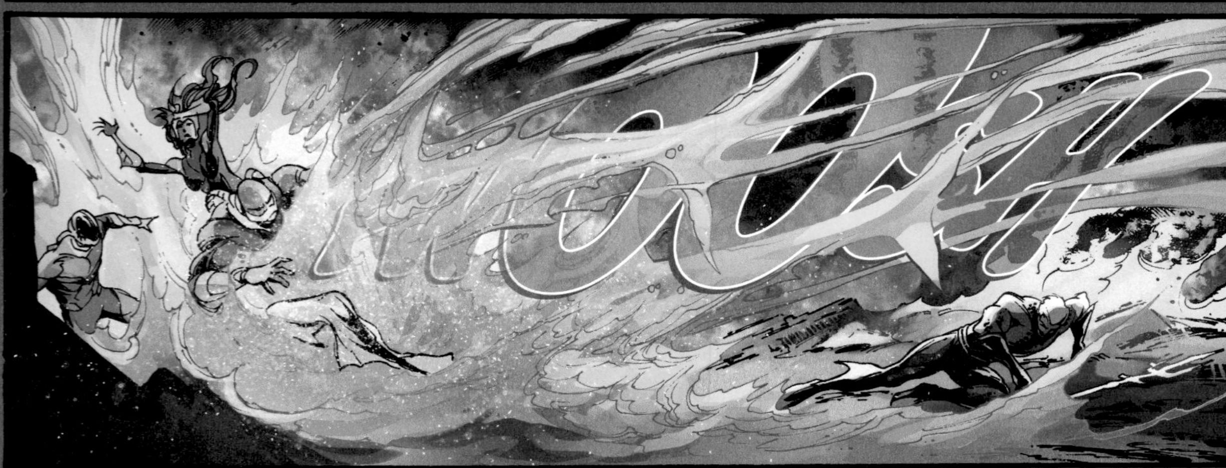

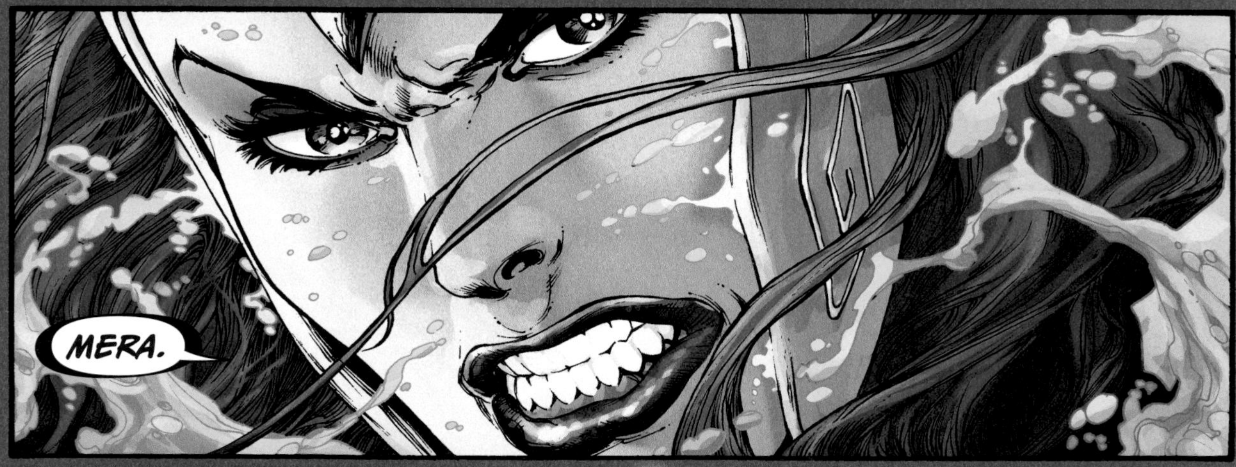
MERA.

ARTHUR, WE NEED TO LEAVE!
NOT UNTIL WE FIND OUT WHO THEY ARE.
WE CAN'T STAY. THEY WON'T BE ALONE FOR LONG.
BUT--

YOU HAVEN'T TOLD HIM, HAVE YOU?
COME ON!

CRA-KOOOM
"WHEREVER WE ARE..."

ELSEWHERE.
...HAVING WINGS IS OBVIOUSLY GOING TO BE A BIG PLUS.
...YES... I GUESS SO...
THERE'RE DOZENS OF LAND MASSES--
--BUT ONLY ONE SEEMS TO BE INHABITED.
WE'RE STRANGERS IN A STRANGE LAND.
WE NEED TO SCOUT THIS AREA, SHIERA--GATHER INTEL ABOUT THIS PLACE BEFORE--
WHAT WE SAW BACK THERE--WHEN WE WENT THROUGH THE GATE...
...REMEMBERING OUR PAST LIVES IS ONE THING, CARTER, BUT I JUST FELT LIKE I EXPERIENCED ALL OF OUR DEATHS AGAIN RIGHT TO THE CORE OF MY SOUL.

...I COULD EVEN HEAR HATH-SET LAUGHING AND SMELL HIS PUTRID BREATH AS HE WHISPERED IN MY EAR.
WHAT DID THE BASTARD SAY?
"WITHOUT LOVE THERE IS NO LIFE."
WE'RE GOING TO GET HIM, SHIERA. WE'RE ON HIS HEELS AND WE'RE GOING TO MAKE HATH PAY FOR WHAT HE'S DONE TO US. I PROMISE.
BUT THAT'S NOT GOING TO END THE CURSE, CARTER.
WHAT'S HAPPENING-- WHAT'S WRONG WITH US, CARTER?
NOT SURE... FELT SOMETHING SIMILAR BACK INSIDE THE MUSEUM WHEN WE KISSED...
...I SAW OUR PAST LIVES STANDING IN FRONT OF ME--LIKE THEY WANTED TO TELL ME SOMETHING-- WARN ME--
ARE WE DYING INSIDE...
...IS THE BLACK LANTERN STILL--

RAARGH!
RRRGN!

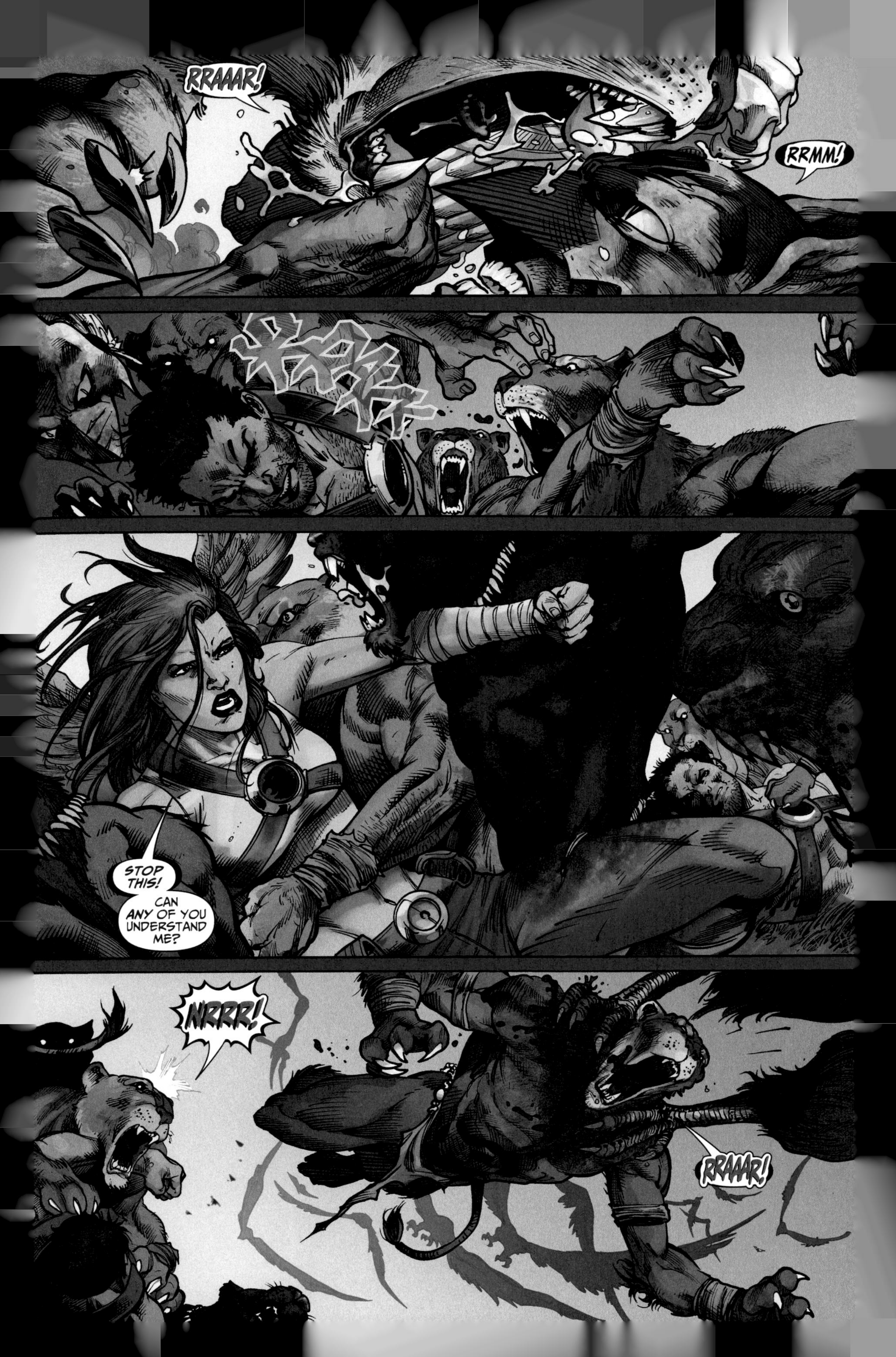
RRAAAR!
RRMM!
KRAK
STOP THIS!
CAN ANY OF YOU UNDERSTAND ME?
NRRR!
RRAAAR!

LOOKS LIKE WE'RE STUCK IN THE *MIDDLE* OF A WAR!
WHOSE SIDE SHOULD WE BE ON?!?
RIGHT NOW, WE'RE ON *OUR*--

AAGH!
CARTER!
SHIERA!
GET YOUR DAMN DIRTY CLAWS OFF ME!
LET HER GO RIGHT--
SKREEEEE!
SKREEEE!
--UGNNN!

UNNFF!
WHERE ARE THEY TAKING HER?!
RRARRR!
SHIERA!
SKREEEEE!
SKOOOM
"DON HALL OF EARTH--"

--WILL NOT RISE.
BOSTON?!

I... I SAW HIM.
WHAT?
YOU SAW WHO? DON? MY BROTHER?

NOT EVERYONE...

...NOT MY SISTER.

BOSTON... YOU SHOULDN'T BE DOING THIS.

SKRUNCH
KRUNCH
SKRUNCH
KRUNCH
HNNN--WHAT THE--
SKRUNCH
KRUNCH
ABOUT TIME YOU WOKE UP.
WHO ARE YOU--? WHERE THE HELL AM I?
WELCOME TO HAWKWORLD. HUMAN
HOPE YOU LAST LONGER THAN YOUR MATE.

MERA, STOP!
NOT UNTIL I KNOW WE HAVEN'T BEEN FOLLOWED.
WE HAVE TO GO BACK AND CLEAN THIS MESS UP WHETHER THEY'RE IN OUR WAY OR NOT.
WHO WERE THEY, MERA?
DID THEY APPEAR WHILE I WAS DEAD AND BURIED? ARE THEY ATLANTEANS?
NO.
THEY HAD WEAPONS MADE OF HARD WATER. LIKE YOUR CONSTRUCTS. ARE THEY FROM YOUR WORLD?
I KNEW THIS DAY WOULD COME. AND THAT THIS FAIRY TALE WOULD END.
WHAT ARE YOU TALKING ABOUT?
ARTHUR...

...I WAS SENT HERE TO KILL YOU.

BRIGHTEST DAY 6
Cover by David Finch, Scott Williams
and Peter Steigerwald

DEAD ZONE

BIG HENDY PARK.
CALIFORNIA.
ALL THE PSYCHOLOGICAL AND PHYSICAL EXPERIENCES SHE HAS YET TO ENCOUNTER CAN BE MINE...
...I WANT THEM...
...I NEED THEM...
HER LIFE SMELLS SO WONDERFUL...
...HER YOUTHFULNESS SIMPLY INTOXICATING.
ENOUGH! YOU HAVE MORE IMPORTANT THINGS TO THINK ABOUT.
THIS MAY BE YOUR LAST CYCLE BEFORE IT PASSES AWAY FOREVER.
J'ONZZ IS BACK AMONG THE LIVING, AND HE IS THE LAST ONE.
DO YOU REALLY THINK NOW IS THE TIME TO DISAPPEAR--SUBMERGE YOURSELF INSIDE THEIR MEAT AGAIN?
BUT I AM STILL SO EMPTY--ALL THOSE YEARS OF LONELINESS--A LIE OF THE MIND TO REMAIN SANE--
WHAT THE HELL--
--OMIGOD--
NOW IS THE TIME YOU MUST RISE AND DO WHAT THE CORE OF YOUR BEING DEMANDS--YOU MUST BE FULFILLED.
AND I WILL BE.
BUT IF I CAN'T HAVE THESE LIVES AT THIS MOMENT, THEN I'LL SIMPLY TAKE THEM.

SINCE YOUR LAST SUBMERSION THERE'S BEEN THE APPEARANCE OF ANOTHER.
SOMEONE WHO MAY CAPTURE HIS ATTENTION--HIS AFFECTIONS--BEFORE WE DO.
THAT WON'T HAPPEN.
HOW CAN YOU BE SO SURE?
BECAUSE I'LL PAY HER A VISIT.

THE REMAINS OF PROFESSOR ERDEL'S LABORATORY.
THERE MUST BE SOME FURTHER EVIDENCE HERE...
...TO HELP CONFIRM MY SUSPICION OF THE KILLER'S IDENTITY BEFORE I--
ALL OF THE OVERGROWN GREEN RETREATS AT MY TOUCH...
...EVERYTHING IN THIS LAB...
...THAT I COME IN CONTACT WITH...

...IS DYING.
"I THINK YOU BROKE IT."

GEORGETOWN.

I DIDN'T BREAK IT.
IT'S NOT GLOWING ANYMORE.
MAYBE IF YOU SHUT UP FOR ONE SECOND, I CAN GET IT TO. I'M TRYING TO CONCENTRATE. LIKE A GREEN LANTERN.
A GREEN LANTERN? YOU'RE NO GREEN LANTERN, BUDDY.
BOSTON'S RING IS OBVIOUSLY DIFFERENT FROM THEIRS, HANK. MAYBE WILLING THE RING TO WORK ISN'T WHAT'S GOING TO GIVE YOU CONTROL OVER IT.

YOU SAY IT'S BEEN TELEPORTING YOU AROUND THE WORLD--
THE UNIVERSE.
AND WHEN IT TOOK ME ON A TOUR OF QWARD TO GET SOME QUALITY FACE-TIME WITH THE ANTI-MONITOR IT REMINDED ME I WAS ALIVE AGAIN--AND THE POINT WAS I'M SUPPOSED TO STAY ALIVE.
OR THE POINT IS YOU NEED TO EMBRACE LIFE AGAIN. WHAT DID YOU ENJOY WHEN YOU WERE LIVING AND BREATHING?
IT'S BEEN SO LONG...

...I DON'T REMEMBER.
THERE HAS TO BE SOMETHING. YOU WERE AN AERIALST, RIGHT?
FOR THE PAYCHECK.
WHAT ABOUT...SOMEONE SPECIAL?

HE LOVED CHEESE-BURGERS.

"HE LOVED CHEESEBURGERS"? WHAT THE HELL DOES THAT HAVE TO DO WITH ANY--?

HOLLY GRANGER
FWAAAASHHHH

YOU SHOULD HAVE LEFT ME ALONE!
GIVE ME THAT RING! TAKE ME TO THE LANTERN!
HOLLY?
NO. GET OFF!

DESPITE WHAT OTHERS HAVE SAID.
FWAAAASHHHH
DEAD ISN'T DEAD.
AAIEEE!

WHAT HAPPENED? WHERE'D DOVE'S SISTER GO?
HOLLY'S GRAVE ISN'T DISTURBED.
HOLLY GRANGER
RIP
BECAUSE SHE DIDN'T REALLY "RISE," DAWN. I THINK IT WAS JUST--
A WARNING.
A WARNING ABOUT WHAT? TRYING TO RAISE THE DEAD?
THAT'S EXACTLY WHAT YOU DID WHEN YOU BROUGHT ME AND DEADMAN BACK, RING! WHY? WHY NOT MY BROTHER? WHY NOT DAWN'S SISTER?
TELL US SOMETHING, DAMMIT!

EAT A CHEESE-BURGER.

UH... **WHAT?**

GGRRRRRR
WHAT'S WRONG WITH ME NOW?

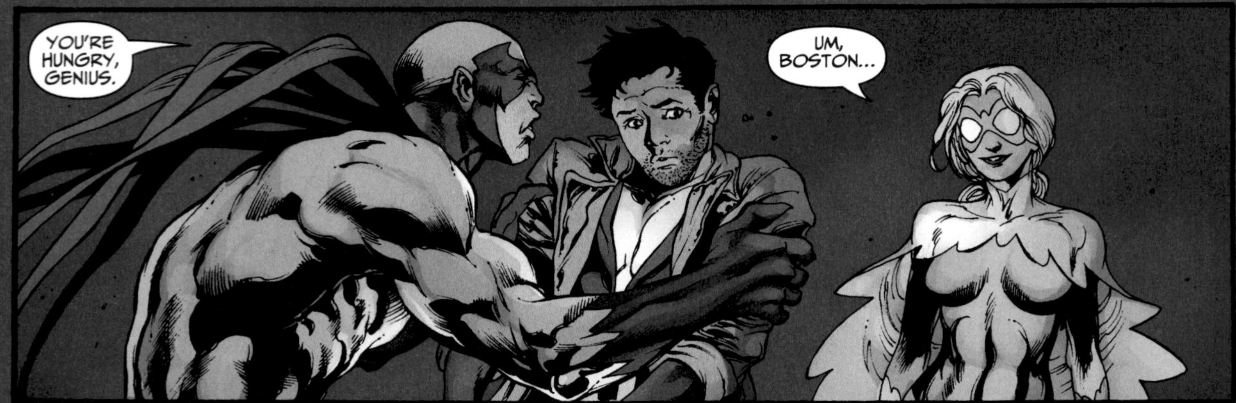
YOU'RE HUNGRY, GENIUS.
UM, BOSTON...

HAVE YOU **EATEN** SINCE YOU'VE BEEN BACK?
ACTUALLY, BEYOND BEING LED AROUND BY THIS RING...

"...I HAVEN'T DONE MUCH OF ANYTHING."
PITTSBURGH UNIVERSITY.
JASON?
JASON, HI. I'M KELLY. FROM THE CHEMISTRY CLUB. I SAT BEHIND YOU LAST WEEK. I BROUGHT THOSE CUPCAKES. YOU DIDN'T WANT ONE, BUT I'M BRINGING CINNAMON ROLLS NEXT TIME.
I WONDERED IF MAYBE YOU WANTED TO STUDY.
WE DON'T HAVE OUR TEST FOR TWO WEEKS.
IT'S NEVER TOO EARLY, IS IT?
THANKS, BUT I STUDY BETTER ALONE.
IF YOU CHANGE YOUR MIND, I'M ON FACEBOOK, OKAY?
OKAY. THANKS.
'BYE.
HEY, JASON?
WHAT?

WHAT'S THE ATOMIC STRUCTURE OF BUBBLE GUM?
THE GIRDERS--?!
WHAT'S HAPPENING TO THEM?!
SOUND THE EMERGENCY ALARM!
OH, NO.
SOMEONE NEEDS TO HELP. SOMEONE...
...ME.
RONNIE.
HUH?
TIME TO WAKE UP, SPORT!

OWWW!!!
FZZHMM
MY HEAD'S KILLING ME. SOMETHING'S WRONG.
THAT'S MY BAD. LATE NIGHT.
ARE YOU HUNG OVER?
I THINK I MIGHT STILL BE DRUNK. MAN, WHY'D YOU DO THIS SO EARLY ON A TUESDAY?
IT'S NOON. AND IT'S WEDNESDAY.
AHHHH!!

WHAT ARE YOU WAITING FOR?! FLY!
WHAT? WHERE?
UP!
I DON'T KNOW HOW IT HAPPENED, BUT...THAT CRANE TURNED INTO BUBBLE GUM. THAT GUY FELL OUT.
YOU MEAN THOSE TWO GUYS.
--WHOOPS.
WHOOPS?!
WHAT ARE YOU WAITING FOR? GO AFTER HIM!
TO THE RIGHT! FLY TO THE RIGHT!
HEY, I GOT THIS. I'VE BEEN FLYING SINCE I WAS FIFTEEN--
OH, YEAH! YEAH!

OKAY, UH, I'M NOT THAT FAST. JUST NEED TO MAKE SOMETHING...A GIANT BOWL OF ICE CREAM?
WHAT'S THE ATOMIC STRUCTURE OF ICE CREAM?
HOW ABOUT AN AIR BAG?
BETTER!
FUMP
IS HE OKAY?
HEY, MAN, ARE YOU... NNGG.
WHAT'S WRONG NOW?
I DON'T FEEL SO--
--HHNNNNNGGH.
AAAHHH

YOU JUST THREW UP ON HIM.
WHAT'S THE ATOMIC STRUCTURE OF MOUTHWASH?
AREN'T YOU GOING TO APOLOGIZE? RONNIE?
HEY!
YOU'RE AN IDIOT, RONNIE!
I'M NOT...
NOT? NOT WHAT?
RONNIE! WHERE ARE YOU GOING?
AWAY. I CAN'T... I CAN'T FLY STRAIGHT...
HOW TOTALLY TRAGIC.
YOU CAN'T HIDE HOW PATHETIC YOU'VE BECOME--
UNNFFF!
--OR HOW FAR YOU'VE FALLEN!

YOU WERE THE YOUNGEST DUDE THE JUSTICE LEAGUE EVER OFFERED MEMBERSHIP TO.
I KNOW.
WHAT DID THEY EVER SEE IN RONNIE RAYMOND BESIDES A KID WHO CAN'T DEAL WHEN THE DEALING GETS TOUGH?
IF YOU STOPPED YELLING AT ME, I COULD FOCUS AGAIN. I COULD BE WHAT EVERYONE TAUGHT ME TO BE. WHAT I WAS. A GOOD GUY. BUT AFTER WHAT I DID...
WHAT YOU DID?
I DON'T WANT TO THINK. ALL I THINK ABOUT IS H-HER. WHAT I DID TO GEHENNA.
RONNIE? YOU REMEMBER IT?
HOW? NO ONE ELSE REMEMBERS WHAT THEY DID WHEN THEY WERE USED BY THE BLACK RINGS--
I CAN'T GET IT OUT OF MY HEAD. SHE WAS SO SCARED AND I'M SO...I'M SO SORRY JASON.
YEAH, HE'S SORRY, JACE. BUT ME? NOT SO MUCH.
WHO SAID THAT?
YOU HEARD THAT?
YEAH.
I THOUGHT I WAS GOING CRAZY.
RONNIE...
...I THINK SOMEONE ELSE IS IN HERE.

"WE NEED TO FIND PROFESSOR STEIN."
SOUTHERN COAST OF THE UNITED STATES.
WHAT ARE YOU TALKING ABOUT?
I WAS SENT HERE TO KILL YOU.
I HEARD YOU THE FIRST TIME, MERA.
ARTHUR, PLEASE... GIVE ME A CHANCE TO EXPLAIN.
WHAT DO YOU THINK I'M DOING?
WE'VE BEEN THROUGH TOO MUCH TOGETHER FOR ME NOT TO.
SO PLEASE, MERA. TELL ME THE TRUTH.
THE TRUTH IS...
...I'VE LIED TO YOU FROM THE VERY FIRST DAY WE MET.

WORLD SEALED OFF FROM THIS ONE.
"IT'S A PENAL COLONY.
"OR THAT'S WHAT IT STARTED OUT AS CENTURIES AGO WHEN A GROUP OF SEPARATISTS WAS BANISHED FROM ATLANTIS DURING ONE OF THEIR MANY CIVIL WARS.
"THOUSANDS WERE SEALED OFF IN THE ATLANTIC BEHIND AN IMPENETRABLE INVISIBLE FIELD.
"FOR CENTURIES, THEY FOUGHT TO ESCAPE WHAT MOST TODAY CALL THE BERMUDA TRIANGLE.
"BUT THEY FAILED.
"MY FATHER, OUR KING, TRAINED ME FROM BIRTH TO BE HIS ULTIMATE WEAPON. TO BE HIS INSTRUMENT OF HATE AGAINST THE ATLANTEANS.
"AND I EMBRACED THAT HATE WITHOUT QUESTION OR HESITATION.
"WHEN A FISSURE IN THE FIELD WAS DISCOVERED A FISSURE THAT WOULD ONLY ALLOW ONE OF US THROUGH BEFORE IT WAS SEALED OFF MY FATHER CHOSE ME.
"HE CHOSE ME TO FIND THE KING OF ATLANTIS AND ASSASSINATE HIM.

"BUT THEN I MET YOU.
"AND I LEARNED THE KING OF ATLANTIS WASN'T ANYTHING LIKE WHAT I HAD BEEN TOLD.

"I DID MY BEST TO BURY WHO I WAS AND WHERE I CAME FROM.
"AND FOR THE FIRST TIME IN MY LIFE...I WAS HAPPY.

"UNTIL BLACK MANTA MURDERED OUR SON.
I BLAMED YOU.
BUT IT WAS AS MUCH MY FAULT AS ANYONE'S.
BLACK MANTA KNEW OF MY PEOPLE, ARTHUR. HE MET THEM BEFORE HE EVER MET AQUAMAN.
OUR CHILD'S DEATH WAS AS MUCH REVENGE ON YOU AS IT WAS ON ME.
THE ONES THAT ATTACKED US ON THE OIL RIG--
XEBEL SOLDIERS. LED BY MY REPLACEMENT AS LEADER OF THE DEATH SQUAD.
SIREN.
"MY YOUNGER SISTER."

I AM RELIEVED TO SEE YOU, LITTLE ONE.
I THOUGHT ANY LIVING ORGANISMS IN CLOSE PROXIMITY TO ME WOULD CONTINUE TO DIE.
BY THE GRACE OF H'RONMEER, THAT IS OBVIOUSLY NOT THE CASE.
BUT THE GREEN MATTER WITHIN A CERTAIN RADIUS OF MY PRESENCE DOES CONTINUE TO DIE UNABATED.
LET'S JUST HOPE ONE OF MY WORST FEARS IS NOT REALIZED.

THE STILL ZONE.

COMPUTER, PLEASE PERFORM A DIAGNOSTIC SECURITY AND ATMOSPHERIC CHECK ON ALL LEVELS OF THIS WHITE MARTIAN MOTHERSHIP.
PRIME CODEWORD REQUESTED.
T'ANN T'AZZ.
CODEWORD CONFIRMED. THANK YOU, J'ONN J'ONZZ.
PROCEEDING WITH DIAGNOSTICS CHECK.
ALL WHITE MARTIANS IN STASIS CHAMBER ACCOUNTED FOR.
STATUS GREEN. ALL SECURITY FULL POWER AT THIS TIME.
EXCELLENT. THANK YOU.

GOTHAM CITY.
THE BATCAVE.
I APPRECIATE YOUR HELPING ME WITH THIS MATTER, MISS GORDON.
I REALIZE IT'S LATE, BUT I RECALLED YOUR HOURS BEING TIED INTO THE NOCTURNAL ACTIVITY OF BIRDS AND BATS.
NOT A PROBLEM, J'ONN, THE NIGHT TIME IS USUALLY THE FIGHT TIME, AND PLEASE, CALL ME BARBARA.
THERE SEEMS TO BE A LOT OF FIREWALLS I NEED TO GO THROUGH, BUT I SHOULD HAVE SOMETHING UP ON THE SCREEN IN JUST A FEW--
AH, HERE IT IS, THERE HAVE BEEN OVER A DOZEN MURDERS THAT FIT THE METHOD OF KILLING YOU DESCRIBED IN DETAIL.
I APOLOGIZE FOR THE GRAPHIC NATURE OF MY REQUEST.
NO NEED TO, J'ONN.
AFTER WHAT MY FATHER AND I WENT THROUGH AT POLICE HEADQUARTERS A FEW MONTHS BACK WITH THOSE HORRIFIC BLACK LANTERNS, NOT MUCH CAN FAZE ME ANYM--
OH, THAT WAS--I APOLOGIZE--I FORGOT THAT YOU WERE--UM--YOUR BODY WAS PUT INTO A DREADFUL SITUATION THAT--
THERE'S NO NEED TO APOLOGIZE EITHER, BARBARA, PLEASE CONTINUE.
OKAY, WELL, THE TIMING OF EACH OF THESE MURDERS STARTS PRETTY SOON AFTER THE DATE YOU GAVE ME FOR YOUR ARRIVAL HERE ON EARTH, AND THE VICTIMS' SKINS HAVE NEVER BEEN ACCOUNTED FOR.
WHY HASN'T THERE BEEN MORE PRESS REGARDING A DECADES-LONG KILLING SPREE?
SUB FILES.
SUB FILES?
YES, THESE ARE CASES BURIED AS DEEP AS A SUBMARINE UNDER THE OCEAN CAN GO, NO PUBLIC SCRUTINY, NEED-TO-KNOW BASIS, VERY HUSH-HUSH.

AND WHY IS THAT?
THESE CASES GET TAGGED THIS WAY WHEN THERE'S A HINT OF META-POWERED INVOLVEMENT, OR WHEN IT SCARES THE FEDS SO BADLY BECAUSE THEY HAVE NO IDEA WHAT THE HELL HAPPENED.
SO THEY COME UP WITH A COVER STORY FOR THE BRUTAL MURDERS.
HOME FIRES, CAR CRASHES, DROWNING--AS YOU CAN SEE ON THE SCREENS, THEY'VE EXPLAINED AWAY ALL THESE DEATHS WITH MUNDANE, EVERYDAY ACCIDENTS THAT CAN BE ACCEPTED BY RELATIVES AND OTHERS MORE EASILY THAN THE ACTUAL OUTCOME.
HMM?
WHAT IS IT, J'ONN?
THE *METHOD* BY WHICH THESE PEOPLE HAVE BEEN KILLED HAS A CERTAIN *RESONANCE*...
A POSSIBLE *PAST* CASE?
I HAVE *NEVER* SEEN ANYTHING LIKE THIS BEFORE, BUT I CANNOT IGNORE THE NAGGING *FAMILIARITY*.
CAN YOU PLEASE CONTACT TITANS TOWER?

TITANS TOWER, THIS IS ORACLE. I HAVE J'ONN J'ONZZ HERE.
WHAT'S UP, ORACLE? HEY THERE, J'ONN, WHAT CAN WE HELP YOU WITH?
HELLO, SUPERBOY. I NEED A TELEPATH OF IMMENSE STRENGTH TO AID ME IN A SITUATION. COULD YOU PLEASE LINK ME IN WITH M'GANN M'ORZZ AT HER CURRENT LOCATION.
MISS MARTIAN'S GONE WALKABOUT.
SHE'S ON THE RESERVE ROSTER--LEFT FOR HER PLACE IN TANAMI, AUSTRALIA TO UNPLUG--GET A LITTLE REST AND RELAXATION BEFORE SHE'S ON ACTIVE DUTY AGAIN.
WALKABOUT?
I'M SENDING OVER A DOC WITH THE LAT AND LONG WHERE SHE'S HOLED UP.
TELL M'GANN TO GIVE US A SHOUT, WE MISS HER. NIGHTY-NIGHT.
I WILL, AND THANK YOU, SUPERBOY.
AND THANK YOU, BARBARA.
YES, I HOPE SO.
IT'S GOOD TO HAVE YOU BACK, J'ONN.
"I HOPE SO"?
THE TANAMI DESERT. AUSTRALIA.

SORRY TO INTRUDE, M'GANN, BUT I HAVE BEEN TRYING TO CONTACT YOU FOR THE LAST SEVERAL HOURS TELEPATHICALLY WHILE EN ROUTE WITH NO--
M'GANN!

BRIGHTEST DAY 7
Cover by David Finch, Scott Williams and Peter Steigerwald

THE SECRET OF LIFE

GEORGETOWN.

ORDER UP!
BIG BELLY BURGER
BIG BELLY BURGER
BIG BELLY BURGER

TWO CHEESEBURGERS WITH THE *WORKS* AND AN EGG SALAD SANDWICH.

THANK YOU.
OH, UH, *THANKS.*
YOU'RE BOTH VERY WELCOME. ENJOY NOW.

WELL?
WELL, WHAT?
THE RING REVEALED YOUR DEEP, DARK SECRET LOVE FOR CHEESEBURGERS.
WHAT ARE YOU WAITING FOR?

HM.

AS GOOD AS YOU REMEMBER?
BETTER ACTUALLY.
THANKS FOR BRINGING ME HERE, DAWN.
HANK SAYS IT'S THE BEST CHEESEBURGER IN TOWN SO YOU CAN THANK HIM.
OH.

SO TELL ME SOMETHING ABOUT YOURSELF.
I, UM, I THINK I'VE TOLD YOU EVERYTHING. USED TO BE DEAD.
NOW I'M NOT.
BEFORE ALL THAT.

MY LIFE WASN'T ANYTHING SPECIAL.
I WASN'T.
EVERYONE'S SPECIAL IN THEIR OWN WAY, BOSTON.

DO YOU THINK THAT RING BROUGHT YOU TO ME FOR A REASON?
A... REASON?
I THOUGHT, MAYBE IT WAS LOOKING FOR HANK, BUT THE VOICE FROM THE RING IS THE SAME VOICE I HEARD WHEN NEKRON WAS ON EARTH.
I THINK I'M CONNECTED TO YOU. TO IT, I MEAN.

I JUST WISH I KNEW WHY IT PICKED ME.
YOU DON'T REALLY SEEM HAPPY TO BE GETTING A SECOND CHANCE AT LIFE.
NEITHER DOES YOUR BOYFRIEND.
HANK'S NOT MY BOYFRIEND. HE'S MY PARTNER.
PARTNER IN WHAT?

"WE WERE GIVEN OUR RESPECTIVE POWERS BY A FORCE FROM BEYOND OUR WORLD.
"HANK BECAME THE AVATAR OF WAR. I BECAME THE AVATAR OF PEACE."
HOW ARE WAR AND PEACE SUPPOSED TO WORK TOGETHER?
SOME HAVE THEORIZED IT'S A GREAT COSMIC EXPERIMENT. OTHERS, LIKE MYSELF, SEE IT MORE AS A FORCE FROM BEYOND GUIDING ME THROUGH A PERSONAL JOURNEY.
I'M HERE TO HELP HANK CONTROL HIS ANGER AND FIND A BALANCE IN HIS LIFE.
AND WHAT'S HAWK DO FOR DOVE IN RETURN?
I PROTECT HER.
I DON'T NEED PROTECTION.
THE JUKEBOX IS BROKEN.
IT WAS JUST PLAYING THE DIXIE CHICKS.
THAT'S WHY I BROKE IT.
LOOK, AS MORONIC AS IT IS THAT THE RING SAID TO "EAT A CHEESEBURGER," HURRY UP AND DO IT.
IT'S OUR ONLY LEAD IN UNRAVELING THE BIG, BAD MYSTERY OF WHY WE'RE BOTH BACK.
I HOPE YOU ENJOYED YOUR MEAL.

SILVER CITY, NEW MEXICO.
BOSTON BRAND OF EARTH.
YOU ARE READY.

JACKSON, LOOK! I TOLD YOU IT WAS WORTH COMING TO SEE THIS THING.
SUPERHEROES!

HEY, YOU STAY AWAY FROM THAT! WE'RE UNDER STRICT ORDERS FROM GREEN LANTERN--
THIS GUY'S WEARING A RING THAT MATCHES THE LANTERN. WE GOT IT COVERED, OFFICERS.
THAT'S ALL WELL AND GOOD, BUT WE SHOULD CALL GREEN LANTERN BEFORE YOU GO ON AND DO ANYTHING.

HAWK, WE DON'T KNOW IF WE CAN TRUST THE... LANTERN.
WELL, LET'S AT LEAST LOOK AT-- NNNGGGHHF.
DAMN THING'S STUCK.

NO. IT'S NOT.
BOSTON, WAIT. WE DON'T KNOW WHAT THIS COULD DO TO YOU.
I NEED TO KNOW, DOVE. I NEED TO KNOW WHY WE'RE BACK.

JACKSON? ARE YOU ALL RIGHT?
I FEEL... WEIRD, MARIA...

"...LIKE I JUST PUT MY FINGER IN AN ELECTRICAL SOCKET."

ALL RIGHT, LANTERN, WHY DID YOU BRING US BACK?

BOSTON BRAND OF EARTH.

YOU NEED TO EMBRACE LIFE.

BOSTON--!
NO! ST-STAY BACK, DOVE.
I NEED TO KNOW... WHO ARE YOU?
I AM THE ENTITY AND I HAVE WATCHED OVER THIS WORLD FROM THE BEGINNING OF EXISTENCE.
BUT I AM DYING.
A REPLACEMENT MUST BE CHOSEN.
EACH ONE OF YOU HAS RETURNED TO PROTECT THIS WORLD UNTIL THE ARRIVAL OF ITS NEW CHAMPION.
AAAHHHH!
HANK HALL OF EARTH.
YES.
TELL ME.

"WHY DID YOU BRING ME BACK?!"
TANAMI DESERT. AUSTRALIA.
M'GANN-- STAY WITH ME-- I NEED YOU TO FOCUS.
FOCUS ON MY VOICE.
...J-J'ONN...
GOOD GIRL.
NOW OPEN YOUR MIND, M'GANN.
FOCUS ON MY THOUGHTS-- HANG ON TO THEM--
--LET THEM GIVE YOU THE STRENGTH TO REGAIN--
UNNN
J'ONN J'ONZZ OF MARS.

BURN IT.
BURN IT DOWN.

"I THINK THERE'S ANOTHER MARTIAN OUT THERE."
PITTSBURGH UNIVERSITY.
I TOLD YOU FORMING FIRESTORM WAS DANGEROUS, RONALD. I TOLD BOTH OF YOU.
A MAN ALMOST DIED, PROFESSOR. WHAT CHOICE DID WE HAVE?
LOOK, TELL HIM I DID IT IF YOU NEED TO.
HE CAN'T BE MAD AT ME FOREVER.
I'M NOT MAD AT EITHER ONE OF YOU. I'M...
WHAT IS IT, PROFESSOR?
SOMETHING'S BOTHERING HIM. ASK HIM--
THIS IS ALL MY FAULT.
WHAT IS? THE VOICE WE'RE HEARING?
THE EXPLOSION. THE PROBLEMS THAT HAVE PLAGUED EACH ONE OF YOU SINCE YOU'VE BECOME BONDED WITH THE FIRESTORM MATRIX.
THE VOICE IS MOST LIKELY A MANIFESTATION OF THE THIRD AND FINAL STAGE OF FIRESTORM...
THIRD AND FINAL STAGE OF FIRESTORM?
WHAT'S THAT MEAN?

I NEED TO SHOW YOU BOTH SOMETHING...AND I HOPE YOU CAN FORGIVE ME--
RONALD RAYMOND OF EARTH, YOU NEED TO STUDY.
WHAT?
AARRGGHHH!
JASON RUSCH OF EARTH, YOU NEED TO GET YOUR HEAD OUT OF THE BOOKS.
LEARN FROM EACH OTHER SO YOU CAN STOP HIM.
THEY CAN'T! HAHAHA!
DON'T LET HIM DESTROY ME.
RONALD?! JASON?!
DID YOU SEE THAT?
I DON'T KNOW...I THINK...
WHOA.
IF YOU THINK YOU CAN HOLD ME IN HERE MUCH LONGER, YOU'RE WRONG!

"SOON I'LL BE FREE TO DESTROY THAT WHITE LANTERN."
HAWKWORLD
WHAT THE HELL ARE YOU TALKING ABOUT?! THERE'S NO SUCH THING AS HAWKWORLD.
I BEG TO DIFFER.
YOU'RE GOING TO BE BEGGING FOR MERCY UNLESS YOU TELL--
THAT'S WHERE YOU ARE, BOY--HAWKWORLD--AND BY THE LOOKS OF THOSE WINGS I'D SAY YOU FIT RIGHT IN HERE.
WHERE IS SHE?
I TAKE IT YOU'RE REFERRING TO THE GIRL WHO WAS SMASHING MY BRETHREN'S HEADS IN.
YOU WERE TRYING TO EAT US.
THAT'S TRUE, POINT TAKEN, AND YOU DIDN'T SHOW ANY ALLEGIANCE TO THE MANHAWKS WHEN THEY ATTACKED SO THAT'S IN YOUR FAVOR AT THE MOMENT.
YOUR WOMAN IS WHERE THEY TAKE EVERYONE, MY WINGED FRIEND--
--UP THERE!
THEN THAT'S WHERE I'M--

CARTER HALL OF EARTH.

UNNN!

DON'T LET THEM LEAVE THIS WORLD.
STOP THE QUEEN.

THAT WHITE LIGHT!
WHO ARE YOU?
DON'T YOU REALIZE, IT IS THE PROPHECY.

HAWKWORLD."
THE NTH CITY.
PREPARE HER FOR THE ARENA!
WE'RE UNDER ORDERS TO GET THOSE WINGS OFF HER!
THEY AREN'T EVEN REAL. SHE'S A PRETENDER.
ZZRAP
AGHHH!
I DON'T NEED WINGS--
SKRAAAAW
--TO TAKE CARE OF YOU!
SHIERA HALL OF EARTH.
NNN!

IF YOUR LOVER DIES HERE, THERE IS NO MORE RESURRECTION.
SAVE HIM FROM HATH-SET.
HAWKGIRL.
HATH...
...THAT LITTLE DEMONSTRATION OF POWER WAS QUITE INTERESTING. THE QUEEN WILL BE VERY PLEASED.
YOUR QUEEN?
WHO THE HELL IS SHE?

"SHE IS THE LOVE OF MY LIFE, AND THE END OF YOURS."
ARTHUR.
I NEVER WANTED TO HURT YOU.
I KNOW, MERA.
AND HONESTLY, IT CHANGES NOTHING BETWEEN US.
WE'VE BEEN THROUGH FAR TOO MUCH TOGETHER.
ARTHUR, WE NEED TO GO TO ATLANTIS. YOU NEED PROTECTION FROM MY SISTER AND HER MERCENARIES.
WHATEVER THEY HAVE PLANNED AGAINST THE SURFACE WORLD GOES *BEYOND* ASSASSINATING YOU--
ARTHUR CURRY OF EARTH.

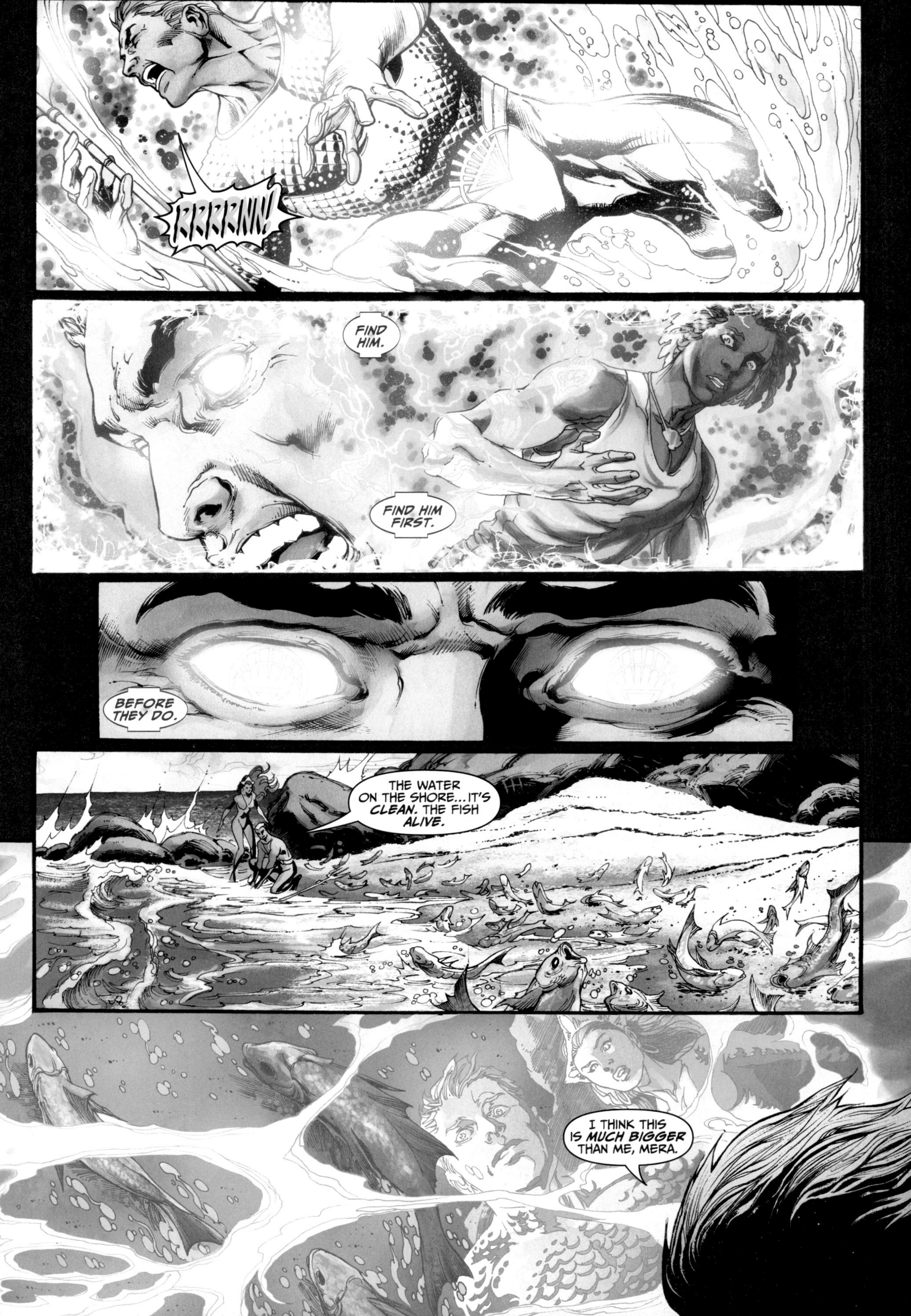
RRRRRNN!
FIND HIM.
FIND HIM FIRST.
BEFORE THEY DO.
THE WATER ON THE SHORE... IT'S CLEAN. THE FISH ALIVE.
I THINK THIS IS MUCH BIGGER THAN ME, MERA.

"I THINK THIS IS AFFECTING EVERYONE."
DIGGER HARKNESS OF EARTH.
THROW THE BOOMERANG AT HER.

JENNIE-LYNN HAYDEN OF EARTH.
BALANCE THE DARKNESS.
YOUR BROTHER WILL SAVE YOUR FRIENDS.

AMON TOMAZ OF EARTH.
FREE THE GODDESS OF NATURE.
FREE YOUR SISTER.
FREE ISIS.

MAXWELL LORD OF EARTH.
MAGOG WILL PLUNGE THIS WORLD INTO WAR.
STOP THE WAR BEFORE IT STARTS.

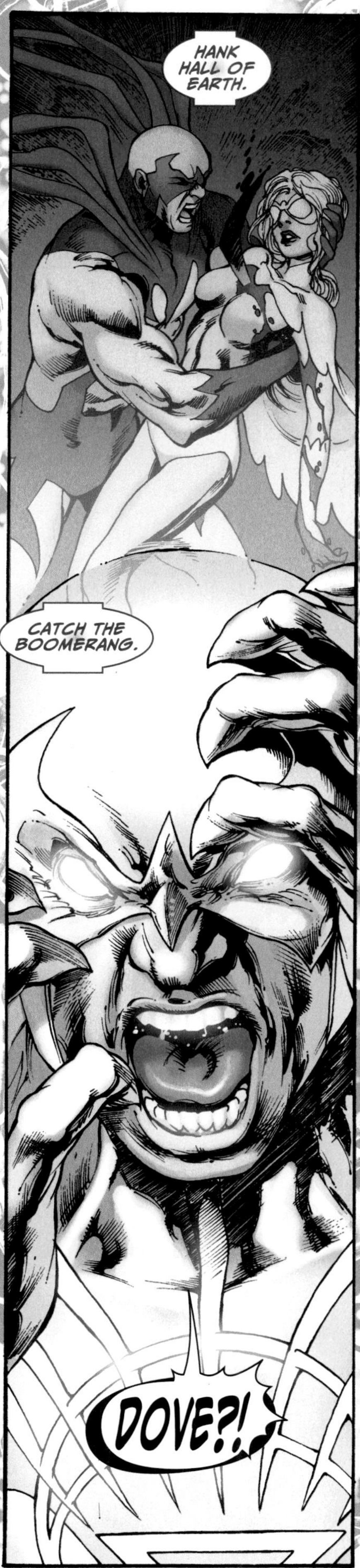

AAARR!

IF YOU WANT TO TRULY LIVE AGAIN, HELP ME.

WHAT DO YOU MEAN IF WE WANT TO "TRULY LIVE"?
LIFE IS A GIFT, BOSTON BRAND.
THE CHOSEN ONE KNOWS THAT BETTER THAN ANYONE.
BUT WHO IS IT? WHO IS... THE CHOSEN ONE?

A NEW PROTECTOR OF EARTH MUST RISE.
AND LIKE EVERY GOOD RING SCANNING FOR A SENTIENT REPLACEMENT, BOSTON BRAND OF EARTH--
--YOU WILL FIND THEM.

BRIGHTEST DAY 8
Cover by David Finch

DEFIANCE

SILVER CITY, NEW MEXICO.
I KNOW WHY WE'RE BACK.
I SAW VISIONS OF EVERYONE.
THAT'S BECAUSE I TOLD YOU, BOSTON BRAND.
MARTIAN MANHUNTER, FIRESTORM, MAXWELL LORD--
WHO'S MAXWELL LORD--?
MAXWELL LORD MUST STOP THE WAR BEFORE IT STARTS.
HOLD UP, DEADMAN. THE LANTERN SAID WE WERE BACK TO HELP THE ARRIVAL OF ANOTHER HERO?!
I'M NOT A PUPPET. I'M NOT BACK TO HELP SOME OTHER GUY.
OR WOMAN.
I'M BACK TO GET A SECOND CHANCE AT WAGING WAR AGAINST CRIME.
MAYBE SO, HAWK. BUT THE WHITE LANTERN NEEDS YOU TO HELP SET THE STAGE FOR SOMEONE ELSE.
I DON'T LIKE IT ANY MORE THAN YOU, BUT IF CARRYING OUT THESE MISSIONS IS THE ONLY WAY TO GET THIS WHITE RING OFF MY FINGER--
--I DON'T HAVE A CHOICE.

WHAT'D THE LANTERN SAY TO YOU, HAWK?
IT SAID I WAS BROUGHT BACK TO PROTECT YOU.
FROM WHAT?
BOSTON, ASK THE RING WHY I NEED PROTECTION.
RING, WHAT'S DOVE NEED PROTECTION FROM?
WE ALL NEED PROTECTION. AND WE NEED A NEW PROTECTOR.
SO START SEARCHING.
AND AS SOON AS I FIND THE "CHOSEN ONE" YOU'LL CUT ME LOOSE, RIGHT? YOU'LL LET ME GET ON WITH...WHATEVER I'M GOING TO GET ON WITH.
IF ANYONE CAN GIVE ME SOME POINTERS ON FINDING THE PERSON WHO'S SUPPOSED TO TAKE MY PLACE, IT'S GREEN LANTERN.
DEADMAN, WAIT--
YOU BOTH HAVE DONE ENOUGH, DOVE. REALLY.
RING, TAKE ME TO HAL JORDAN!
DOVE!
DOVE?

NAMI DESERT, AUSTRALIA.
I WAS DYING-- AND YOU HEALED ME, J'ONN--
--YOU BECAME SOMETHING... BRIGHT... INTENSE...
IT SEEMS I BECAME A WHITE LANTERN.
YEAH, I COULD FEEL YOUR LIGHT BURNING THROUGH ME, BUT IT DIDN'T HURT--I DON'T UNDERSTAND, HOW DID--
THERE ARE MANY QUESTIONS THAT NEED ANSWERS SINCE MY... RESURRECTION, BUT RIGHT NOW THE MOST IMPORTANT ONE IS--
WHO DID THIS TO YOU, M'GANN?
A MARTIAN.
YOU ARE THE ONLY WHITE MARTIAN LEFT ON THE PLANET. I CHECKED THE STASIS CHAMBER IN THE STILL ZONE, ALL THE WHITE MARTIANS ARE ACCOUNTED--
NO. SHE WAS A GREEN MARTIAN, J'ONN.
THAT'S NOT POSSIBLE-- WHOEVER IT WAS MUST HAVE MANIPULATED THEIR FORM TO DECEIVE--
IT WAS NO TRICK, J'ONN-- I PENETRATED HER THOUGHTS BEFORE SHE BLOCKED ME OUT.
I AM THE LAST OF MY KIND. THE PLAGUE WIPED OUT EVERYONE. THE ONLY ANSWER IS THAT ANOTHER WHITE MARTIAN MUST HAVE ELUDED THE JLA AND ASSIMILATED ITSELF INTO THE POPULATION. BUT WHY LIE DORMANT FOR SO LONG--
I'M OPENING MYSELF TO YOU-- MY MIND IS YOURS, J'ONN.
BE ME...
...AND SEE WHAT YOU CAN SEE...

DID YOU REALLY THINK YOU COULD HIDE FROM ME, GIRL?
WHO ARE YOU?!

IS THAT YOUR IDEA OF TRYING TO GET INSIDE MY MIND?
YOU SHOULD BE ASHAMED OF YOURSELF. YOU DISHONOR YOUR MARTIAN HERITAGE WITH SUCH A COARSE PSYCHIC INTRUSION.
A MARTIAN TODDLER COULD TRAIPSE ACROSS MY MINDSCAPE WITH MORE FINESSE THAN YOU DEMONSTRATE HERE TODAY.
HERE, LET ME SHOW YOU HOW IT'S DONE.
AAGHHH!
AH, SENT FROM MARS BY ROCKET TO THE VEGA SYSTEM TO ESCAPE THE CIVIL WAR BETWEEN THE GREENS AND WHITES, WERE YOU?
...G-GET OUT OF M-MY H-HEAD...
AND THIS PLACE--THIS "OUTBACK" AS YOU CALL IT--MAKES YOU FEEL COMFY, HMM, REMINDS YOU OF HOME AND ALL THAT YOU LEFT BEHIND?
WELL, LET ME REMIND YOU THAT--
WAIT--IT'S ALL A LIE!
YOU'RE A LIE!
YOU DARE POSE AS A GREEN, WHEN ALL YOU ARE IS A WARMONGERING--
--AND LOATHSOME--
--VILE--
WHITE MARTIAN!

DID YOU REALLY THINK HIDING UNDER THIS DISGUISE MAKES YOU WORTHY OF HIS ATTENTION?
YOU AND J'ONN WOULD HAVE AS MUCH IN COMMON PSYCHICALLY AND PHYSICALLY AS THIS ROCK!
YOU AND YOUR KIND COULD NEVER BE A TRUE COMPANION! YOU WILL NEVER GIVE HIM WHAT A TRUE GREEN MARTIAN CAN!
YOU ARE BENEATH ME...
...YOU ARE BENEATH US.
I LEAVE YOU TO DIE HERE ALONE!
NO.
IT'S TRUE.
BY THE GRACE OF H'RONMEER...
...THERE IS ANOTHER GREEN MARTIAN...

"...I AM NOT THE LAST."
HAWKWORLD.
WHERE ARE WE GOING?
YOU SAID YOU WANTED TO KNOW EVERYTHING THERE IS TO KNOW, SO THAT'S WHERE WE'RE GOING.
HE IS THE LIGHT.
I SAW SOMETHING-- A CITY OF GREEN, A FOREST, BEING RIPPED INTO THE AIR--!
HE IS THE ONE.
ENOUGH, DAMMIT! I AM NOT A GOD-- I HAVE NO IDEA WHAT HAPPENED BACK THERE!
YOU SURE ABOUT THAT, EARTHMAN?
IT'S NOT EVERY DAY WE GET A VISITOR HERE WHO SUDDENLY ERUPTS WITH BRIGHT WHITE LIGHT AND HEALS EVERYONE AROUND HIM.
AT LEAST I TAKE IT FROM YOUR TONE YOU BELIEVE ME.
I DON'T BELIEVE IN GODS. I JUST BELIEVE IN ME.
I AM TONRARR, THE LEADER OF THIS LIONMANE PRIDE.
"LIONMANE," I'VE MET YOUR KIND BEFORE.
WHERE?
ON THE OTHER SIDE OF THE GATEWAY.
IMPOSSIBLE, NO PRIDE MEMBERS HAVE EVER LEFT HAWKWORLD.
SOMEONE HAS. OR SOMEONE LIKE YOU.

I NEED TO FIND SHIERA AND FIND OUT WHAT THE HELL THAT VISION MEANT.
WATCH OUT.
SKRAK
THIS IS WHAT WORKING IN THE NTH METAL MINES GETS YOU.
AFTER YOU'RE KIDNAPPED YOU'RE SENT TO SLAVE AWAY REMOVING NTH ORE. WHEN YOU'RE TOO WEAK TO CONTINUE YOU'RE TOSSED AWAY LIKE GARBAGE.

THE *ONES ABOVE* ALWAYS THROW THE BODIES *HERE* TO MAKE A POINT.
THESE *STATUES*-- WHO ARE THEY?
THEIR TRUE NAMES ARE LOST TO THE AGES...

FOLLOW ME.
WHERE?
INTO THE LEG.

I GIVE YOU... THE HISTORY OF HAWKWORLD.
THIS CAVE DRAWING AND THE ORAL HISTORY PASSED FROM GENERATION TO GENERATION IS ALL THAT REMAINS OF IT.
BUT WHAT WE DO KNOW IS THAT HAWKWORLD IS A BRIDGE BETWEEN PLANETS. EARTH AND THANAGAR.
HUMANS FROM YOUR WORLD CAME HUNDREDS OF THOUSANDS OF YEARS AGO--THEY PEACEFULLY COEXISTED WITH EVERY RACE HERE FOR EONS... EXCEPT THE HAWKS.
THE TRUST BETWEEN THE EARTHLINGS AND THE HAWKS WAS STRAINED--
--AND ONLY MADE WORSE WHEN NTH METAL WAS DISCOVERED BY THE EARTHLINGS. THEY COVETED IT-- ESPECIALLY THE ABILITY TO FLY.

...AND LEFT THIS ONE IN CHAOS FOR ANOTHER HUNDRED THOUSAND YEARS ALONG WITH THE HIDDEN SECRETS OF THE NTH METAL UNDER OUR FEET.
THEN AS THE STORY GOES, SUDDENLY, ONE DAY, ANOTHER EARTHLING APPEARED, A FEMALE, WHO TOOK COMPLETE CONTROL OF THE MANHAWKS AND BUILT AND RAISED THE NTH CITY INTO THE CLOUDS.

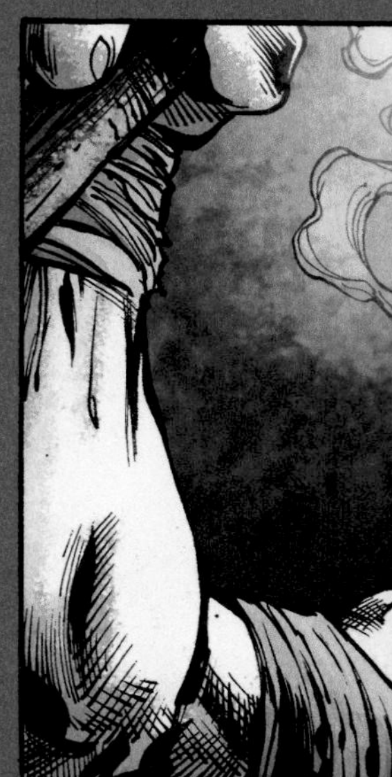

AH, WE HAVE ARRIVED.

WINGS MEANT ***POWER.*** THE HUMANS EMBRACED THE IDEA PUT FORTH BY A SMALL GROUP OF EARTHLINGS THAT THEY WERE MEANT TO RULE BY BIRTHRIGHT.

SO THAT'S WHAT THEY DID USING FEAR AND FORCE, THEY GOVERNED US BY TURNING ALL THE RACES AGAINST EACH OTHER TO KEEP US FROM UNITING AND REBELLING.

BUT AS TIME PASSED SOME OF THE HUMANS GREW TIRED OF WAGING A NEVER-ENDING WAR. THEY ALLOWED THE BLOODLINES TO MERGE, AND THAT WAS WHEN THE SECRET PORTAL TO THANAGAR WAS DISCOVERED.

IT GAVE THE RESTLESS ONES A NEW CAUSE. ARMED WITH NTH METAL AND LOYAL BLOOD-RELATIVE MANHAWKS IN TOW, THEY RACED TO CONQUER A NEW WORLD...

IT IS THERE, TO THIS DAY, THAT THIS QUEEN SHRIKE SUPPOSEDLY STILL RESIDES FOR OVER TWO THOUSAND YEARS--

BRING OUT THE HEALER!
BRING OUT THE HEALER!
BRING OUT THE HEALER!
SOUNDS LIKE OUR HISTORY LESSON IS BEING CUT SHORT.

YES, IT SEEMS WORD HAS SPREAD QUICKLY OF YOUR ARRIVAL...
...AND A WORLD OF OPPRESSED SOULS WANTS YOU TO SHINE YOUR LIGHT ON THEM.
NO. I DON'T SEE OPPRESSED SOULS, TONRARR...

...I SEE AN ARMY.
"TAKE HER WINGS."

HIGH ABOVE THE CLOUDS OF HAWKWORLD.
THE NTH CITY.
BACK THE HELL OFF!

HNNFF!
I HAVE TO ADMIT, I FELT CHEATED THAT THOSE BLACK LANTERNS HAD THE PLEASURE OF HEARING YOUR DEATH RATTLE INSTEAD OF ME.
YOU WANT ME TO FIGHT FOR YOUR QUEEN'S AMUSEMENT, HATH-SET?

YES.
FINE.
BUT LET'S MAKE THIS FIGHT BETWEEN YOU--
--AND ME!

SO YOU'RE HATH-SET'S GIRLFRIEND?
WHO ARE YOU?
SHE IS KNOWN IN HAWKWORLD AS QUEEN SHRIKE.
AND SHE HAS RULED THIS PATHWAY BETWEEN EARTH AND THANAGAR FOR CENTURIES.
I'VE LEFT YOU AND HAWKMAN A TRAIL OF CRUMBS, AND LIKE THE HUBRISTIC BIRDS YOU ARE, YOU FOLLOWED THEM STRAIGHT HERE.
ONCE I CAPTURE YOUR BRUTE OF A MATE, EVERYTHING WILL BECOME CLEAR.
I DON'T CARE WHAT YOU'RE HERE TO DO OR WHAT YOU WANT WITH US, HATH.
THIS TIME YOU DIE FIRST!

SHRAK
SHIERA.
I ALWAYS SAID YOU HAVE YOUR FATHER'S RAGE.

AND YOUR MOTHER'S RESOLVE.
MOTHER?!
SKLANG
...THE BRIGHT LIGHT MY DAUGHTER BATHED US IN WAS QUITE TANTALIZING, HATH.
I NOTICED THAT EVEN THE ANCIENT SCAR ON MY BODY HAS COMPLETELY DISAPPEARED.
YES, MY QUEEN, OLD WOUNDS HEALED...
"...AND NEW ONES TO INFLICT."

TIME IS OF THE ESSENCE--HER *PSYCHIC DEFENSES* MAY BE DOWN--WE MUST *JOIN* OUR MINDS AND LOCATE A TELEPATHIC SIGNATURE THAT COULD GIVE US A LEAD.

TANAMI DESERT.

ARE YOU UP TO THIS, M'GANN?

YOU BET I AM, J'ONN.

FOCUS THEN-- ACROSS THE GLOBE-- HUNT FOR ANY *TELEPATHIC ANOMALY* THAT INDICATES A DEPARTURE FROM THE NORM.

I THINK I SENSE SOMETHING...
YES, I'VE LOCKED ON IT ALSO.
THERE'S A *TELEPATHIC BLACK HOLE*...

"...IN THE CENTER OF...
"...STAR CITY."

BRIGHTEST DAY 9
Cover by David Finch

LOST & FOUND

THE ATLANTIC.
THE WHITE LIGHT GAVE YOU A VISION--
OF A BOY I'VE NEVER SEEN BEFORE. WITH SOME KIND OF EEL TATTOO SPIRALING AROUND HIS ARM.
EEL TATTOO? ARTHUR, I--
HELLO, AQUAMAN.
MMMFF!
AHHH--!
I ASK FOR THE RING TO TAKE ME TO GREEN LANTERN AND IT DUMPS ME UNDERWATER?
DO YOU REMEMBER CAMP BRIGHTON, BOSTON?
WHAT?

YOU USED TO LOVE SWIMMING.
I THOUGHT I WAS GETTING THE HANG OF USING THIS RING, BUT IT'S STILL GOT A MIND OF ITS OWN. I MEAN, NO OFFENSE, AQUAMAN, BUT I'M NOT EXACTLY SURE WHY IT BROUGHT ME TO YOU INSTEAD OF GREEN LANTERN.
MAYBE IT WASN'T JUST ME YOU WERE DRAWN TO, DEADMAN. THE OIL SPILL SEEMS LIKE SOMETHING A PROTECTOR OF EARTH WOULD BE DRAWN TO.
OR MAYBE THIS IS WHY EARTH NEEDS ANOTHER PROTECTOR?
THOSE WERE THE EXACT WORDS THE RING USED, DOVE?
CLOSE, I'D GUESS. THE GIST OF IT WAS THAT DEADMAN, AQUAMAN, HAWK AND ALL THE OTHERS WERE RESURRECTED TO PLAY A PART IN PREPARING FOR THE ARRIVAL OF SOMEONE ELSE.
MAYBE IT WAS THAT GUY YOU SAW IN YOUR VISION?
HAWK'S WAS.
BUT YOU SAID ALL THE VISIONS WERE DIFFERENT.
WHAT DID YOU SEE, DEADMAN?
NOTHING. LOOK, I JUST WANT WHOEVER THIS OTHER HERO IS--
--AND I'M GUESSING IT'S THE PERSON WHO'S SUPPOSED TO BE WEARING THIS RING--TO STEP UP AND TAKE IT--
NOT UNTIL THE TWELVE DO WHAT THEY'VE BEEN ASKED TO DO.
THEN THAT'S WHAT WE DO. DEADMAN, YOU GO TO EVERYONE AND TELL THEM WHAT YOU'VE TOLD US.
BUT--
IF THERE'S SOMEONE ELSE OUT THERE MEANT FOR THAT RING, WE NEED TO FIND THEM.
THE WORLD NEEDS ALL THE HEROES IT CAN GET.
IN THE MEAN-TIME, I NEED TO FIND THIS BOY.
ARTHUR...
...I KNOW WHO HE IS.

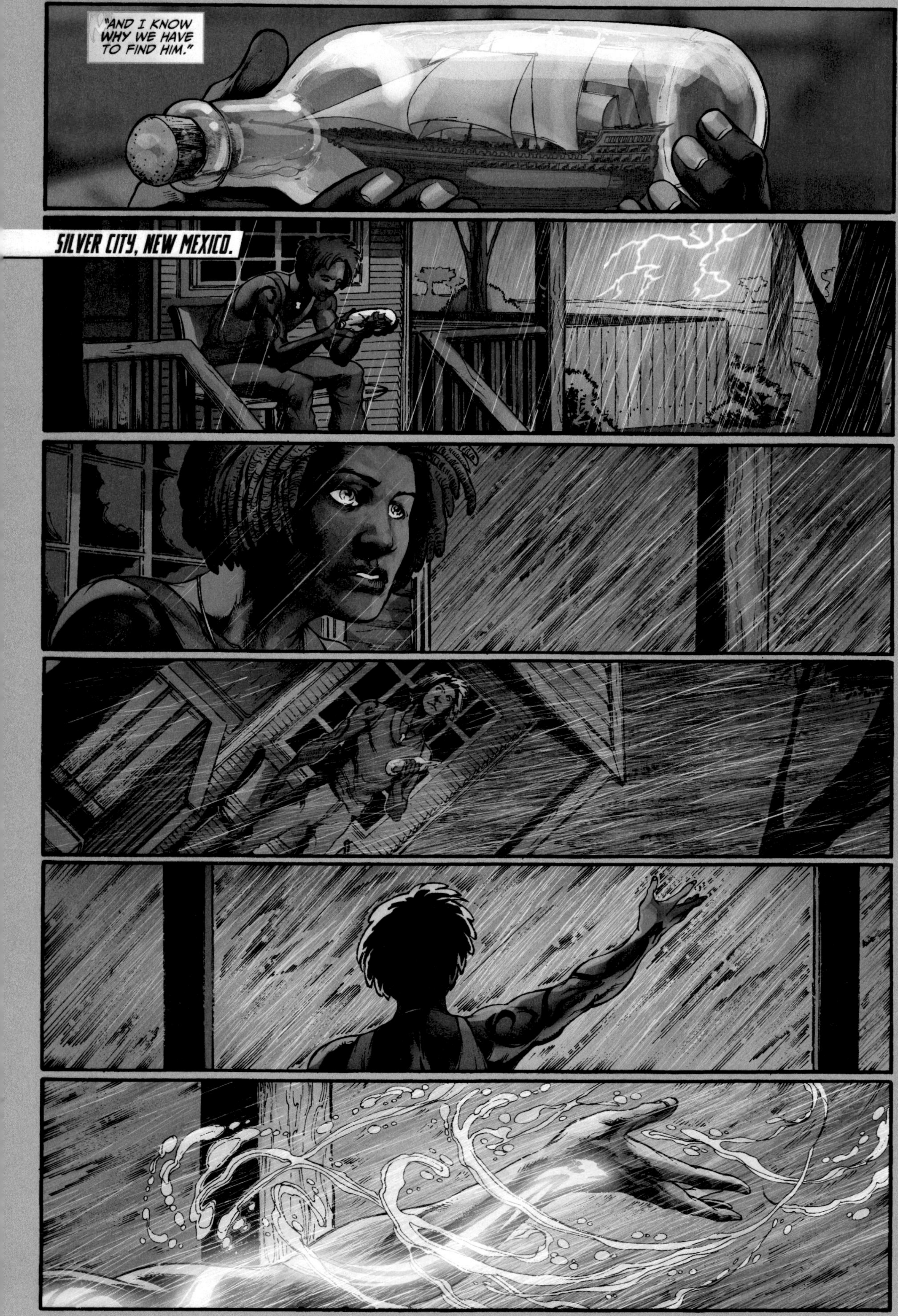

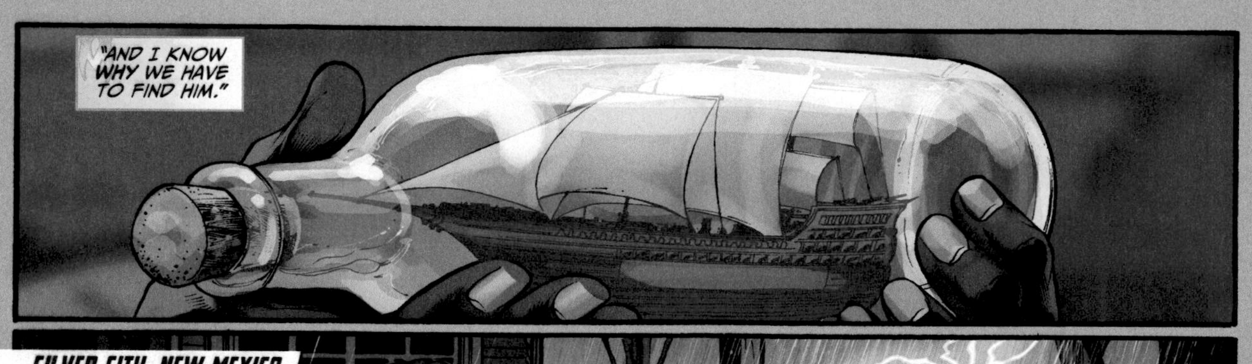

"AND I KNOW WHY WE HAVE TO FIND HIM."

SILVER CITY, NEW MEXICO.

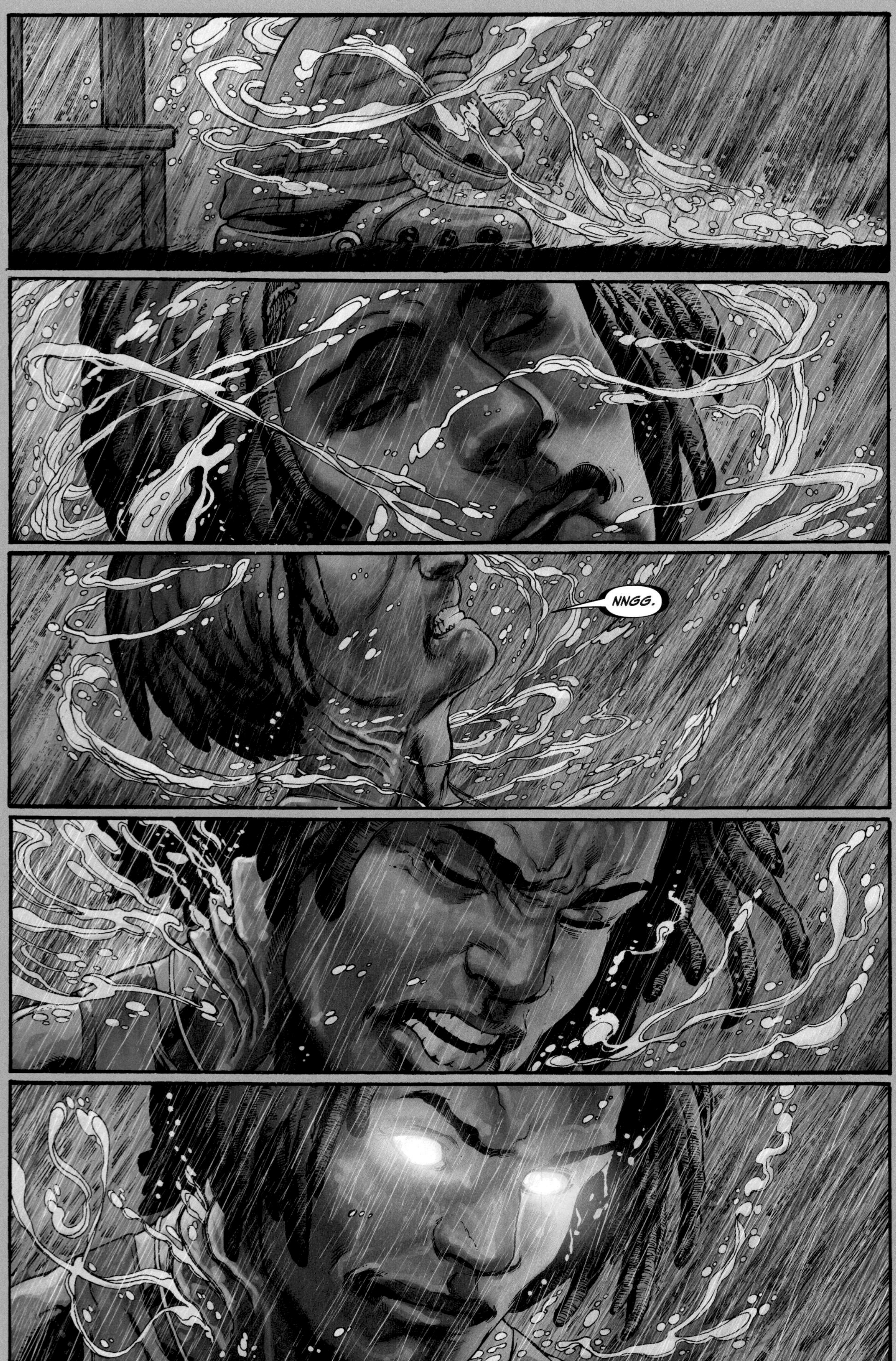
NNGG.

JACKSON!

KRRKKSHH

JACKSON, WHAT ARE YOU DOING?
NO ONE WAS AROUND, DAD. I--
SON, YOU *KNOW* WE CAN'T TAKE RISKS LIKE THIS. YOU *KNOW* THAT.
I...

YOUR MOTHER AND I DON'T WANT TO LOSE YOU.
YOU *WON'T*, DAD.
JACKSON, IT'S NOT THAT SIMPLE.
WE *LOVE* YOU.

I...I'M SORRY, DAD. I'VE BEEN FEELING SO *PENT UP*.
I FEEL LIKE I'M GOING TO EXPLODE, BUT...

...I WON'T DO IT AGAIN.
OKAY, SON.
OKAY.

BUT I THINK IT'S TIME.
TIME FOR *WHAT*, DAD?

"TIME FOR THE TRUTH."

STAR CITY.

ASTOUNDING.

SIMPLY ASTOUNDING.

BUT IF THE ***VISION*** I WAS GIVEN BY THE ***WHITE LANTERN*** IS CORRECT...

...I WILL HAVE TO ***BURN*** DOWN THIS PLACE OF MIRACULOUS GROWTH...

...TO ***DESTROY*** THE ONLY OTHER ***GREEN MARTIAN*** LEFT IN THE UNIVERSE.

BUT THERE IS NO WAY I WILL ALLOW MYSELF TO BE CONTROLLED BY SOMETHING I DO NOT COMPLETELY UNDER--

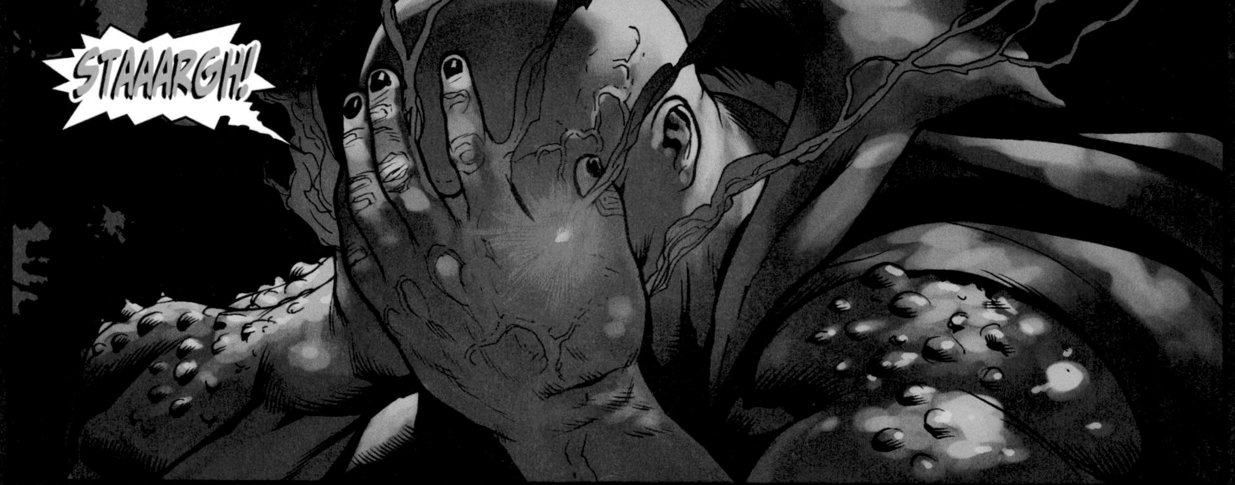

ELSEWHERE.
REMEMBER, SHOPPERS, A HALF GALLON OF NICKY'S VANILLA FUDGE TWIRL IS ON SALE FOR A SPECIAL BONUS CLUB PRICE OF $1.99!
FINEST MEATS
HEY, MOMS! DON'T GO HOME WITHOUT CHECKING YOUR BABY BUCKS ACCOUNT!
WE HAVE A WIDE VARIETY OF PRODUCTS ON SALE THIS WEEK FROM DINO DIAPERS TO LULU'S BABY FOOD!
WE'RE PROUD OF OUR NEW EXPANDED ORGANIC FOOD SECTION! DON'T FORGET TO STOP BY AND TAKE A LOOK!

WHAT YOU EAT!"
--TELEPATHY --CAN'T CONTROL--
--CACOPHONY-- OF THOUGHTS--
--FROM ACROSS THE EARTH--
THE GREEN MUST DIE.
--BOMBARDING ME--
--RAINING ON ME--
--EVERYONE--
YOU MUST BURN IT AWAY.
--EVERYONE WANTS SOMETHING--
--WANTS NOTHING--
--WANTS SOMEONE--
YOU HAVE RETURNED FOR A REASON.
RRARGHHH
--TO SAVE--TO BE SAVED--
--TO KILL--TO BE KILLED--
--TO LOVE--TO BE LOVED--
--TO HATE--TO BE HATED--
YOU HAVE RETURNED FOR A PURPOSE.
YOU'RE A BIG FELLA.

--AND I LIKE BIG TARGETS!
THIS PLACE CONTINUES TO HAVE PLENTY OF SURPRISES.
GREEN ARROW A.K.A. OLIVER QUEEN.
Powers: Master archer and highly trained martial artist.
AARGHH!
SHUNK
SHUNK
YOU MUST CHOOSE.
CHOOSE LIFE.
CHOOSE DEATH.
ISOLATION.
DESOLATION.
UNNN!
FWAM

TRAAAGH!
UNN...DAMN TREE'S...DRAWING ALL KINDS OF ATTENTION...
FOCUS.
FOCUS YOUR THOUGHTS.
AHHLLIEE...
DO NOT DEVIATE.
ASSUME CONTROL.
J'ONN?
IS THAT YOU?
EMBRACE ME.
EMBRACE YOU.
LET LIFE WIN.
LET DEATH WIN.
THIS IS NOT THE GREEN YOU WILL BURN.
THIS IS NOT THE FOREST YOU WILL RAZE.
--LIFE--
--LIFE ON MARS--
--LIFE--
--ON--
--MARS--
--LOVE--
--ON--
--MARS--

HOLES IN SOULS.
--SOULS IN HOLES--
CLIMB OUT.
HERE AT SHOPPERS' DELIGHT WE ALWAYS APPRECIATE YOUR BUSINESS AND YOUR FEEDBACK!
YAAAGH!
YAAAGH!
...I DID IT... I BROUGHT MARS TO LIFE...
...BUT AT WHAT COST?...
...FORSAKE EARTH, J'ONN...
BRING IT BACK...BRING MARS BACK FOR US...
TAKE HOLD.
LET GO.
--WAKE UP--
DREAM THE DREAM.
--LOVE IS VENGEANCE--
--VENGEANCE IS LOVE--

...MARS... IT'S ALIVE...
DROP A SUGGESTION INTO THE MANAGER'S BOX AND AUTOMATICALLY ENTER YOURSELF TO WIN A ROMANTIC GETAWAY FOR TWO TO BERMUDA COURTESY OF POSEIDON CRUISES!

AND DON'T FORGET OUR SALE ON NEW DOUBLE-STUFF CHOCOS!
REMEMBER, LADIES, THE WAY TO A MAN'S HEART IS THROUGH HIS STOMACH!
GET CHOCO YUM
$3.99! SALE

WHAT THE HELL'S HAPPENING, J'ONN?!?

WHY ARE YOU DOING THIS?!?

GET AWAY FROM THE TREE!
YOU'RE KILLING IT--
I AM JOHN JONES!
YOU ARE NOT JOHN JONES.
--YOU'RE KILLING EVERYTHING--
I AM JOSH JOHNSTONE!
YOU ARE NOT JOSH JOHNSTONE.
--YOU'RE DESTROYING THE WHOLE DAMN FOREST!
I AM A BLACK LANTERN!
YOU ARE NOT A BLACK LANTERN.
FIGURED THIS TREE MIGHT NEED SOME PROTECTING--
--JUST NEVER THOUGHT IT'D HAVE TO BE FROM AN OLD FRIEND!
YOU ARE J'ONN J'ONZZ, THE MARTIAN MANHUNTER.
SORRY TO GO ALL "RET OF THE JED J'ONN--
--BUT I KNOW YOU CAN TAKE IT!

HEY, WHITE LANTERN TREE OF LIGHT!
BOOOOM
KOOOM
IF YOU GOT ANY MAGIC THAT COULD HELP ME LIFT A THREE HUNDRED AND FIFTY POUND MARTIAN YOU MIGHT WANT TO TOSS SOME MY WAY--
--OTHERWISE THIS WHOLE FOREST IS GOING TO BE TOAST!

KRAKKK
C'MON, DAMN IT-- WAKE UP, J'ONN!
I COULD USE A LITTLE HELP HERE!
SKRAK
THEN MIGHT I SUGGEST LETTING GO OF MY ARMS, OLLIE...

...SO WE CAN EFFECT A NEW STRATEGY.
WHICH IS WHAT EXACTLY?

KROOOM
SKRASHH
TO RUN OUT OF HERE AS FAST AS WE CAN.

HELLUVA PLAN THERE, J'ONNY BOY!
SO MUCH FOR LIVING UP TO YOUR JLA MASTER TACTICIAN STATUS!
THAT TREE OF LIGHT WITH THE WHITE LANTERN SYMBOL--WHAT DO YOU KNOW ABOUT IT?!

NOT MUCH--EXCEPT THAT IT MAY HAVE SOMETHING TO DO WITH SCREWING UP THE POWERS OF ANYONE WHO ENTERS THIS FOREST!
ONCE I LANDED HERE IT WAS AS IF MY MIND AND BODY WERE AT *WAR* WITH EACH OTHER!--THATS WHY I'M UNABLE TO FLY AT THE MOMENT.
YEAH, TELL ME SOMETHING I DON'T ALREADY KNOW!

THE SAME WHITE LANTERN THAT RESURRECTED ME ALSO SPOKE TO ME HOURS AGO-- SHOWED ME A *VISION* OF A FOREST ENGULFED IN FLAMES--AND *I* WAS THE ONE *BURNING* IT DOWN.
SO YOU WHAT, ROLLED SOME DICE AND PICKED *THIS* FOREST?!
SKKRRRKKOOOMM

IT WAS THE *ONLY* SPOT ON EARTH, OLIVER, WITH A *TELEPATHIC BLACK HOLE* THAT I--
COULDN'T READ ANY MINDS IN SO YOU MADE IT A DAMN TARGET!
IT IS NOT THE FOREST FROM THE VISION--THAT IS WHAT THE WHITE LANTERN SYMBOL ON THE TREE *REVEALED* TO ME--I HAVE NO INTENTION OF DESTROYING IT NOW!
SURE AS HELL DOESN'T LOOK THAT WAY TO ME!

SINCE MY RETURN IT SEEMS I BRING A CERTAIN LEVEL OF TOXICITY TO ALL PLANT LIFE IN MY IMMEDIATE VICINITY.
THAT'S A DAMN GOOD REASON TO FINALLY GET YOUR GREEN-PLAGUED ASS--
--OUT OF MY FOREST RIGHT NOW!
FASCINATING. COMPLETE REGENERATION.
UNFREAKING-BELIEVABLE.
AND MY TELEPATHIC POWERS ARE ONCE AGAIN BACK TO NORMAL.
THAT'S GOOD TO HEAR, BUT FEEL FREE TO HOLD OFF ON PAYING ME ANY VISITS UNTIL YOU FIX THIS KILLING ALL PLANT LIFE THING, J'ONN.
OF COURSE. THE SOLITUDE OF SUCH A BEAUTIFUL PLACE CAN BE QUITE TEMPTING. I WOULD NEVER WILLFULLY JEOPARDIZE SOMETHING YOU HOLD SO DEAR, OLIVER.
GET OUT OF MY HEAD, J'ONN--YOU KNOW I HATE IT WHEN YOU USE YOUR TELEPATHIC--
I WAS NOT IN YOUR HEAD. IT WAS AN OBVIOUS OBSERVATION OF BOTH OF OUR... SITUATIONS.

I HAVE BEEN GIVEN A SECOND CHANCE AT LIFE...
...AND I HARDLY BELIEVE IT WAS SO THAT I COULD HIDE AWAY FROM THE REST OF THE WORLD.
I HOPE THAT TREE HUG CAN HELP YOU MORE WITH THE VISIONS YOU'RE HAVING.
IT DID.
I AM GOING BACK.
BACK WHERE?
HOME.

MNESTY BAY.
WHERE IS HE?
THOMAS CURRY R.I.P.
WHERE IS YOUR SON?
KRAKKSKHH
LOOKING FOR AQUAMAN?
sktch

WE'RE LOOKING FOR YOU.
RRAGH!
KRAZZZZTTT
WHO ARE YOU?

THE WARNINGS ABOUT YOU WERE EXAGGERATED, SURFACE DWELLER.
YOU CUT EASY.
YAAAARR!
AND YOU--
YAAAA
--BURN EASY!

YOU'RE FISH.
FISH COME OUT OF THE WATER AND THEY DIE.
SPLTCHHH
ENOUGH.
IT'S BEEN A LONG TIME DAVID.

WE'RE NOT HERE TO RESTART OUR WAR. WE NEED TO WORK TOGETHER.
WE NEED TO FIND YOUR SON.

BRIGHTEST DAY 10
Cover by David Finch
FINCH

A CHANGE IS GONNA COME

PITTSBURGH UNIVERSITY.
THE LABORATORY OF PROFESSOR MARTIN STEIN.
I'M TESTING A THEORY.
CAN YOU AND RONALD TRANSMUTE THAT FOOTBALL?
INTO WHAT?
WHAT DID YOU HAVE IN MIND?
HOW ABOUT A GLOBE OF THE EARTH? A PLASTIC GLOBE?
PLASTIC? SURE, I CAN--
FZZZZMM
WHAT'S GOING ON? I KNOW THIS.
OF COURSE, YOU DO, JASON--
--BUT DOES RONALD?

DO I KNOW THE MOLECULAR STRUCTURE OF PLASTIC?
I'D GATHER YOUR POWERS AREN'T FULLY FUNCTIONAL BECAUSE THEY'RE NOW BEING FUELED BY THE MIND IN CONJUNCTION WITH THE BODY. SO WHATEVER RONALD KNOWS, OR IN SOME CASES DOESN'T--
I'M GUESSING "NO."
SOME CASES?
PLASTIC IS BAD FOR THE ENVIRONMENT ANYWAY.
HEY, HOW ABOUT WATER? I KNOW WATER!
FZAM
WHY WOULD THE POWERS CHANGE?
THE FIRESTORM MATRIX BONDED WITH RONALD MUCH MORE THAN IT EVER DID MYSELF. IN A WAY IT EVEN REJECTED ME, TRANSFORMING ME BRIEFLY INTO A FIRE ELEMENTAL. MAYBE TO DISTANCE ME FROM RONALD. IT SAW SOMETHING IN HIM...
...AND THEN THE MATRIX SAW SOMETHING IN YOU TOO, JASON, DIDN'T IT? IT CHOSE YOU.
AND NOW THAT THE MATRIX IS FULLY BONDED TO YOU BOTH, FIRESTORM IS GOING THROUGH YET ANOTHER METAMORPHOSIS. A FINAL STAGE, I MENTIONED.
YOU'RE BECOMING MORE POWERFUL THAN YOU COULD IMAGINE.
BUT ALSO AS UNSTABLE AS NITRO-GLYCERIN.
TAKE OFF YOUR GLOVE.
WHAT THE HELL IS GOING ON?

WHOA.

LET GO OF ME, JASON! SEPARATE!
NOT UNTIL PROFESSOR STEIN GIVES US THE OKAY TO TRY.
JUST DO IT, JASON! SOMETHING'S WRONG!
RONNIE, CALM DOWN!

BOYS, PLEASE! YOU CAN'T ARGUE!

WHAT DO YOU MEAN WE "CAN'T"?
WHAT IS IT, PROFESSOR?
YOU COULD UPSET THE MATRIX.
UPSET THE MATRIX? I THOUGHT THE MATRIX WAS JUST...A BONDING FORM OF ENERGY OR SOMETHING. LIKE THE FORCE KEEPING ATOMS TOGETHER.
THE TRUTH IS, I NEVER THOUGHT THROUGH THE ACCIDENT THAT TRIGGERED THE CREATION OF FIRESTORM. I THOUGHT IT CREATED THE MATRIX, BUT...
...I WAS ARROGANT LIKE THE REST OF THEM. AND MOST LIKELY WRONG.
WHEN RONALD AND I FIRST MET, I WAS ATTEMPTING TO VALIDATE MY THEORIES ON THE EXISTENCE OF THE BIG BANG.
THAT THERE WAS AN ACTUAL SPARK THAT PRECEDED THE EXISTENCE OF THE UNIVERSE. AND I THINK THAT DAY I NOT ONLY PROVED THE EXISTENCE OF THAT SPARK--
-- I CAPTURED IT.
IS THAT THE VOICE WE'VE BEEN HEARING?
IT'S POSSIBLE.
BUT YOU'RE SAYING THE MATRIX IS--
THE BIG BANG. THE TRIGGER FOR STARTING THE UNIVERSE. OR RESTARTING IT IN THIS CASE.
RE-STARTING IT?

THE UNIVERSE IS AN ENDLESS CYCLE OF EXPANSION AND CONTRACTION. IT LIVES AND GROWS FOR BILLIONS OF YEARS. AND THEN IT COLLAPSES AND STARTS AGAIN.
ACCORDING TO COUNTLESS SCIENTISTS, INCLUDING THE ATOM, *THIS* UNIVERSE'S EXPIRATION DATE IS LONG OVERDUE.
THE BURDEN OF THIS CREATION...OF WHAT YOU ARE...
WHAT?
WHAT ARE WE, PROFESSOR STEIN?
TOGETHER, YOU'RE THE MOST ***DANGEROUS*** BEING IN THE UNIVERSE.

"YOU WERE SENT HERE TO KILL ME.
"BLACK MANTA HAS A SON WHO'S THE KEY TO STOPPING YOUR PEOPLE FROM DESTROYING THE SURFACE WORLD."
WHAT ELSE HAVEN'T YOU TOLD ME, MERA?
THAT'S EVERYTHING.
AND IF WE CAN GET TO MANTA'S SON WE CAN STOP MY SISTER BEFORE--
I'LL FIND HIM, BUT I'LL DO IT MYSELF.
ARTHUR--
I NEED TO PROCESS EVERYTHING, MERA.
AND YOU NEED TO FIND SOMEONE ELSE TO HELP YOU HOLD BACK YOUR PEOPLE UNTIL I FIND MANTA'S SON.
WE CAN'T DO EVERYTHING TOGETHER RIGHT NOW. THE STAKES ARE TOO HIGH. AND QUITE HONESTLY--
"--I NEED SOME TIME ALONE."

THE RIO GRANDE, NEW MEXICO.
HOW MUCH FARTHER, DAD?
WE'RE HERE, JACKSON.
AND WHERE'S HERE EXACTLY?
THE PLACE YOUR MOTHER AND I ALWAYS KNEW WE'D HAVE TO BRING YOU.
THE COTTAGE.
THE COTTAGE? I DIDN'T KNOW WE HAD A COTTAGE.
DAD?
WHAT'RE WE DOING?
WHY WAS MOM SO UPSET WHEN WE LEFT?
BECAUSE SHE KNEW THIS DAY WOULD COME.
AND SO DID I.

DAD, JUST TELL ME WHAT YOU NEED TO TELL ME.
YOU KNOW HOW MUCH YOUR MOTHER AND I HAVE TRIED TO PROTECT YOU.
BECAUSE I CHANGE WHEN I HIT WATER.
MORE THAN THAT. MORE THAN I PROBABLY CAN IMAGINE.
WHAT THE HELL IS THAT?
A CHEST.
"A WOMAN GAVE IT TO ME AND YOUR MOTHER FIFTEEN YEARS AGO."
"IT BELONGS TO HER?"
"NO, JACKSON."
IT BELONGS TO YOU.
IT BELONGS TO ME?
JACKSON...
...YOU'RE NOT OUR SON.

"A WOMAN ROSE UP FROM THE SEA WITH YOU IN HER ARMS. THAT WAS THE FIRST TIME YOUR MOTHER AND I LAID EYES ON YOU. SHE SAID YOUR REAL PARENTS WEREN'T FIT TO RAISE YOU. SHE ASKED US TO.
"SHE SAID THAT YOU WOULD SAVE THE WORLD FROM A WAR BETWEEN LAND AND SEA."

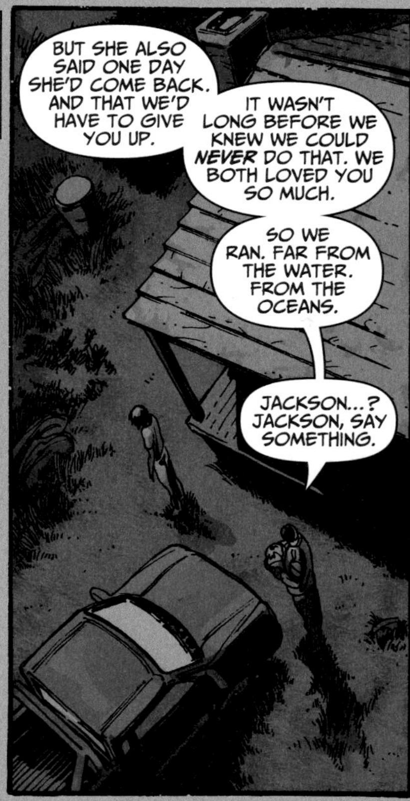
BUT SHE ALSO SAID ONE DAY SHE'D COME BACK. AND THAT WE'D HAVE TO GIVE YOU UP.
IT WASN'T LONG BEFORE WE KNEW WE COULD NEVER DO THAT. WE BOTH LOVED YOU SO MUCH.
SO WE RAN. FAR FROM THE WATER. FROM THE OCEANS.
JACKSON...? JACKSON, SAY SOMETHING.

IS JACKSON EVEN MY REAL NAME?

WHO AM I, DAD? IS IT IN THIS CHEST?
IS EVERY SECRET LOCKED AWAY?

I DON'T KNOW.
YOUR MOTHER AND I TRIED TO OPEN IT, BUT THE WOMAN SAID ONLY YOU WOULD BE ABLE TO--
YOU TOLD ME I WAS BORN DIFFERENT, BUT YOU DON'T REALLY KNOW THAT EITHER, DO YOU? YOU DON'T KNOW WHY I AM THE WAY I AM.
WILL WHAT'S IN THE CHEST TELL ME?

DAD? WHAT'S HAPPENING?
KRAKKLL
YOUR POWERS ARE BEING ACTIVATED BECAUSE YOU'RE BEING TRACKED.

BY ME.
THUNK
GET IN THE TRUCK, JACKSON!
NOW!

BUT, DAD, I CAN'T--
YOU CAN DRIVE. JUST GET *IN!*

GO!

DAD, WHAT DO WE *DO?*
FOR ONCE--

--WE HEAD *TOWARDS* THE WATER.

I KNEW SOMETHING WAS HAPPENING--THE PONDS DRYING UP AROUND TOWN--THE RAINFALL AND LIGHTNING TEN TIMES WHAT'S NORMAL.
I KNEW SOMETHING WAS COMING BUT I WAS TOO SCARED TO DO ANYTHING.
DAD, STOP! WE'RE HEADING TOWARDS THE CLIFF! IT'S *SUICIDE!*
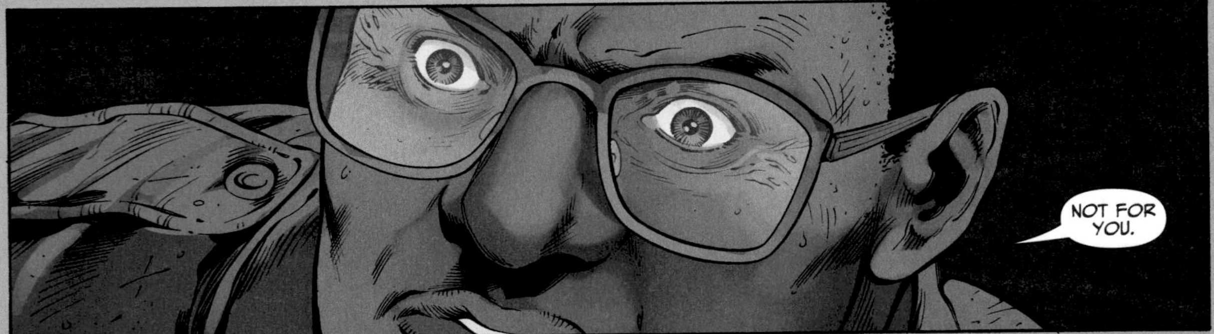
NOT FOR YOU.

VRRRRRR

TELL YOUR MOTHER I LOVE HER.
AND KNOW HOW MUCH I LOVE YOU.

DAD--

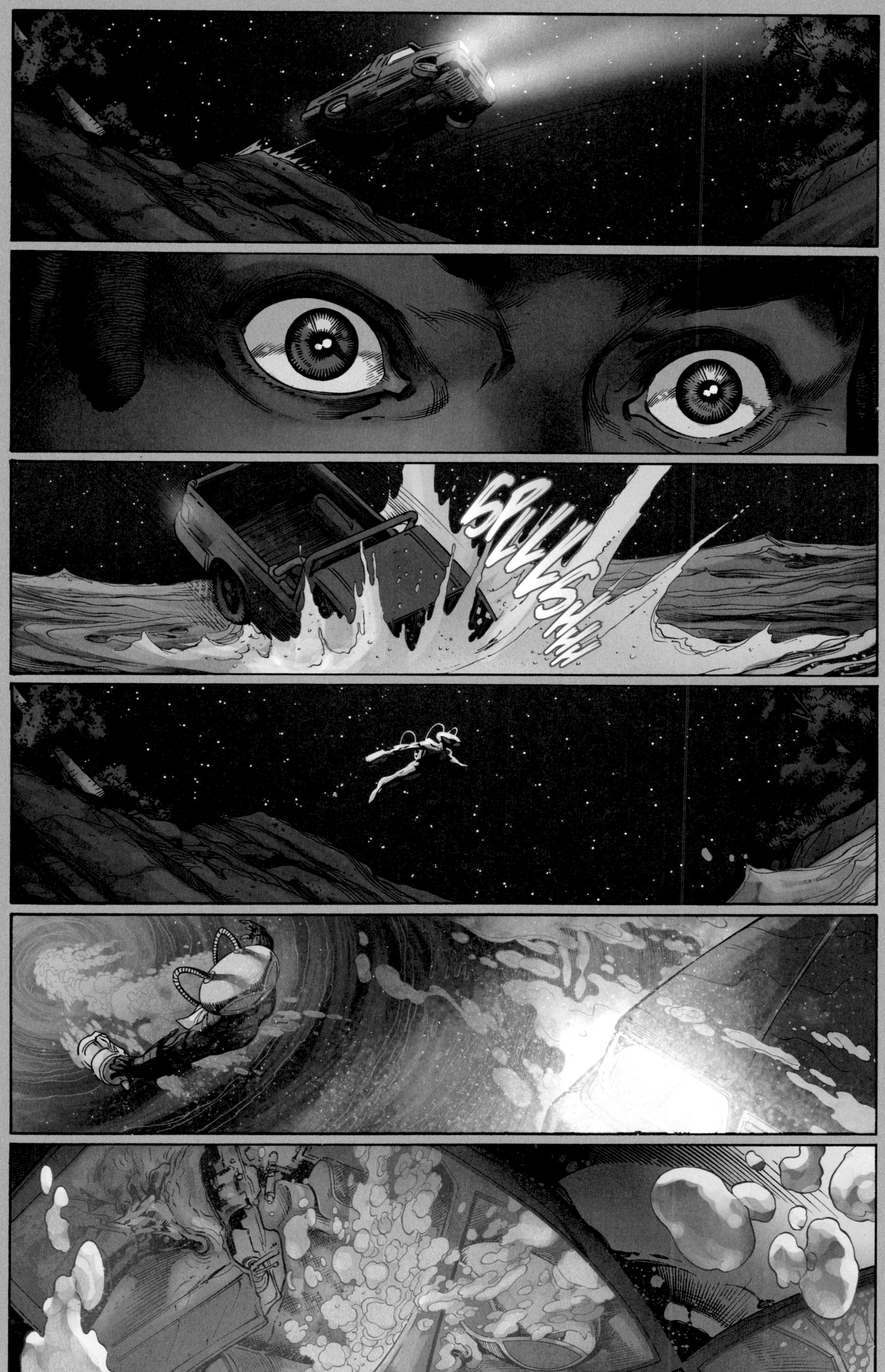
SPLUUSHHH

KAANNG
LEAVE US ALONE!

HN.

UNEXPECTED.
AAAHH--!

WHAPP

BUT INTERESTING.
AAAH!
KRAAK

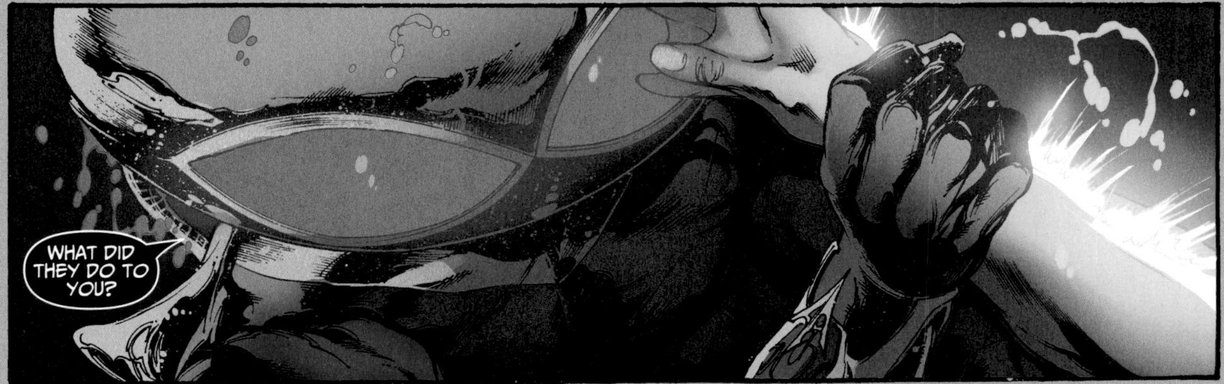
WHAT DID THEY DO TO YOU?

BACK OFF!

BOOOSHHH

HNNN?
DAD, WE'RE GETTING OUT OF HERE RIGHT--

WHAMM
NNFF!
YOUR SON IS MORE ADEPT THAN I WOULD'VE SUSPECTED, MANTA.

IT'S SURPRISING.
IT'S DISAPPOINTING, SIREN.
YOU MADE HIM LIKE YOU.
NO. HE'S *DIFFERENT* FROM US.

STAY AWAY! LEAVE MY DAD ALONE!

HE IS *NOT* YOUR FATHER.
HE IS NOTHING BUT ANOTHER MAN I'VE KILLED.
VOOOKK

WHAPP

AQUAMAN.
SNNPP
MANTA.

"I'VE BEEN WAITING FOR THIS."
PITTSBURGH.
THE LABORATORY OF PROFESSOR MARTIN STEIN.
THINK OF YOURSELVES AS A LIVING VERSION OF THE LARGE HADRON COLLIDER UNDERNEATH THE FRANCO-SWISS BORDER.
THE WHAT?
THERE WERE RUMORS OF HOW DANGEROUS IT WAS--SOME SAID EVERY TIME IT WAS USED THERE WAS A ONE IN TEN BILLION CHANCE OF TURNING THE UNIVERSE INSIDE OUT.
YES. RUMORS. MAYBE UNFOUNDED. MAYBE NOT.
BUT THE FACT HERE IS: EVERY TIME YOU AND RONALD ARGUE YOU'RE CAUSING A DESTABILIZATION IN THE MATRIX.
THE MORE YOU'RE AT EMOTIONAL ODDS, THE HIGHER THE CHANCES OF TRIGGERING A NEW BIG BANG.
AND WHAT ARE THE CHANCES OF THAT, PROFESSOR?
AT AN EMOTIONAL EQUILIBRIUM, NEAR ZERO.
BUT AGITATED? ONE IN A MILLION. MAYBE ONE IN A HUNDRED THOUSAND.
SO WE'RE BASICALLY ONE GIANT CONTROL/ALT/DELETE BUTTON FOR THE UNIVERSE?
YOU TWO BLOW UP, AND EVERYTHING IN EXISTENCE WILL BE DESTROYED.
LEAVING ONLY THE TWO OF YOU.
ONLY US?
AND ME. RIGHTEOUS!

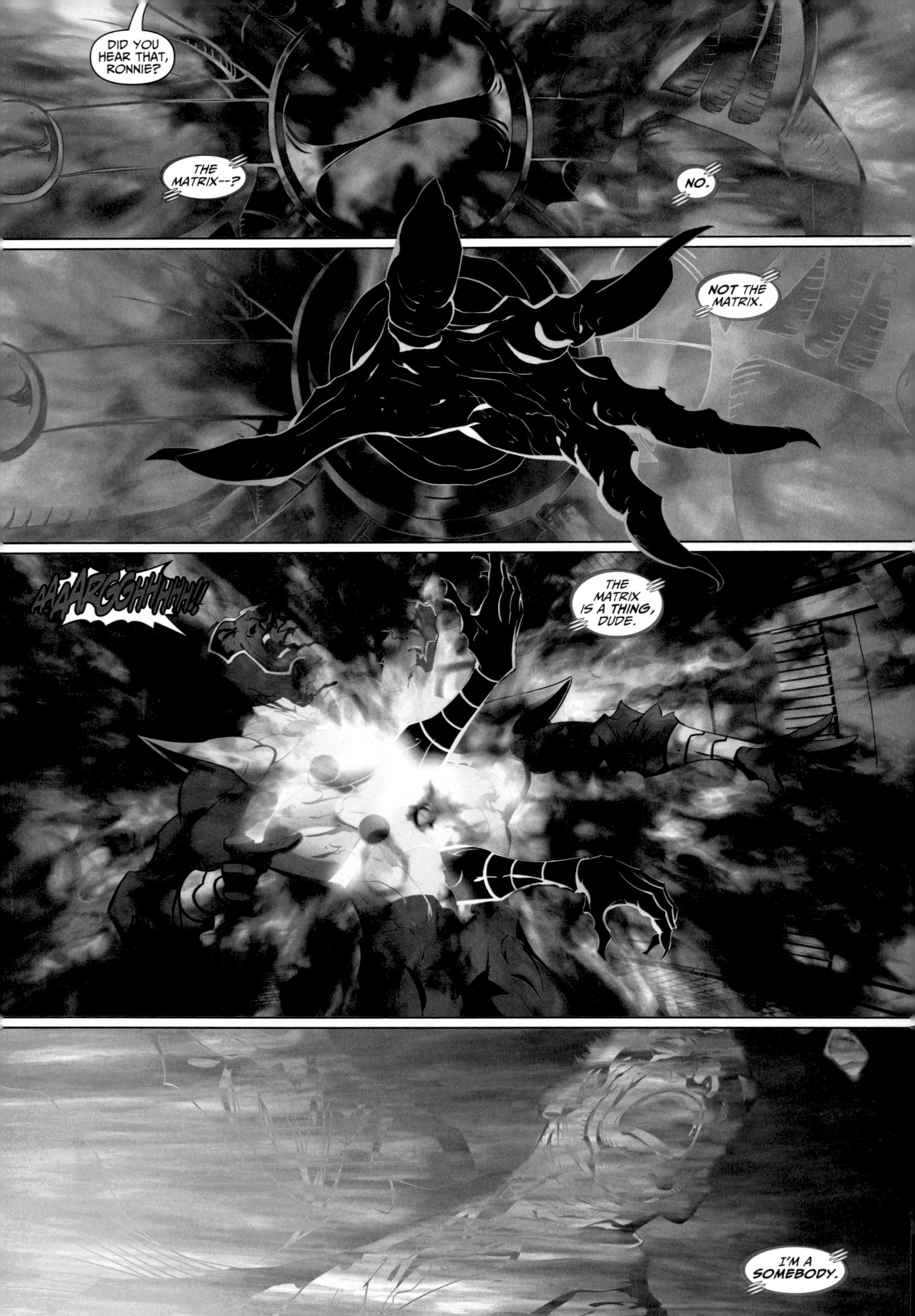
DID YOU HEAR THAT, RONNIE?
THE MATRIX--?
NO.
NOT THE MATRIX.
AAAARGGHHHHH!!
THE MATRIX IS A THING, DUDE.
I'M A SOMEBODY.

JASON RUSCH.
RAGE. LOVE. HOPE.

RONNIE RAYMOND.
WILL. FEAR. AVARICE.

AND PROFESSOR STEIN.

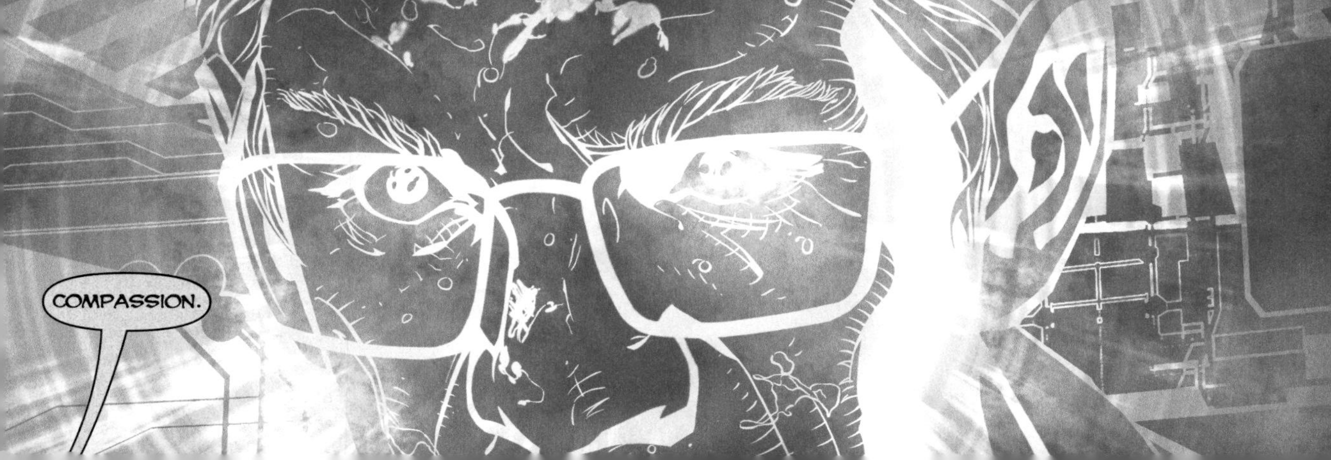

THIS IS GONNA BE SO BOSS.

BRIGHTEST DAY 11
Cover by David Finch

FATHERS' DAY

PITTSBURGH.
THE LABORATORY OF PROFESSOR MARTIN STEIN.
PLEASE! DON'T KILL THEM!
CHILL, PROFESSOR. I'M NOT GONNA KILL THEM. I'M GOING TO HURT THEM.
I'M GOING TO PUT RONNIE AND JASON THROUGH SO MUCH EMOTIONAL TORTURE.
I'M GOING TO MAKE THEM HATE EACH OTHER.
YOU ALREADY KNOW WHAT THAT'LL DO. YOU TOLD THEM. THEY GET TOO UPSET WITH ONE ANOTHER AND--
--KA-BOOM!
THERE GOES THE NEIGHBORHOOD. AND THAT'S ALL I WANT, OLD DUDE. THE DEATH OF EVERY LIVING THING.
WHAT ARE YOU?
OH, MAN, AM I GLAD YOU ASKED.

YOU CAN CALL ME...
FZZAAMM
DEATHSTORM
HOW HARDCORE IS THAT?
TH-THEY'RE GOING TO STOP YOU.
I'M UNSTOPPABLE. I'M DEATH PERSONIFIED. AND I'M STILL AROUND BECAUSE JASON AND RONNIE WON'T LET ME GO.
THEY CREATED ME.
LET ME TELL YOU THE SECRET OF THE UNIVERSE, PROFESSOR.
THERE'S NO GOOD OR EVIL.
THERE'S ONLY DEAD OR ALIVE.

I DON'T BELIEVE THAT. THEY DON'T BELIEVE THAT.
YEAH. YOU KNOW RONNIE BETTER THAN ME, DON'T YOU?
YOU KNOW EVERY FAILURE AND INSECURITY HE HAS FESTERING INSIDE HIM THAT'S TURNED THIS MORON FROM A HERO INTO A ZERO.
I'M NOT GOING TO KILL YOU, PROFESSOR. AFTER ALL...
NN.
AAAARRHHH!
PROFESSOR...?
A MIND'S A TERRIBLE THING TO WASTE.

NEW MEXICO.
ALONG THE RIO GRANDE.

I'M SURPRISED TO SEE YOU HERE, AQUAMAN.
BUT I'M PLEASED.
WHERE IS SHE? WHERE'S MERA?

RUN, KID!
GET TO THE ROAD.
DAD? BLACK MANTA. HE'S--
JUST RUN, JACKSON!
YOU CAN'T KEEP ME AWAY FROM THAT BOY.
THOOOM
AFTER ALL...
...YOU KNOW HOW IMPORTANT SONS CAN BE TO THEIR FATHERS.

DON'T WORRY ABOUT PROFESSOR STEIN, RONNIE. I BROUGHT HIM ABOARD THE DEATH TRAIN.
CHOO CHOO!
DAMN, THIS IS A GOOD BRAIN TO PICK THROUGH. SURE THE SCIENTIFIC STUFF IS AS ABOUT AS INTERESTING AS WATCHING SAVED BY THE BELL RERUNS, BUT IT'S GOING TO BE USEFUL.
ALMOST AS USEFUL AS THE PERSONAL ANECDOTES.
THE PROFESSOR ALWAYS SAW YOU LIKE A SON. THAT'S WHY HE'S SO DISAPPOINTED IN WHAT YOU'RE DOING NOW.
GET OUT OF MY HEAD!
IF YOU'RE GOING TO LIVE LIFE HIDING FROM IT IN THE BOTTOM OF A BOTTLE, WHY LIVE LIFE AT ALL?
YOU'RE RIGHT. LET HIM GO! PLEASE! TAKE ME INSTEAD--
YOU? YOU DON'T KNOW JACK ALL, RONNIE.
HOW ABOUT THIS? KILL JASON AND I LEAVE YOU AND THE PROF ALONE. I PROMISE. JASON HATES YOU ANYWAY. HOW COULD HE NOT AFTER WHAT WE DID TO HIS GIRLFRIEND?
HE DIDN'T DO ANYTHING.
THAT WAS YOU. THE BLACK LANTERN FIRESTORM.
IT'S DEATHSTORM, DUDE!
WHATEVER.
C'MON, JASON.
YOU LIKE RAGE, "DUDE"?
WAPP

HOW ABOUT THE FURY OF FIRESTORM?

I STILL REMEMBER THE SOUND YOUR SON MADE WHEN I GUT HIM LIKE A FISH.
A *WHIMPER.*
YOU CAN'T HURT ME ANYMORE, MANTA.
THERE'S NO ONE *ELSE* YOU CAN USE LIKE THAT.
WHAT ABOUT *MERA?* OR IS THAT *OVER?*
IF YOU'RE HERE, THAT MEANS SHE FINALLY TOLD YOU THE *TRUTH* I'VE ALWAYS KNOWN.
ABOUT WHAT HER PEOPLE DID TO *ME.*
ABOUT WHAT THEY WANTED TO DO TO *YOU.*

FTTCH
NNGG
YOU WERE THE LAST TO KNOW.
YARGGGH!
KAAZZZZTTT
HOW SAD.

DETROIT.

HOME OF ALVIN RUSCH.

HOW'D YOU GET SO DAMN SMART?

HAD TO BE YOUR MOTHER. BECAUSE ALL YOU GOT FROM ME WAS *GRIEF* AND *ANGER.*

I'VE NEVER BEEN THERE WHEN YOU NEEDED ME, JASON. I'VE ALWAYS BEEN WORRIED ABOUT MYSELF.

DAD?!
LOOK OUT, PEOPLE! DADDY RUSCH IS IN THE HOUSE!
I BROUGHT YOU HERE BECAUSE I'M GOING TO NEED A LITTLE HELP SCREWING WITH JASON TOO, POPS.
YOU TWO HAVE NEVER GOT ALONG, RIGHT? TELL ME WHY!
AARGHHH!
MR. RUSCH?!
STEIN? WHAT'S GOING ON? WHAT'S--
C'MON, KIDS!
ROAD TRIP!

NO ATLANTIS. NO TEMPEST. NO MERA.
WHAT DO YOU HAVE LEFT TO LIVE FOR?

DAD! THERE'S A TRUCK!
IT'S NOT SLOWING DOWN!

AARGHH!

ME.

OOONNNNKKKK

EERRRRRRRTTT
WE NEED A LIFT.
GET IN.
VRRRRRRR
SO, AH... WHERE WE GOING?

"JUST DRIVE. FAST."
WE CAN'T LET HIM GET AWAY! HE CAN'T--
A GIANT LASSO?
THAT'S WEAK, DUDES.
HE'S RIGHT, JASON. A FREAKING ROPE LASSO?
PROFESSOR STEIN AND MY DAD ARE FUSED WITH HIM, RONNIE. WHAT AM I SUPPOSED TO THINK OF?
SOMETHING HE WON'T LAUGH AT.
DESTINATION: ARRIVED!
ARRGHHH!
JASON...DO YOU REMEMBER THAT VISION WE SAW?

THE... WHITE LANTERN.
THE SOURCE OF ALL LIFE ON EARTH! RADICAL!
MAN, IT'S HEAVY.
KRAKKLLL
BUT NOT WHEN IT'S INFECTED A LITTLE, HUH?
I DESTROY THIS THING AND I DESTROY ALL LIFE ON EARTH--
NO.
YOU WILL NOT DESTROY THE WHITE LANTERN.
WHO IS THAT? STEIN?
YOU WILL BRING THE WHITE LANTERN TO ME.
I DON'T--

AND YOU WILL BRING ME AN ARMY.
THE TWELVE WHO LIVE MUST BE STOPPED.
THE NEW SAVIOR MUST NEVER BE CHOSEN.
THE POWER OF LIFE WILL BELONG TO ME.
YOU HEARD HIM, DUDES.

RISE

NOW LEAVING
NEW MEXICO

GIVE ME YOUR HAND.
WHAT--?

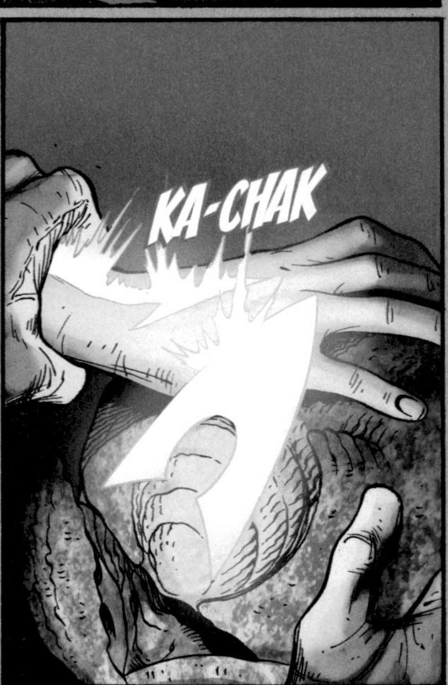
KA-CHAK

WHAT'S IN IT?

SOMETHING THAT TELLS US...

"...WHERE WE NEED TO GO NEXT."

MARS.

BRIGHTEST DAY 12
Cover by David Finch, Scott Williams
and Peter Steigerwald

ALL THIS USELESS BEAUTY

MARS.
THE FOURTH PLANET FROM THE SUN.
I CAN HEAR YOU.
EVERY THOUGHT.
EVERY BREATH.
EVERY BEAT OF YOUR HEART.
AND I KNOW THAT YOU CAN HEAR MINE.
I AM COMING FOR YOU...

...I AM COMING TO END YOU, *D'KAY D'RAZZ.*
J'ONN, THAT'S *NOT* TRUE, WE BOTH KNOW YOU'RE *LYING* TO YOURSELF.
ENDINGS ARE NOT ON YOUR MIND. IT'S THE CHANCE OF *BEGINNINGS* THAT HAVE TAKEN ROOT IN YOUR HEART.
YOU'RE NO LONGER DESTROYING THE GREEN, YOU'RE CULTIVATING IT.
IT'S TIME FOR US TO SAVE MARS *TOGETHER.*

I KNOW YOU WANT TO DROP TO YOUR KNEES AND CRY WITH JOY FOR ALL THIS BEAUTY.
SO DO I.
PLEASE, TAKE MY HAND, J'ONN...
...HOW LONG HAS IT BEEN SINCE WE'VE BOTH FELT THE WARMTH OF ANOTHER GREEN MARTIAN'S SKIN?
YOUR DEEPEST AND STRONGEST WISH IS NOW A REALITY, THIS COLD, DEAD WORLD IS ALIVE AND GREETS YOU AGAIN-- SURROUNDS YOU WITH ITS TOUCH-- ITS SMELL--
THE ONLY SMELL YOU'VE BROUGHT HERE IS DEATH.
DO YOU RECOGNIZE THESE SCARS?
I DO.
AT FIRST I THOUGHT THEY WERE TOO ABSTRACT, BUT I SHOULD'VE REALIZED THAT YOU, A MANHUNTER, WOULD SEE THROUGH THESE SCARS FOR WHAT THEY ARE.
THE MARTIAN SYMBOLS OF LOVE AND HATE.
YES, A PURE REMINDER OF ALL THAT I FEEL FOR MY SACRED HOME, THE BIRTHPLACE OF MY TORMENT.
DO YOU LIKE THEM? I CARVED THEM MYSELF.
IF YOU WISH, I CAN CARVE THEM INTO YOUR SKIN TOO SINCE YOU'RE AS MUCH A WALKING CONTRADICTION AS I AM.
I AM NOTHING LIKE YOU, D'KAY.

J'ONN, REMEMBER, I CAN HEAR EVERY THOUGHT OF YOURS LOUD AND CLEAR--THERE ARE NO SECRETS BETWEEN US--
--YOU HATE ME FOR THE INNOCENTS I HAVE MURDERED--YOU WANT TO KILL ME, AND I CAN UNDERSTAND THAT...
YOU DON'T UNDERSTAND ANYTHING ABOUT ME.
OH, BUT I DO, BECAUSE THERE'S A SMALL PIECE OF YOUR SOUL THAT WANTS TO LOVE ME, J'ONN--WANTS TO YELL OUT "THANK HRONMEER I AM NOT ALONE ANYMORE, ANOTHER GREEN MARTIAN HEART FINALLY BEATS IN THIS UNIVERSE BESIDE MINE."
YOU ARE QUITE DELUSIONAL.
AND YOU'RE USING THIS TIME WISELY--LOOKING FOR WEAKNESS--FLIPPING THROUGH MY BRAIN CELLS LIKE A DEFT SEARCH ENGINE WHILE YOUR RAGE BATTLES YOUR LOVE.
I CAN NEVER LOVE SOMEONE AS TWISTED AS YOU.
BUT YOU MAY COME TO LOVE THE IDEA OF ME-- OF WHAT WE CAN DO TOGETHER--OF A WORLD THAT WE CAN CREATE AS HUSBAND AND WIFE, FATHER AND MOTHER--
KKRRKK
ALL YOU ARE IS A CRACKED FOUNDATION--WHAT MAKES YOU THINK I WOULD BUILD A WORLD WITH YOU, D'KAY?!

THERE IS NOTHING WORSE THAN BEING ALONE! NO ONE HAS SURVIVED THE PRIVATIONS WE HAVE--THE HOPELESSNESS--THE ISOLATION!

THE TWO LONELIEST BEINGS IN THE UNIVERSE HAVE FINALLY FOUND EACH OTHER! WHO ARE YOU TO STAND IN THE WAY OF FATE--OF THE BIRTH OF A NEW WORLD?!?

YOU DARE STAND HERE IN MY ANCESTRAL HOME AND DESECRATE IT WITH YOUR FANATICAL RAMBLINGS--
--IN THIS PLACE--WHERE I STOOD AND WATCHED MY WIFE AND CHILD BURN BEFORE MY EYES AS THEY PLEADED WITH ME TO SAVE THEM--TO HOLD THEM IN THEIR FINAL MOMENTS--
SHOOOM

I SAW THE WHITE LANTERN SYMBOL--I FELT ITS IMMENSE POWER THROUGH YOUR MIND--YOU CAN'T TURN YOUR BACK ON WHY YOU WERE RESURRECTED!
IT'S MARS' TIME NOW--EARTH HAS HAD ITS DAY--WE'RE BOTH HERE AT THIS MOMENT FOR A REASON!
I CAN LOVE YOU, J'ONN! I WANT TO LOVE YOU--WE'RE CONNECTED--THAT'S WHY YOU MUST LOVE ME IN RETURN!

"MUST"?!? WHY MUST I LOVE YOU, D'KAY?!?
BECAUSE YOU'RE A MARTIAN--BECAUSE YOU'RE GREEN?!?
IT'S NOT A GOOD ENOUGH REASON--I WISH IT WERE--BUT IT'S NOT! YOU HAVE MADE THAT POSSIBILITY IMPOSSIBLE BY YOUR HORRENDOUS DEEDS!
DAMN YOU FOR SQUANDERING THE GRACE AND PROMISE WE COULD HAVE SHARED BY BEING A MONSTER INSTEAD OF A MARTIAN I COULD CHERISH AND RESPECT!
I MOURN FOR WHAT COULD HAVE BEEN!
IT'S NOT OFTEN A CHILD EMBRACES A SPECIFIC GOAL SO EARLY IN LIFE.
BUT WHEN I DISCOVERED THE EXISTENCE OF MARTIANS WHO COULD ONLY READ MINDS BUT NOT BE READ BY OTHER MARTIANS MY PURPOSE BECAME CLEAR.
I SHOULD CURE THEM--FIX THEM ALL--SO THEY COULD BE LIKE THE REST OF US.
NO SECRETS. NO LIES. OPEN MINDS AND OPEN HEARTS.
SO I UNDERTOOK A MERCY MISSION--A MISSION TO BRING THESE CEREBRALLY ISOLATED MARTIANS WHO WERE NOT PART OF THE COLLECTIVE MIND INTO THE FOLD.
THE PROCEDURE WAS QUICK AND PAINLESS. SOME SURVIVED, SOME DID NOT.
IF ALL OF US AS A RACE WERE NOT CONNECTED TELEPATHICALLY, THEN NONE OF US WERE.
BUT IT GREW MORE DIFFICULT TO LOCATE THE ISOLATIONISTS, SO I PROPOSED A PURGING STRATEGY THAT WOULD RID MARS OF THEIR SECRETIVE NATURE ONCE AND FOR ALL.
THE MANHUNTERS AND THE HIGH COUNCIL DIDN'T SHARE MY OPINION.
NO ONE UNDERSTOOD THE GREATER GOOD I WAS TRYING TO SERVE.
I WAS DECLARED A DEVIANT, AN ENEMY OF MARS, AND SECRETLY LOCKED AWAY IN A TELEPATHIC DAMPENING CELL DEEP UNDER THE GROUND.
ONE DAY THE MANHUNTER ASSESSMENT VISITS SUDDENLY STOPPED.
I HAD NO CONTACT WITH ANYONE.

AND I REJOICE IN WHAT WILL BE!
FWAM
THE LONELINESS WAS UNBEARABLE AS TIME SLIPPED AWAY.
I STOPPED COUNTING THE DAYS AFTER TWO HUNDRED YEARS.
THEN SALVATION ARRIVED IN A FLASH OF LIGHT...
...AND I WAS BROUGHT TO EARTH BY ERDEL'S TRANSPORTER BEAM.
UNFORTUNATELY FOR HIM AND HIS DAUGHTER I WAS IN NO MOOD FOR CONVERSATION--
--ESPECIALLY SINCE I FOUND MYSELF SUDDENLY BOMBARDED BY THE WAKING THOUGHTS OF BILLIONS OF NEW LIFE FORMS.
I ALWAYS FOUND MY TELEPATHY TO BE A BLESSING--I NOW FOUND IT TO BE A CURSE--I NEEDED TO SHUT OUT ALL THE VOICES IN MY HEAD.
AFTER WHAT OUR OWN PEOPLE DID TO ME I DECIDED TO FORSAKE ALL THINGS MARTIAN--AND WITH GREAT DIFFICULTY WIPED MY OWN MIND AND BODY CLEAN OF ALL MARTIAN MEMORIES --IT WAS TIME TO ASSIMILATE--
AND THE ONLY WAY TO EMBRACE THIS NEW LIFE WAS TO INHABIT A HUMAN LIFE UTTERLY AND COMPLETELY.
THE DIVERSITY OF LIVES TO CHOOSE FROM WAS ASTOUNDING.
I WAS LOST IN THE EXPERIENCE OF BEING HUMAN.
SO LOST THAT I NEVER EVEN RECOGNIZED ANOTHER MARTIAN PRESENCE ON EARTH...
...THAT IS UNTIL I WAS SUDDENLY HIT BY THE MASSIVE TELEPATHIC BURST YOU FIRED WHEN YOU WERE KILLED--
--IT PENETRATED MY PSYCHIC WALL, BUT NOT ENOUGH TO PULL MY CONSCIOUSNESS COMPLETELY FROM THE HUMAN I HAD INHABITED.
THAT FINALLY OCCURRED WHEN I SAW THE IMAGES ON TELEVISION OF YOUR RESURRECTION.
SEEING ANOTHER MARTIAN ALIVE AND WELL SHOOK ME FROM MY SELF-INDUCED SLUMBER AND RETURNED ME TO FULL AWARENESS OF WHO AND WHAT I WAS.

THIS IS WHAT PEOPLE WHO CARE ABOUT EACH OTHER DO, J'ONN--
--THEY SHARE.
THEY SHARE THEIR DOUBT AND PAIN. THEY SHARE THE DARKNESS SO THEY CAN CRAWL TOWARDS THE LIGHT TOGETHER.
IT WAS YOU--YOU SENT THAT PSYCHIC FLASH TO ME ON MARS--SHOWED ME I WASN'T THE ONLY MARTIAN THAT ERDEL BROUGHT TO EARTH--THAT YOU WERE THE FIRST--

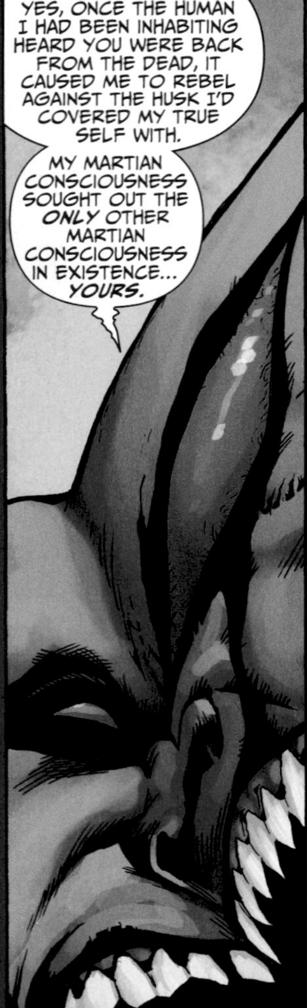
YES, ONCE THE HUMAN I HAD BEEN INHABITING HEARD YOU WERE BACK FROM THE DEAD, IT CAUSED ME TO REBEL AGAINST THE HUSK I'D COVERED MY TRUE SELF WITH.
MY MARTIAN CONSCIOUSNESS SOUGHT OUT THE ONLY OTHER MARTIAN CONSCIOUSNESS IN EXISTENCE... YOURS.

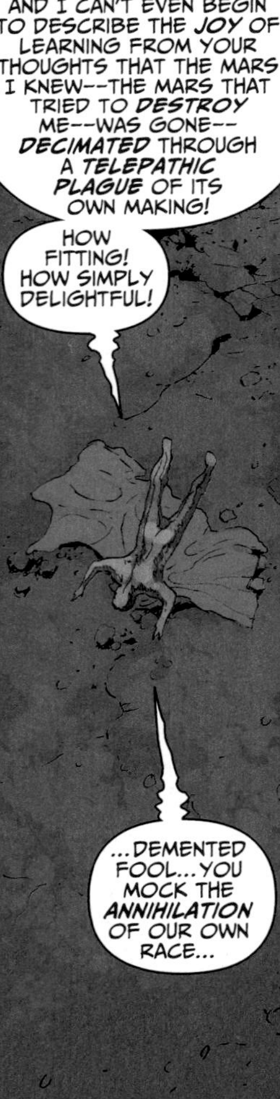
AND I CAN'T EVEN BEGIN TO DESCRIBE THE JOY OF LEARNING FROM YOUR THOUGHTS THAT THE MARS I KNEW--THE MARS THAT TRIED TO DESTROY ME--WAS GONE--DECIMATED THROUGH A TELEPATHIC PLAGUE OF ITS OWN MAKING!
HOW FITTING! HOW SIMPLY DELIGHTFUL!
...DEMENTED FOOL...YOU MOCK THE ANNIHILATION OF OUR OWN RACE...

OPEN YOUR EYES, J'ONN J'ONZZ, LOOK AT THE OPPORTUNITY IN FRONT OF US, THERE'S A CLEAN SLATE HERE...
...YOU'VE ALREADY STARTED THE REGENERATION OF MARS, AND AS THE EARTHLINGS SAY, IT CAN BE A GARDEN OF EDEN AND WE ITS ADAM AND EVE!
YOU HAVE MISCONSTRUED THAT PARTICULAR STORY, D'KAY...YOU ARE NOT EVE...

...YOU ARE THE SERPENT!
AAAGHHH
YOUR SOUL IS REPULSIVE!
AND YOUR SOUL, J'ONN, IS DIVIDED...
...JUST LIKE YOUR ALLEGIANCE!

DID YOU REALLY THINK WE WOULDN'T NOTICE YOU WERE TERRAFORMING MARS BY SUCKING THE LIFE FROM EVERY BLADE OF GRASS, FLOWER AND TREE ON EARTH?
OUR WORLD ACCEPTED YOU--GAVE YOU A HOME TO CALL YOUR OWN, AND HOW DO YOU REPAY US--BY STEALING THE VERY ECOSYSTEM THAT SUSTAINS US!
IS THAT ALL THE EARTH REALLY MEANS TO YOU--A LAYOVER UNTIL YOU CAN BRING MARS BACK? COME ON, MAN.

DON'T YOU SEE, J'ONN, HOPE'S KEPT YOU FROM LIVING A FULL LIFE!
HOW LONG ARE YOU GOING TO LET YOURSELF BE TORN BETWEEN TWO WORLDS?
YOUR FAMILY'S GONE--YOUR PEOPLE ARE GONE--DUST IN THE WIND FOR HUNDREDS OF YEARS, NOTHING LEFT TO HOLD ON TO EXCEPT YOUR FUTILE AND PATHETIC OBSESSION!
THERE IS NOTHING FUTILE ABOUT HOPE!
YOU CAN'T ALWAYS GET WHAT YA WANT, J'ONNY. YOU CAN HAVE ONE OR THE OTHER, BUT YA CAN'T HAVE BOTH!
IF WE HAVE TO BURY YOU AGAIN UP HERE TO SAVE OUR PLANET, WE'LL DO IT!

SILVER CITY, NEW MEXICO.

"YOU ARE BETTER OFF DEAD, J'ONN."

UP, UP AND *AWAYYYY!*

THAT DEATHSTORM THING JUST CREATED HIS OWN *BLACK LANTERN CORPS.* WHAT THE HELL ARE WE SUPPOSED TO DO NOW?
WE GO AFTER THEM, THAT'S WHAT!
SO *FLY!*

THAT THING HAS MY DAD TRAPPED INSIDE HIM--AND YOUR DAD--
PROFESSOR STEIN'S NOT MY DAD--
YOU MIGHT NOT SEE IT THAT WAY, RONNIE, BUT HE DOES.
WHY DO YOU THINK HE'S SO WORRIED ABOUT YOU?
BECAUSE I CAN'T GET MY $#@% TOGETHER.
YOU CAN. YOU HAVE BEFORE.
I DID A TON OF RESEARCH ON YOU WHEN I WAS FIRST BONDED WITH THE MATRIX. I KNOW WHAT YOU DID WHEN YOU WERE FIRESTORM.
NEXT TO BATMAN AND THE FLASH, YOU HAD MORE SUPER-VILLAINS TARGETING YOU THAN ANYBODY ELSE. AND YOU BEAT THEM.
YOU WERE THE YOUNGEST MEMBER TO EVER JOIN THE JUSTICE LEAGUE. AND THEY WENT AFTER YOU.
YOU STOPPED NUCLEAR WARS, RONNIE. AND--
I DON'T WANT A PEP TALK RIGHT NOW, JASON!
I JUST WANT YOU TO THINK OF A WAY TO HELP PROFESSOR--

WHAT'S WRONG?
MAYBE WE'RE UPSETTING THE MATRIX. I DON'T THINK WE'RE SUPPOSED TO BE ARGUING.
THAT'S ARGUING?
WE'RE SCREWED IF THAT'S ARGUING.
WE JUST HAVE TO STAY IN SYNC, RONNIE.
STAY IN SYNC?
WHEN HAVE WE BEEN IN SYNC?
HEY, NIGHT OF THE FLYING DEAD! WAIT UP!
YOU REALLY HAVE BALLS, GUYS. TWELVE ON TWO? FINE WITH US.
OKAY. YOU GOT THEIR ATTENTION. NOW WHAT?
YOU'RE THE ONE THAT'S SUPPOSED TO DO THE THINKING.
STOP! BRING ME THE WHITE LANTERN. NOW!
THAT VOICE. I'VE HEARD IT SOMEWHERE BEFORE.
ALL RIGHT, ALL RIGHT! FUN LATER. WORK NOW. C'MON, CREW.
WE'RE OUT.
FZZAMM
WHAT'S HAPPENING? WHERE'D THEY GO?
I DON'T KNOW.

"BUT I THINK THIS JUST GOT BIGGER THAN THE TWO OF US, RONNIE. I THINK IT'S TIME WE GO FIND THE JUSTICE LEAGUE."
GOTHAM CITY.
THE WATCHTOWER.
WHAT'S WRONG, BOSTON?
HNN.
JUST HAD A SHIVER RUN UP MY SPINE. I HAVEN'T FELT THAT SINCE... THE WHITE RING BROUGHT ME BACK TO LIFE.
DO YOU THINK IT MEANS ANYTHING?

"IT'S PROBABLY NOTHING."

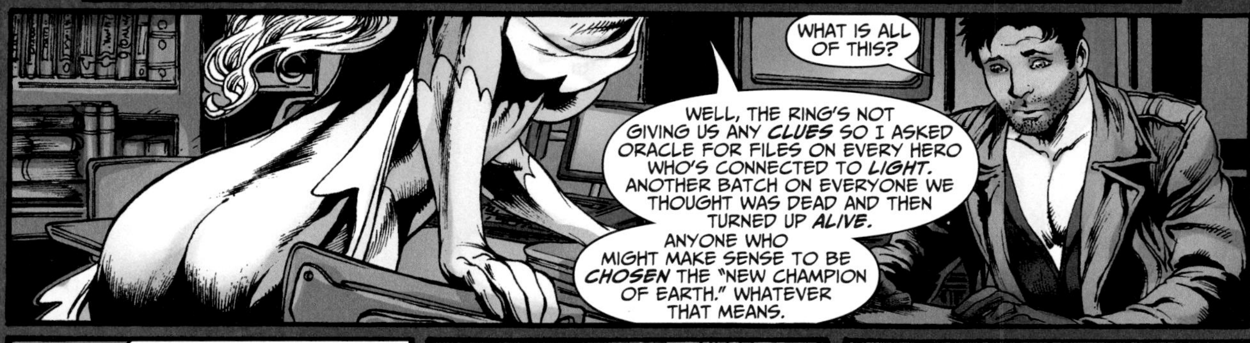
WHAT IS ALL OF THIS?
WELL, THE RING'S NOT GIVING US ANY CLUES SO I ASKED ORACLE FOR FILES ON EVERY HERO WHO'S CONNECTED TO LIGHT. ANOTHER BATCH ON EVERYONE WE THOUGHT WAS DEAD AND THEN TURNED UP ALIVE.
ANYONE WHO MIGHT MAKE SENSE TO BE CHOSEN THE "NEW CHAMPION OF EARTH." WHATEVER THAT MEANS.

I FIGURE IF THE SEARCH FOR WHOEVER IS SUPPOSED TO BE WEARING THAT RING IS ON, WE SHOULD START SOMEWHERE.
DOVE, I KNOW YOU'RE GETTING PRESSURE FROM HAWK TO DITCH ME, BUT I REALLY DO APPRECIATE THE HELP.

THANKS.
YOU'RE WELCOME, BOSTON.

SO, UM... WHO DO WE TALK TO FIRST?

"WHO DO WE THINK IS GOING TO BE THE WHITE LANTERN?"
RRAGGHH!
DAMN YOU!
GET OUT OF MY HEAD, D'KAY!

I *KNOW* WHAT YOU'RE TRYING TO DO--

--NONE OF THIS IS REAL!

BUT THIS IS!
YAAGHHH
I WILL NOT ALLOW MYSELF TO DESTROY THE EARTH!

I WILL BRING MARS BACK MY WAY--
UNNN
--NOT YOUR WAY!
LIVE.
LIVE.
LIVE.
POOM
POOM
POOM

LIVE

...I DID IT...
...BY THE GRACE OF H'RONMEER...
...I TRULY DID IT!
J'ONN?
M'YRI'AH...
K'HYM..
DA?
LET ME TOUCH YOU--ARE YOU REAL--IS IT YOU, M'YRI'AH-- IS IT YOU, K'HYM, MY BEAUTIFUL DARLING?
WE'RE HERE, DA. WE'RE HERE.

WHAT HAPPENED, J'ONN? I DON'T REMEMBER ANYTHING AFTER THE PLAGUE HIT.
I HAVE BEEN BLESSED WITH NEW POWERS-- I HEALED MARS AND--
--AND I HEALED YOU!
NOTHING ELSE MATTERS--YOU'RE BACK-- AND EVERYTHING IS ALL RIGHT--
WE'RE TOGETHER AGAIN...A FAMILY...AS IT WAS MEANT TO BE.
I LOVE YOU BOTH TO THE VERY CORE OF MY SOUL.
NOT AS MUCH...

...AS WE LOVE YOU, J'ONN.

BRIGHTEST DAY 13
Cover by David Finch, Ryan Winn and Peter Steigerwald

UNDER A BLOOD RED SKY

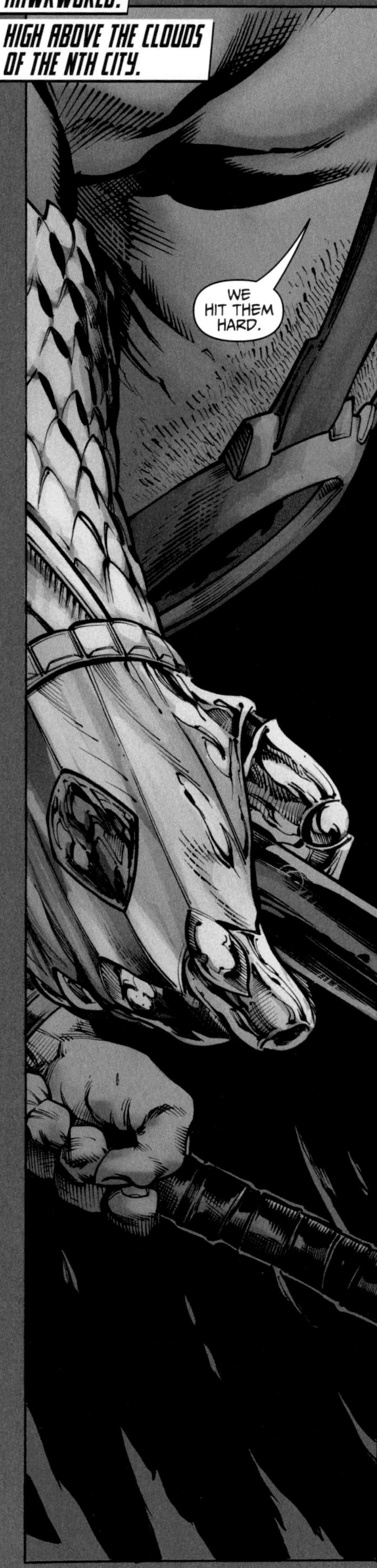
HAWKWORLD.
HIGH ABOVE THE CLOUDS OF THE NTH CITY.
WE HIT THEM HARD.
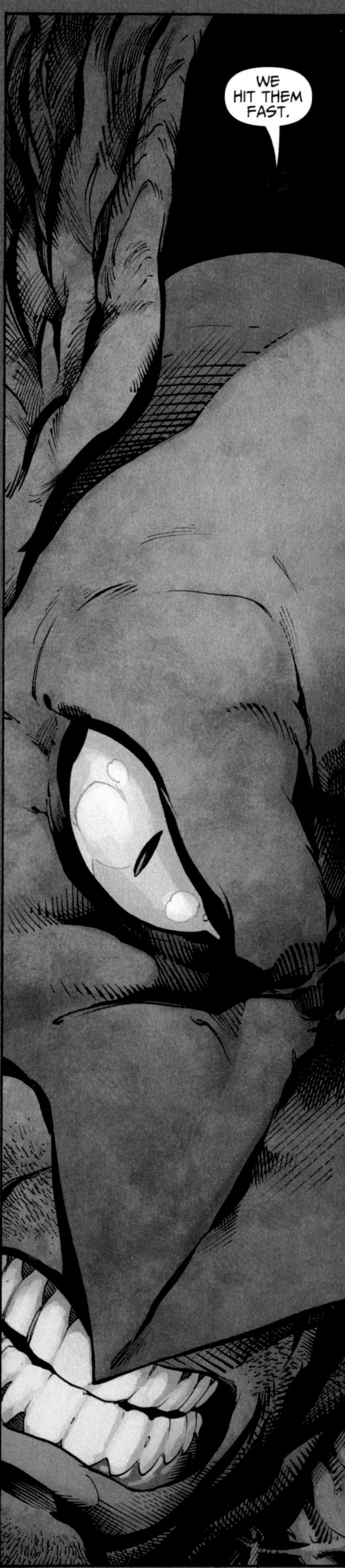
WE HIT THEM FAST.

AND WE DON'T TAKE PRISONERS.

ATTACK!

TAKE THE FIGHT INTO THE CITY WHERE THEY CAN'T MANEUVER--MOVE OUT OF THEIR ELEMENT!

LIONMANES!
REMOVE THE NTH ORE FROM YOUR BACKS AND DROP!

SKREEEEE!

LET'S FIND A PLACE WHERE WE CAN TALK.
SKREEEE!

WHERE IS SHE?!?
WHERE ARE THEY KEEPING HAWKGIRL?!?
SKREEEEE!
WE PROTECT OUR QUEEN--NO MATTER WHAT YOU DO TO ME--I'LL NEVER--
I'LL RALLY MY PRIDE AND THE LIZARDKONS--IF I CAN KEEP US WORKING TOGETHER WE'LL HEAD TO THE CENTER OF THE CITY AND THEN SPREAD THROUGH THE--
DO WHATEVER YOU NEED TO DO, TONARR. YOU'VE GOT YOUR MISSION AND I'VE GOT MINE.
SCRAAW
RRIPPP
SKREEEEE!
I'LL KEEP TEARING YOU LIMB FROM LIMB UNTIL YOU TELL ME WHAT I NEED TO KNOW.
...NO...STOP... I KNOW WHERE SHE IS...
I'M LISTENING.

INSIDE THE NTH CITY.
IT'S BEAUTIFUL, ISN'T IT?
A WORK OF ART IN ITS OWN RIGHT...
...MY WORK OF ART--MY TIMELESS MAGNUM OPUS...
ALL THOSE USELESS LIVES YOU'VE LIVED...
IF I COULD HANG THIS IN A MUSEUM I BELIEVE A FITTING TITLE WOULD BE...
...A LEGACY OF DEATH!

LET'S SEE THOSE PRETTY EYES OF YOURS...
WHAT ARE YOU DOING WITH THE GATE?!?
YOU GOT WHAT YOU WANT-- IT BROUGHT YOU HERE TO HAWKWORLD SO YOU COULD JOIN MY TRAITOROUS MOTHER!
YES, THAT IT DID, HAWKGIRL, BUT THIS WAS ALWAYS MEANT TO BE A ROUND TRIP FOR BOTH THE QUEEN AND ME.
I WOULDN'T COUNT ON EATING THAT CHEESE JUST YET, HATH-SET, THE BEST LAID PLANS OF MICE AND MEN ARE--
I JUST REALIZED WHEN THE BLACK LANTERNS KILLED YOU IT WAS THE FIRST TIME IN OVER TWO THOUSAND YEARS THAT BOTH OF YOU DIDN'T ACTUALLY DIE AT MY HANDS.
MUST'VE BEEN A REAL SAD DAY TO HAVE YOUR STREAK END LIKE--
THERE'S SOMETHING QUITE ENCHANTING ABOUT YOUR FALSE BRAVADO THAT I'LL MISS ONCE I'M HOLDING THE STILL-BEATING HEARTS OF HAWKMAN AND HAWKGIRL IN MY--
SPTOO

KRAK
UNNN
THE ONLY THING YOU'RE GOING TO BE HOLDING, HATH, IS YOUR OWN WARM GUTS WHICH WILL FINALLY END THIS CURSE OF YOURS FOREVER.
THE ONLY THING FINALLY COMING TO AN END, HAWKGIRL--
WHAK
--IS YOU.

ENOUGH TAUNTING, HATH.
THE ATTACK'S BEGUN, AND SO HAS OUR FINAL JOURNEY TO A NEW WORLD.
GOOD HE'S SAVED US THE TROUBLE OF HACKING THROUGH THAT ACCURSED JUNGLE BELOW TO LOOK FOR HIM.
ATTACK-- WHAT ATTACK?
AH, IT SEEMS LIKE ONLY YESTERDAY YOU WERE A BABY AND I WAS WIPING MY MILK FROM YOUR LIPS...
YOUR BELOVED KHUFU--OR CARTER--HAS RAISED HIMSELF AN ARMY OF PUTRID LIONS AND LIZARDS AND IS NOW STRIKING AT THE HEART OF MY CITY SEARCHING FOR YOU.
WHICH MEANS WE'LL SOON HAVE BOTH KEYS IN HAND.
YES, BUT IT'S NOW TIME TO INSERT THE FIRST ONE.
PLACE HER ON THE GATE, HATH.
AND MAKE SURE MY DAUGHTER SCREAMS AS LOUDLY AS POSSIBLE.
YOUR WISH IS MY COMMAND, MY QUEEN.

AAGHH!
WE'VE COME FULL CIRCLE, CHAY-ARA.
SHUNK SHUNK

AAGHH!
I HEAR YOU, SHIERA!

MY PLEASURE.
AAGHH!
SHUNK SHUNK

AAGHH!
RRAGHH!
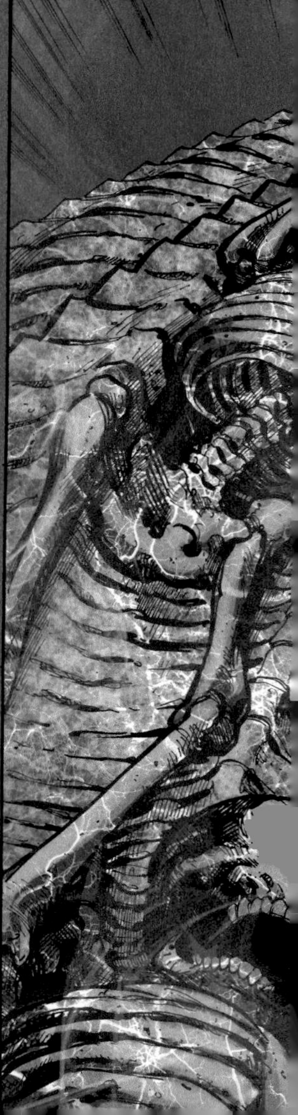

I SCREAMED IN PAIN GIVING BIRTH TO YOU AND NOW, IN A STRANGE WAY, ONCE YOU POWER UP THE GATE AND I FINALLY LEAVE THIS PLACE YOU'LL BE GIVING **BIRTH** TO ME.

WHAT A WONDERFUL... ***MATERNAL INSTINCT*** YOU HAVE... ***MOTHER.***

TURN UP HER VOLUME, HATH.

I'M ***SURE*** YOUR ***SOUL MATE,*** KHUFU, HEARD ***THAT.***

IT MUST BE ***TEARING*** HIS HEART APART KNOWING HE CAN'T GET TO YOU IN YOUR MOMENT OF DESPERATION.

SO, WHILE WE WAIT FOR HIM, I'M SURE YOU HAVE MANY QUESTIONS YOU'D LIKE TO HAVE ANSWERED...

"AS YOU KNOW, MY DARLING, IT WASN'T LONG AFTER THE PHARAOH LOST HIS WIFE THAT WE LOST YOUR FATHER TOO, THE PHARAOH'S YOUNGEST BROTHER, TO THAT VILE PESTILENCE WHICH TORE THROUGH OUR CITY THAT DARK YEAR.

"I NEVER TOLD YOU THIS, CHAY-ARA, BUT I MARRIED THE PHARAOH WITH THE UNDERSTANDING THAT PRINCE KHUFU WOULD ASK FOR YOUR HAND IN MARRIAGE...

"...NOT THAT THE PRINCE NEEDED ANY PRODDING FROM HIS FATHER, SINCE BOTH OF YOU LOVED EACH OTHER DEEPLY FOR MANY YEARS AND YOUR UNION WAS INEVITABLE.

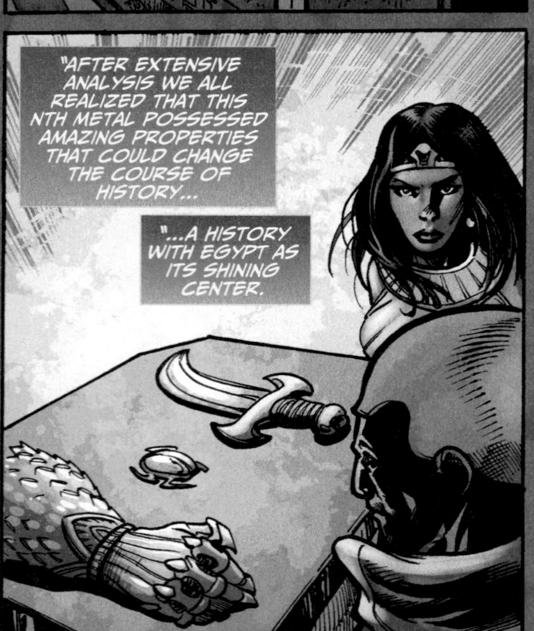
"AFTER EXTENSIVE ANALYSIS WE ALL REALIZED THAT THIS NTH METAL POSSESSED AMAZING PROPERTIES THAT COULD CHANGE THE COURSE OF HISTORY...
"...A HISTORY WITH EGYPT AS ITS SHINING CENTER.

"BUT YOUR STEPFATHER WAS A PHARAOH WITHOUT ASPIRATIONS--WITHOUT VISION.
"HE WAS A MAN TALENTED AT MANAGING MATTERS OF STATE--ANYTHING BEYOND THE HORIZON LINE DIDN'T CONCERN HIM.
"HE WAS CONTENT.
"I WAS NOT.

"WHAT I DID, I DID FOR EGYPT, CHAY-ARA."
"YOU DID IT FOR YOU, MOTHER. NO ONE ELSE."

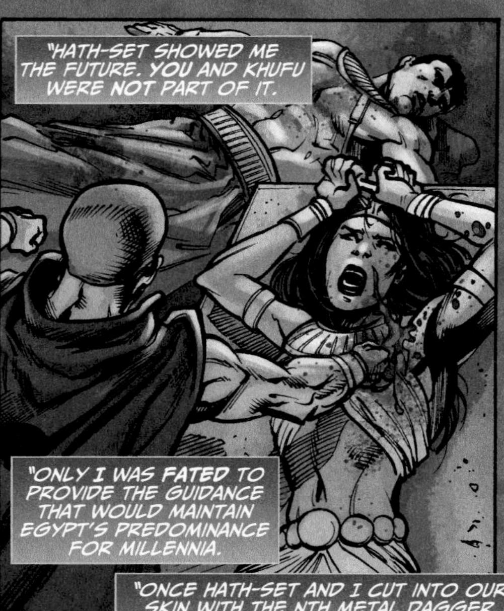
"HATH-SET SHOWED ME THE FUTURE. YOU AND KHUFU WERE NOT PART OF IT.
"ONLY I WAS FATED TO PROVIDE THE GUIDANCE THAT WOULD MAINTAIN EGYPT'S PREDOMINANCE FOR MILLENNIA.
"ONCE HATH-SET AND I CUT INTO OUR SKIN WITH THE NTH METAL DAGGER COVERED IN YOUR SACRIFICIAL BLOOD IT WAS PROPHESIED THAT WE WOULD THEN BECOME IMMORTAL."

"BUT OUR WORLD CHANGED THE DAY THAT NABU, THE PHARAOH'S TRUSTED ADVISOR'S PROPHECY CAME TRUE AND THE THANAGARIAN SHIP WAS DISCOVERED...

"...ALONG WITH THE STRANGE SUBSTANCE CALLED NTH METAL THAT POWERED THE ALIEN VESSEL.

"HATH-SET'S LOVE AND VISIONS WERE INSPIRING.
"YOUR STEPFATHER DID NOT AGREE."

"SO BECAUSE THE PHARAOH DIDN'T HAVE CONQUEST ON HIS MIND, YOU KILLED HIM?"
"HE HAD NTH METAL AT HIS FINGERTIPS AND DID NOTHING BUT PHILOSOPHIZE ABOUT WHY IT SHOULD NEVER BE WEAPONIZED.

"...SO I'D SAY IT WAS HIS LACK OF WILL THAT KILLED HIM."
"IT SURE AS HELL WASN'T UNBEARABLE GRIEF OVER THE DEATH OF HIS LAST WIFE LIKE IT SAID IN THAT SUICIDE LETTER YOU LEFT FOR US TO FIND."

"ALL YOU PROVIDED WAS REGICIDE AND A COUP. YOU BETRAYED ME--YOU BETRAYED YOUR HUSBAND--YOU BETRAYED EGYPT."
"ONE PERSON'S COUP IS ANOTHER PERSON'S DIVINE MISSION, CHAY-ARA...

"...BUT AFTER MANY LONG YEARS OF RULING EGYPT I CRAVED AN ADVENTURE.
"...SO I FINALLY WENT IN SEARCH FOR THE SOURCE OF NTH METAL...
"...AND FOUND A WORLD IN DIRE NEED OF A RULER WITH A WOMAN'S TOUCH."

I DO ADMIT, I STAYED HERE LONGER THAN I... ANTICIPATED.
LOOKING AT YOUR FACE AND WINGS, I'D HAVE TO AGREE.

THE DESIRE TO FLY ON HAWKWORLD IS OVERPOWERING. ONE TOO MANY GENETIC EXPERIMENTS, I'M AFRAID.
YOU MUST BE SO PROUD OF EVERYTHING YOU'VE ACCOMPLISHED.
I AM PROUD! THIS CITY WAS BUILT ON MY INSPIRATIONS--THERE WAS NO PHARAOH--SIMPLY ME AND THIS...UNCIVILIZED LITTLE WORLD THAT I HAD TO SHAPE ALL ON MY--

YAARGHH!
OUR GUEST IS ARRIVING.
SHUNK
KRAK

SHUNK
KRAK
CLANG

KRAK
SHUNK
CLANG

...YOU CAN'T BE... NO...

SHIERA!
CARTER!

GET AWAY FROM HER!
AAIIEE
UGGNN

NOW IT'S *MY* TURN, HATH!
WHAT-- NAGHH

I DON'T KNOW *HOW* YOU'RE HERE, QUEEN KHEA, AND *WHY* YOU'RE DOING THIS TO YOUR OWN DAUGHTER--
--BUT RIGHT NOW I DON'T GIVE A DAMN!
AAAGHH!
KOOM

HOW DOES IT FEEL, HATH?!? HOW DO THESE LAST BREATHS TASTE, *HMM*?!
HOW DOES IT FEEL TO KNOW YOU'LL NEVER BE ABLE TO *TEAR* CARTER AND ME APART EVER AGAIN?!
HOW DOES IT FEEL TO *LOSE* IT ALL, HATH?
AGHKK

WHAT--
I GO BY THE NAME QUEEN SHRIKE NOW...

...AND THANKS TO MY PROLONGED EXPOSURE TO NTH METAL HERE ON HAWKWORLD, KHUFU...
RRGH!
...I CAN CONTROL ANYTHING THAT HAS EVEN A TRACE AMOUNT OF IT.

FOR ALL THE PAIN AND MISERY YOU'VE CAUSED--
AACKKK

--DIE, YOU EVIL SON OF A BITCH!
KRAKK

WHEN I'M THROUGH WITH--
ARRGH
SKRAK
AS YOU CAN SEE, IT'S NOT JUST INANIMATE OBJECTS I CAN CONTROL...
YOUR BODIES HAVE ABSORBED A GREAT DEAL OF NTH METAL POWER OVER TIME, HAWKMAN...
RRRNN
...NOT AS MUCH AS MINE, OF COURSE, BUT STILL A SIGNIFICANT ENOUGH AMOUNT THAT I CAN MANIPULATE YOU LIKE PUPPETS ON A STRING.
WE'RE ALL EXACTLY WHERE WE NEED TO BE.
THE ONLY PLACE YOU NEED TO BE IS WITH YOUR LAPDOG HATH IN HELL!

EVEN MY POOR DELUDED HATH DIDN'T REALIZE HE WAS A KEY TO THIS GATE.
BY INITIATING THE CURSE ALL THOSE YEARS AGO HE CURSED HIMSELF--BUT THANK YOU FOR KILLING HIM SO I DIDN'T HAVE TO.
YOU'VE ALL PLAYED YOUR PARTS TO PERFECTION AND JUMPED THROUGH THE HOOPS I HOPED YOU WOULD.

YOUR TWO BODIES, STILL IMBUED WITH LIFE AND ATTACHED TO THIS SIDE OF THE GATE, ARE THE FINAL CIRCUIT KEYS I NEEDED.
...MY STRENGTH'S INCREASING A THOUSAND-FOLD...

NOW OUR JOURNEY CAN TRULY BEGIN.

AARGRHHH
FOLLOW ME, MY MANHAWKS!

IT'S TIME TO DRAG MY DREAM INTO EXISTENCE...

...STARTING HERE ON ZAMARON!

GOTHAM CITY.
THE WATCHTOWER.
YEAH. I DIE. I COME BACK.
WITH A NEW POWER EVERY TIME, MR. SHELLEY?
SOME BETTER THAN OTHERS. LAST WEEK I COULD'VE BEATEN CYBORG IN ARM-WRESTLING. AFTER AN UNFORTUNATE ACCIDENT INVOLVING A GAS LEAK AND MY INABILITY TO QUIT SMOKING, THIS WEEK--
--I CAN TRAVEL THROUGH ELECTRONICS.
AND THAT'S WHAT "RESURRECTS" THE RESURRECTION MAN, RIGHT? ELECTRONICS? NANOTECHNOLOGY?
THAT'S WHAT THE PEOPLE THAT DID THIS TO ME SAY, BUT--
FORGET IT.
IT'S NOT HIM EITHER, DOVE?
NOT ME WHAT? WHAT'S GOING ON? WHO'S THAT?
HOW CAN YOU BE SURE IT'S NOT HIM, BOSTON?
THE RING'S STILL QUIET. AND IF RESURRECTION MAN WAS THE CHOSEN ONE... WHICH JUDGING BY HIS SKETCHY RECORD WOULD'VE BEEN A STRETCH ANYWAY...
...WHY WOULDN'T THE RING FLY OFF ME AND ONTO HIM?
WHAT'S IT WAITING FOR? WHY IS IT JUST...
...WAITING.
BOSTON? WHAT IS IT?
UP IN THE SKY. IT'S BACK ON.
YOU HAVE BEEN WAITING... HAVEN'T YOU, RING?

"YOU'VE BEEN WAITING FOR BATMAN."

BRIGHTEST DAY 14
Cover by David Finch

ACROBATS

BOSTON, WAIT!
I CAN FEEL THE RING URGING ME AHEAD, DOVE. I THINK I'M GOING TO FINALLY GET OFF THIS CRAZY TRAIN RIDE.
I THINK--
A REPLACEMENT HAS BEEN CHOSEN.
YEAH. YOU'RE TALKING ABOUT OLD BAT EARS NOW THAT HE'S BACK, AREN'TCHA? BACK FROM THE GRAVE TO SAVE THE DAY AGAIN BY PUTTING YOU ON, HUH, RING?
FINE BY ME.
HAVEN'T DONE THIS IN AWHILE. A LONG WHILE.
AND I KNOW YOU'VE BEEN TRYING TO TELL ME I NEED TO LIVE LIFE WITH A SAFETY NET.

BUT WHAT FUN IS THAT?

WHAT ARE YOU DOING, BOSTON BRAND?
WHAT'S IT *LOOK* LIKE, RING?

I'M GOING TO FIND--

--BATMAN?!
HEY! WHO THE HELL'S *THAT?*
UH, OH.

HAVEN'T TAKEN DOWN ANY BAD GUYS WITH MY OWN BODY IN, WELL--
--EVER.

AT LEAST WHEN YOU BROUGHT US BACK, RING, YOU BROUGHT US BACK AT THE PHYSICAL PEAK OF OUR LIVES.
AAH!

SIX-ON-ONE?

NOT A PROBLEM.

CHAK
IT'S SEVEN, YOU IDIOT.

IT'S ZERO, FREEZE.

AHH-AHH-AHH--!
BATMAN...
AHH--!
QUIT CRYING, VICTOR.
YOU'LL BE FINE.
WHAT ARE YOU DOING HERE, DEADMAN?
KLANGG
WE'VE ONLY MET WHEN I WAS AN INVISIBLE GHOST TALKING THROUGH OTHER PEOPLE. HOW DID YOU KNOW IT WAS ME?
I'M BATMAN.
TOUCHÉ.
I ALSO KNOW YOU WERE PART OF A GROUP OF PEOPLE, GOOD AND BAD, WHO WERE BROUGHT BACK TO LIFE BY ONE OF GREEN LANTERN'S LIGHT SHOWS.
AND I HEARD THROUGH THE SPANDEX GRAPEVINE THAT YOU WERE RESURRECTED TOO.
I WASN'T DEAD. THANKS TO DARKSEID, I WAS LOST IN TIME.
BUMMER.
BOSTON!

I HEARD GUNFIRE! IS EVERYONE ALL RIGHT?
WHAT'S DOVE DOING HERE?
SHE'S, UH, WITH ME, BATS.
DOVE'S BEEN GIVING ME A HAND DEALING WITH THIS WHITE RING. I WAS THE ONLY MEMBER OF THE *BACK-TO-LIFE CLUB* THAT GOT SADDLED WITH ONE.
I'VE BEEN HOLDING ONTO IT... UNTIL IT FINDS THE *CHOSEN ONE.* THE ULTIMATE CHAMPION OF EARTH.
YOU.
ME?

BOSTON, HOW CAN YOU BE SURE THE WHITE RING WAS MEANT FOR BATMAN?
BECAUSE BATMAN IS THE SMARTEST PERSON ON THE PLANET. THERE'S NO ONE ELSE ON EARTH ANYONE WOULD TRUST MORE WITH THIS KIND OF POWER.
WE DON'T KNOW WHAT KIND OF POWER THE WHITE RING EVEN HAS.
IT CAN RAISE THE DEAD. IT CAN MAKE THE ANTI-MONITOR SHOUT "OW!" MAYBE WE'RE NOT MEANT TO KNOW WHAT ELSE IT CAN DO. MAYBE NO ONE IS EXCEPT FOR THE CHOSEN ONE.
AND IT'S HIM, ISN'T IT, RING?
BOSTON--
GO, RING.
DAMMIT, GO! IT'S BATMAN YOU WANT, HE'LL KNOW WHAT TO DO. HE ALWAYS KNOWS WHAT TO DO.
SO LEAVE ME THE HELL ALONE!

AAARGHHH!
AQUAMAN.
JADE.
CAPTAIN BOOMERANG.
FIRESTORM.
DEADMAN.
HAWKGIRL
HAWKMAN.
OSIRIS.
MARTIAN MANHUNTER.
HAWK.
REVERSE-FLASH.
MAXWELL LORD.

YOU SURE ABOUT THIS?
NO.
LIFE ON EARTH.
IT'S ALL CONNECTED. LIKE TWISTING ROOTS IN THE GROUND.
BUT THE ENTIRE WEB WAS CORRUPTED.
EXCEPT FOR YOU, BOSTON. YOU WERE DEAD. YOU WERE PURE.
HEY!
NNNG?
THAT'S WHY I CHOSE YOU TO GUIDE ME. IT SHOULD BE AN HONOR, BUT YOU SAW IT AS A CHORE. YOU DON'T CARE ABOUT ANYONE'S LIFE BUT YOUR OWN.
SO YOU TRIED TO FORCE THIS BURDEN UPON THIS MAN.
YOU CHOSE POORLY.
CHAK

BLAMMM

BOSTON!

BOSTON?

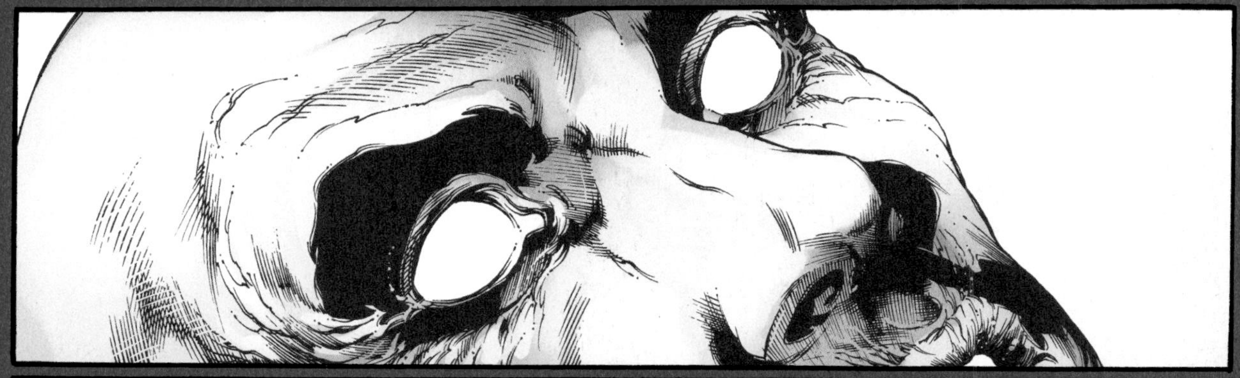

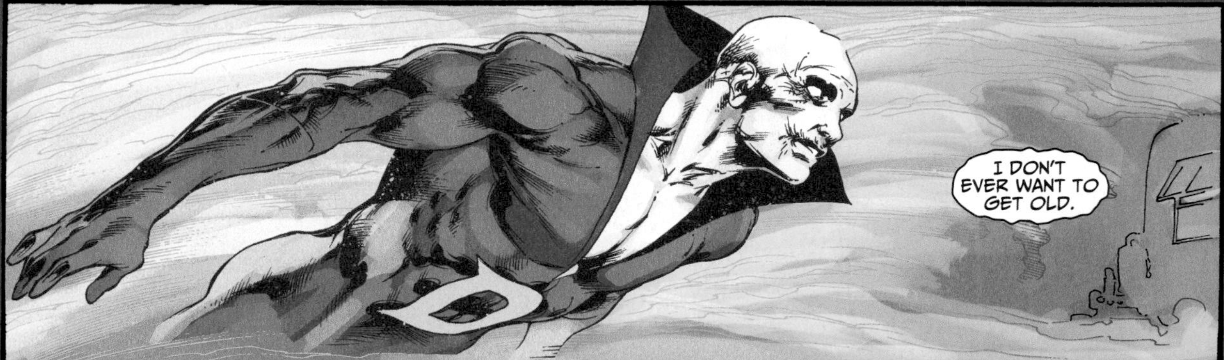
I DON'T EVER WANT TO GET OLD.

NO ONE DOES.
GRANDPA?
AND YOU DON'T WANT TO BE STUCK IN A CHAIR LIKE GRANDPA, HM?

NO.

WHAT IF I TOLD YOU I WASN'T STUCK IN THIS CHAIR, BOSTON?

YOU CAN WALK?
NO. NOT ANYMORE. BUT I DON'T THINK I'M STUCK IN THIS CHAIR.
WHAT? THAT DOESN'T MAKE ANY SENSE.
I'M STILL HERE. I'M STILL ABLE TO TALK TO YOUR MOTHER AND YOU AND YOUR BROTHER.
I'VE BEEN GIVEN MORE TIME THAN YOUR GRANDMOTHER AND YOUR FATHER. I'VE BEEN LUCKY.
IT'S NOT A BAD THING TO GROW OLD. IT'S A PRIVILEGE.

OF COURSE, I WAS LIKE YOU WHEN I WAS YOUNGER. EVERY DAY LASTED A WEEK. EVERY WEEK A YEAR. AND LIFE WASN'T SO PRECIOUS. RECKLESSNESS IS FOR THE YOUNG.
UH HUH.
DID YOU KNOW I HELD THE RECORD FOR LONGEST DISTANCE JUMP ON A HARLEY DAVIDSON FOR NEARLY TWO DECADES?
I'M GONNA SEE WHAT'S ON TV.

GRANDPA?

SCARS ARE THE BULLET POINTS OF LIFE.

DRIVE-IN
BIG BELLY BURGER
I WAS PLAYING HIDE-AND-SEEK WITH MY COUSINS IN A CORNFIELD BY THEIR HOUSE. I TRIPPED AND FELL ON A RAKE.

THAT'S WHY I USUALLY WEAR SKIRTS THAT COVER MY KNEES.

OH.
BOSTON?
WHAT?
DO YOU WANT TO BE HERE?
SURE. I'M HUNGRY.
WITH ME, I MEAN?

WHERE ARE THEY? DOES A CHEESEBURGER REALLY TAKE *THIRTY* MINUTES?
WHAT A TOTAL WASTE OF TIME.

I REMEMBER HER.
AUDREY. SHE GOT SICK AFTER WE GRADUATED. SHE'S DEAD.

AM I DEAD?
WHO WOULD GO TO YOUR FUNERAL?

FRIENDS? FAMILY? DO YOU *HAVE* ANY, YOU #@%@?
JUST BECAUSE *I'M* THE ONE DRAWING THE CROWDS AND EARNING *FOUR* TIMES WHAT YOU MAKE, DOESN'T MEAN YOU GET TO BREAK DOWN MY DOOR IF I'M *LATE* GETTING ON STAGE.
YOU KEEP CALLING ME NAMES, I'LL BREAK MORE THAN THAT!
I'VE GOT THE CROWD ALL WARMED UP, BOSTON.
AND NOW, LADIEEEES AND GENTLEMEN! THE ACT YOU ALL CAME HERE TO SEE!
YOU HEAR THAT, TOBY? I DON'T NEED THEM WARMED UP.
KA-CHAK
THE DEATH-DEFYING!

TINY, PLEASE.
HIS EGO IS THROWING THE ENTIRE NIGHT OFF.
BOSTON BRAND IS KEEPING MY FATHER'S CIRCUS UP AND RUNNING.
LORNA?
DON'T KID YERSELF. HE AIN'T DOIN' IT FOR YOU OR THE CIRCUS. THE ONLY THING BOSTON BRAND IS WORRIED ABOUT--
--IS BOSTON BRAND.
WAIT! STOP ME, TINY! DON'T LET ME GO OUT THERE! PLEASE!
I'M GOING TO GET SHOT! I'M GOING TO GET SHOT AND KILLED TONIGHT!
THE AMAZING!
JERK.
WAIT! BOSTON!
I DON'T WANT TO DIE.
DEADMAN!

BLAMM

NO!

I-I KNOW I NEVER CARED ABOUT ANYONE BUT ME...
NOT UNTIL AFTER I WAS D-DEAD.
UNTIL AFTER I LITERALLY WALKED IN THEIR SHOES.

BUT I DID THAT. EVEN AFTER I SOLVED MY OWN MURDER. EVEN AFTER I WAS PROMISED I COULD MOVE ON. I STAYED HERE. INVISIBLE. A GHOST.
DAMMIT, I DO CARE ABOUT PEOPLE. I JUST WANT TO WALK IN MY OWN SHOES NOW. I MIGHT NOT BE MEANT TO SAVE THE UNIVERSE OR THE EARTH, BUT I CAN MAKE LIFE BETTER FOR OTHERS. AND FOR ME.
WHY IS THAT WRONG? WHY?!

I WANT TO LIVE, DO YOU HEAR ME?!
I WANT MY SECOND CHANCE!
THEN STOP HESITATING, BOSTON BRAND.

AND TAKE IT.
KAAFFF!
YOU WILL NOT FIND THE CHOSEN ONE BY SEARCHING FOR THEM.
LIFE IS NOT WHAT YOU PLAN.
LIFE IS THE UNEXPECTED.
KRKLANG
LIVE LIFE AGAIN THE WAY YOU WISH TO.
AND THE CHOSEN ONE WILL COME TO YOU.
DAMN YOU. DAMN THAT RING. I WAS...I WAS SO SCARED.
SO WAS I.
IS BATMAN--?
SHOCKER.
I'M SURPRISED HE DIDN'T STAY TO ASK MORE QUESTIONS.
MAYBE THE RING ALREADY GAVE HIM THE ANSWERS.
DID IT GIVE YOU ANY?
YEAH.
I JUST HOPE THERE'S MORE TO LIFE THAN A GOOD CHEESEBURGER.
THERE'S PLENTY MORE.

IT'S BATMAN.
WE NEED TO TALK ABOUT MAXWELL LORD.

BRIGHTEST DAY 15
Cover by David Finch

WHATEVER HAPPENED TO THE MANHUNTER FROM MARS?

MARS.
WE'RE HERE TODAY TO CELEBRATE A LIFE.
A LIFE WELL LIVED.
A LIFE WELL IMAGINED...

...AND MOST IMPORTANT, A LIFE WELL SPENT IN THE PURSUIT OF TRUTH, JUSTICE, AND THE UNIVERSAL WAY...
...IT'S THE 25TH ANNIVERSARY SINCE HE USHERED IN A NEW ERA OF TRANQUILITY NOT JUST HERE ON MARS, BUT ALSO ON EARTH.
PEACE IN OUR TIME. PEACE IN MY TIME. I DIDN'T THINK I'D LIVE TO SEE IT.
THANKS TO HIM I DID.
YOU'VE BEEN A SHINING EXAMPLE THAT IT'S NEVER TOO LATE TO START OVER AGAIN, THAT IT'S NEVER TOO LATE TO CARE AND DEMAND MORE OF OURSELVES... OR OTHERS.
YOU'VE BLAZED A TRAIL, OL' BUDDY, AND IT'S BEEN A GREAT RIDE TRYING TO KEEP UP WITH YOU ALL THESE YEARS...
...A TEAMMATE WHO CARED ABOUT NOT ONLY WHAT WAS ABOVE, BUT ALSO WHAT WAS BELOW...
WHAT ELSE CAN I SAY, EXCEPT HE'S SHOWN US THE MOST AMAZING EXPRESSION OF WILLPOWER THIS UNIVERSE HAS EVER SEEN.
I'M PROUD TO NOT ONLY CALL HIM MY FRIEND, BUT ALSO MY SECTOR PARTNER...
...MY FAVORITE MARTIAN, GREEN LANTERN J'ONN J'ONZZ.

GREETINGS MARS.
THE PURE BLISS I FEEL STANDING BEFORE YOU TODAY, HERE IN THE LITERAL HEART OF THE CITY, IS AS STRONG AS IT WAS TWENTY-FIVE YEARS AGO.
EVERY LIVING AND BREATHING THING IN THIS UNIVERSE IS FAMILY.
IT HAS ALWAYS BEEN MY MISSION TO SPREAD THAT MESSAGE THROUGHOUT THE GALAXY.
WE ARE ALL CONNECTED.
WE ARE ONE.
AND TOGETHER WE CAN ACHIEVE ANYTHING.
NONE OF THIS WOULD BE POSSIBLE IF NOT FOR MY WIFE, M'YRIAH, AND MY CHILDREN, FOR THEY ARE THE ROCK I STAND UPON, MY UNWAVERING PARTNERS IN ALL THE JOYS AND CHALLENGES THAT THIS WONDERFUL LIFE HAS TO OFFER.
SO, IF THERE IS ONE THOUGHT I WOULD LIKE TO LEAVE YOU ALL ON THIS SPECIAL ANNIVERSARY, IT IS THIS:
I DID NOT GIVE LIFE TO YOU...
...YOU HAVE GIVEN LIFE TO ME.

SEEMS YOUR FELLOW MARTIANS HAVE ***LITERALLY*** PUT YOU ON A ***PEDESTAL.***

A ***PLACE*** I FIND MYSELF ***NOT*** ENTIRELY COMFORTABLE WITH, DIANA.

KINDA STRANGE TO THINK THE LAST TIME MOST OF US WERE TOGETHER ON MARS IT WAS LIFELESS AND BARREN AND WE HAPPENED TO BE BURYING YOU, J'ONN.

TIME FLIES WHEN YOU ARE HAVING FUN, HAL.

DID J'ONN J'ONZZ JUST CRACK WISE?

NOTHING LIKE HAVING YOUR FAMILY AND ENTIRE PLANET BACK TO HELP PUT A SMILE ON YOUR FACE.
YES, KAL, QUALITY OF LIFE DOES WONDERS FOR THE SOUL.
SO DOES THE QUALITY OF LEGACY WHEN YOU'RE STARING AT YOUR OWN MORTALITY.
I THINK YOU'VE GOT A FEW MILES LEFT IN THE TANK THERE, BRUCE.

I'M CLOSER TO THE END THAN I AM THE BEGINNING, BARRY, AND THAT'S OKAY WHEN YOU'RE JUST MEAT AND BONE.

IT'S THE NATURAL ORDER OF THINGS WHEN YOU'RE NOT A MARTIAN, OR WEARING A POWER RING OR SURROUNDED BY THE SPEED FORCE OR POWERED BY THE SUN ITSELF OR AN AMAZONIAN PRINCESS OR A HALF-HUMAN ATLANTEAN.

BUT NO MATTER WHAT YOU ARE, THERE'S ONLY ONE SIMPLE QUESTION YOU HAVE TO ASK YOURSELF THAT REALLY MEANS ANYTHING, AND THAT IS: ***DID I DO MORE GOOD THAN BAD?***

AND WHAT WAS YOUR ANSWER?
OUR SCALES OF JUSTICE ARE PERSONAL, ARTHUR--WE'VE ALL DONE THINGS THAT'VE HAUNTED US--WE ALL BEAR THE WEIGHT OF THOSE CHOICES DIFFERENTLY.
BUT RIGHT HERE, RIGHT NOW, BETWEEN FRIENDS, BRUCE, WHAT ANSWER COMES TO YOU IN YOUR PRIVATE MOMENTS?

YOU CAN READ MY MIND AND FIND OUT FOR YOURSELF.
I WOULD PREFER YOU SHARE IT WITH US.
MY ANSWER'S AS SIMPLE AS MY QUESTION: I HOPE SO.

THAT'S ALL YOU GOT, "I HOPE SO"?
HOPE IS ALL YOU EVER HAVE IN THE END, ISN'T THAT RIGHT, J'ONN?
YES, BUT NEVER UNDERESTIMATE THE POWER OF WILL.

OUR COMBINATION OF WILL AND HOPE IS WHAT'LL CONTINUE TO MAKE PEOPLE'S LIVES BETTER THROUGH THE YEARS.
IT'S WHAT LETS ME GO TO SLEEP JUSTIFIED.
COME ON, KAL, WE ALL KNOW YOU DON'T SLEEP.

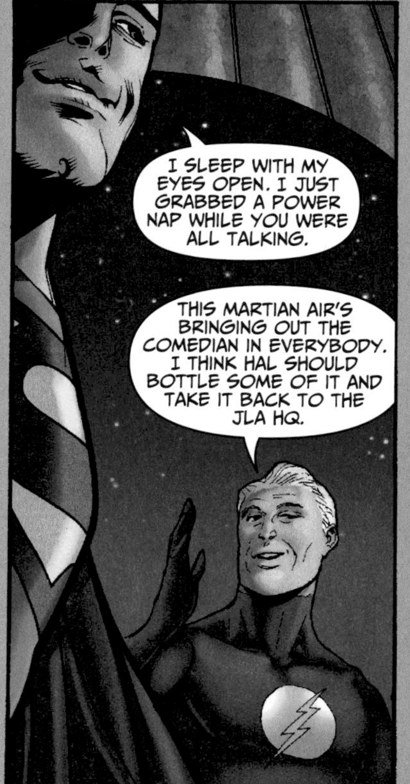
I SLEEP WITH MY EYES OPEN. I JUST GRABBED A POWER NAP WHILE YOU WERE ALL TALKING.
THIS MARTIAN AIR'S BRINGING OUT THE COMEDIAN IN EVERYBODY. I THINK HAL SHOULD BOTTLE SOME OF IT AND TAKE IT BACK TO THE JLA HQ.

WHAT HAL SHOULD TRY TO BOTTLE, BARRY, IS THE HEART, GRACE, WILL, INTEGRITY, NOBILITY, AND ENDURANCE OF THIS GROUP...
...BECAUSE WHAT LEAVES ME JUSTIFIED IS KNOWING ALL OF YOU WILL BE HERE LONG AFTER I'M GONE TO CARRY ON.
I HAVE NOTHING TO ADD TO BATMAN'S HEARTFELT WORDS, EXCEPT TO SAY YOUR PRESENCE HERE TODAY MEANS A GREAT DEAL...

...IT'S BEEN MY HONOR AND PRIVILEGE...

"...TO BE A PART OF THE JUSTICE LEAGUE OF THE PAST, PRESENT, AND FUTURE."

WHAT AN AMAZING DAY IT HAS BEEN, M'YRIAH.
INCREDIBLY POIGNANT AND STIRRING, MY DARLING HUSBAND...
...YOUR FAMILY AND PEOPLE ARE INCREDIBLY PROUD OF YOU...
...BUT NO ONE'S MORE PROUD OF YOU THAN I AM.

IT WAS SO KIND OF YOUR FRIENDS TO JOIN US FOR THIS ANNIVERSARY.
KEEPING THEIR ARRIVAL A SECRET TOOK A GREAT DEAL OF EFFORT.
IT WAS A PLEASANT SURPRISE.
YOU KNEW ALL ALONG, DIDN'T YOU?
OF COURSE NOT, I HAD NO IDEA THEY WERE--

J'ONN J'ONZZ, YOU'RE A TERRIBLE LIAR.
OKAY, YES, I KNEW ALL ABOUT IT.
YOU DO REALIZE YOU'RE SPOILING MELISSA WITH ALL THOSE COOKIES.
THAT'S WHY WE CAN NEVER GET HER TO EAT HER REGULAR FOOD.

RRAAACH

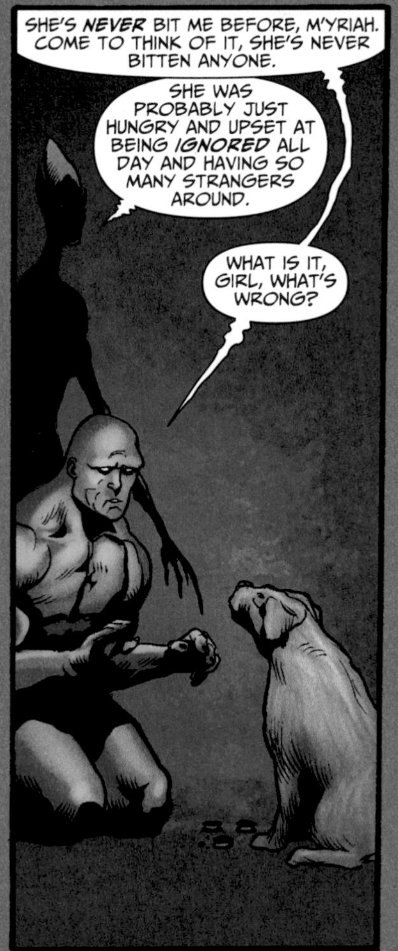
SHE'S NEVER BIT ME BEFORE, M'YRIAH. COME TO THINK OF IT, SHE'S NEVER BITTEN ANYONE.
SHE WAS PROBABLY JUST HUNGRY AND UPSET AT BEING IGNORED ALL DAY AND HAVING SO MANY STRANGERS AROUND.
WHAT IS IT, GIRL, WHAT'S WRONG?

I'M SURE IT'S NOTHING, J'ONN.
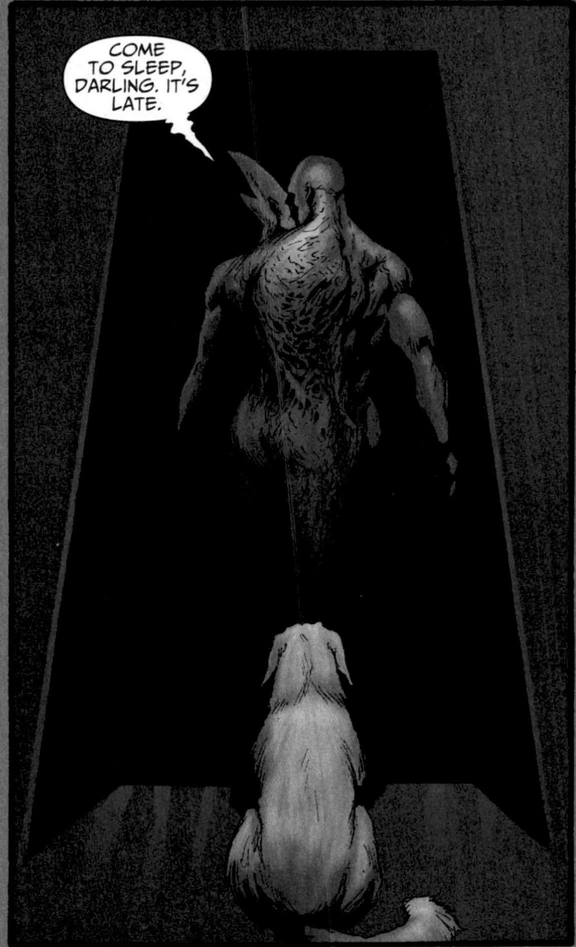
COME TO SLEEP, DARLING. IT'S LATE.
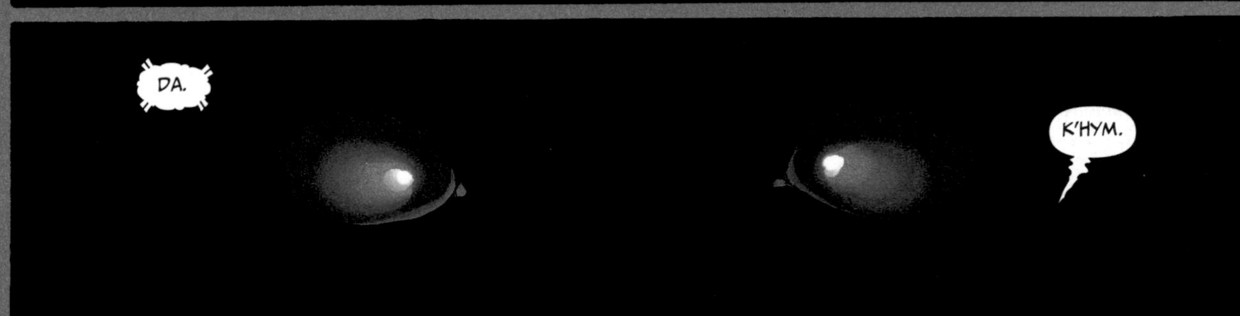

DA.
K'HYM.
YOUR THOUGHTS ARE TANGIBLE. BLOOD HAS BEEN SPILLED. THERE'S BEEN A MURDER.
IT'S EVEN WORSE, DA...

"...IT'S BATMAN."

...BRUCE... NO...

RING. SCAN FOR ALL SIGNS OF ORGANIC AND INORGANIC MATTER AND INDEX IMMEDIATELY.
REQUEST COMPLETE.

WHAT WERE YOU TRYING TO TELL ME, BRUCE?

FORGIVE MY FINAL INTRUSION, OLD FRIEND...
...BUT I AM SURE YOU WOULD WANT ME TO MAKE AN EXCEPTION TONIGHT.
ANY RESIDUAL IMAGERY TO DRAW FROM, DA?

I AM AFRAID NOT, K'HYM.
MAYBE THIS REMAINING PHYSICAL EVIDENCE CAN BE USED TO--

PEARL BULLETS?
THIS WAS PERSONAL.
AND WHOEVER DID IT KNEW I WOULD REALIZE THAT.
IF THEY WERE ABLE TO KILL BATMAN, THEN THE ENTIRE JLA IS AT RISK--

WE MUST WARN THEM QUICKLY WITH A TELEPATHIC--
WHAT IS IT, DA?

--THEY'RE GONE, K'HYM-- I CANNOT SENSE THEM ANYWHERE ON MARS!
WE MUST FIND THEM!

"THERE IS ALWAYS SOMEONE WHO CELEBRATES THE VICTORY OF FEAR.
"THERE IS ALWAYS SOMEONE WHO WANTS TO SHUT OFF THE LIGHT...
"...BY DESTROYING THE GOOD WITHIN US...
"...THE GOOD AMONG US.
"SOMEONE HAS MURDERED MY FRIENDS...
"...AND SPIT ON OUR HARD-EARNED PEACE OF THE LAST TWENTY-FIVE YEARS."

I HAVE ASSEMBLED YOU ALL HERE TO TELL YOU THAT JUSTICE WILL BE SERVED...
...AND THE MANHUNTERS OF MARS WILL BE THE ONES SERVING IT...
...WITH EXTREME PREJUDICE.
I WILL NOW INITIATE A PSYCHIC PROBE THAT WILL PENETRATE EVERY MIND ACROSS MARS.
IT WILL RESULT IN SEVERE PAIN AND A SHORT PERIOD OF DEBILITATION--
--BUT I CONSIDER IT A SMALL PRICE TO PAY FOR HELPING US LOCATE SUPERMAN AND ALSO THE PERPETRATOR OF THESE APPALLING CRIMES.
I FOUND SUPERMAN!
HE'S ALIVE!
WHERE?
DEEP BENEATH MARS...

"...IN THE UNDERGROUND SECURITY BUNKER WHERE OUR MOST POWERFUL ENEMIES ARE HELD CAPTIVE."

THERE HE IS!

IS THIS WHAT I THINK IT--
A KRYPTONITE MASK.

THANK H'RONMEER, HE'S STILL ALIVE AFTER SUCH A LONG EXPOSURE.

YOU SAID ONLY SOMEONE WITH INCREDIBLE POWER COULD TAKE OUT THE ENTIRE JLA--I'LL SCAN HIM--MAYBE HE'S SOMEHOW RESPONSIBLE OR KNOWS--

GET OUT OF HIS MIND, K'HYM!
SUPERMAN'S **NOT RESPONSIBLE** FOR ANY OF THIS INSANITY.
HOW CAN WE BE SURE UNLESS--

SUPERMAN IS ABOVE REPROACH.
NO ONE IS ABOVE REPROACH, DA. IT'S ONE OF THE CENTRAL TENETS I LEARNED WHEN I BECAME A MANHUNTER.
YOU WILL NOT BREACH HIM, UNDERSTOOD?
NO, I **DON'T** UNDERSTAND-- YOU BREACHED BATMAN'S MIND WHEN--

BATMAN WAS DEAD.
A DEEP PROBE IS SOMETHING I DO NOT PERFORM ON THE MINDS OF CLOSE FRIENDS UNLESS THEY GIVE THEIR EXPRESS APPROVAL.

YOU DIDN'T GIVE IT A SECOND THOUGHT WHEN YOU **PERFORMED** IT ON ME, AND EVERY OTHER FELLOW MARTIAN ON THE PLANET.
WHY DIDN'T YOU ASK FOR **OUR** APPROVAL?
WHEN DO **WE** GET THE SAME CONSIDERATION THE EARTHLINGS DO? **WHERE** DO WE RANK, DA?

HOW DARE YOU SAY *THAT* TO ME.
HAVE *YOU* EVER *CONSIDERED* WHAT I HAD TO GO THROUGH TO *RESURRECT* MY PEOPLE-- MY FAMILY?!?

SEE--THAT'S THE PROBLEM, YOU TREAT US SOMETIMES LIKE MINDLESS CHILDREN-- HERE TO *SAY* THINGS-- DO THINGS--EVEN *THINK* THINGS *YOU* WANT US TO THINK BECAUSE--
THAT IS *NOT* TRUE, K'HYM.
IT *IS* TRUE, DA.
WHEN DO YOU FINALLY CUT THE *TIES THAT BIND* YOU TO EARTH SO YOU CAN BE HERE WITH US COMPLETELY IN MIND *AND* SPIRIT?

SUPERMAN'S LIFE WAS IN JEOPARDY-- IT WAS *IMPERATIVE* THAT I PROBE--
I'M YOUR DAUGHTER-- *THOSE* ARE YOUR PEOPLE DOWN THERE-- WHEN DO WE COME FIRST?
I HAVE *ALWAYS* PUT MY FAMILY FIRST.
WHICH FAMILY, DA?
...J-J'ONN...

...THEY USED *KRYPTONITE*... DIDN'T GET A CHANCE TO SEE WHO ATTACKED ME...
JUST *RECHARGE*, KAL, THE KRYPTONITE'S GONE--LET THE SUN'S RAYS GET YOU BACK UP TO FULL POWER, WE'RE GOING TO NEED IT.

WHAT IS IT, J'ONN--I CAN SEE IT IN YOUR FACE?
SOMEONE HAS A *VENDETTA* AGAINST THE JLA...WE ARE THE ONLY TWO LEFT...*ALL* OUR DEAREST FRIENDS HAVE BEEN SLAUGHTERED.
THAT'S NOT POSSIBLE...I WANT TO SEE THEM...
...NOW.

IT'S A NIGHTMARE...ALL OF OUR ENEMIES ARE DEAD--LOCKED AWAY--AND STILL I'M STANDING HERE STARING DOWN AT THE LIFELESS FACES OF... BRUCE, HAL, ARTHUR... OH, POOR BARRY...

...AND DIANA...

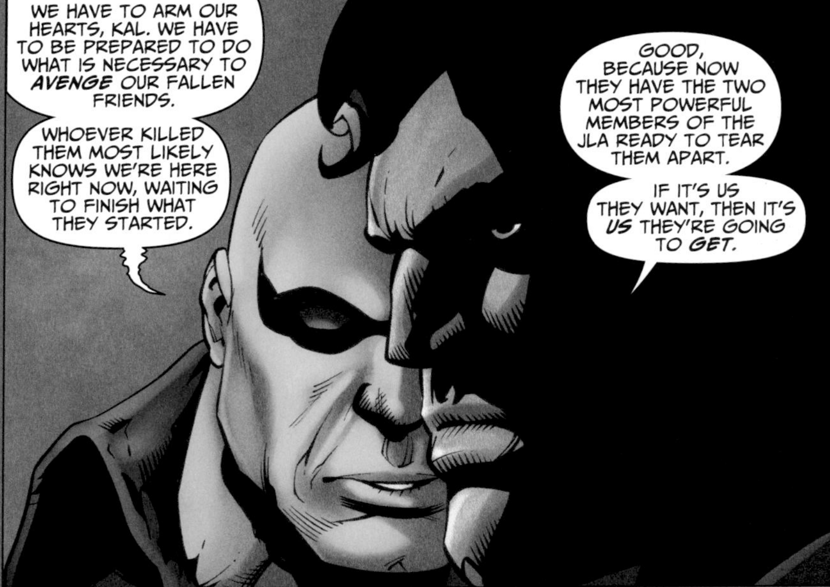
WE HAVE TO ARM OUR HEARTS, KAL. WE HAVE TO BE PREPARED TO DO WHAT IS NECESSARY TO AVENGE OUR FALLEN FRIENDS.
WHOEVER KILLED THEM MOST LIKELY KNOWS WE'RE HERE RIGHT NOW, WAITING TO FINISH WHAT THEY STARTED.
GOOD, BECAUSE NOW THEY HAVE THE TWO MOST POWERFUL MEMBERS OF THE JLA READY TO TEAR THEM APART.
IF IT'S US THEY WANT, THEN IT'S US THEY'RE GOING TO GET.

I ENVY YOU SOMETIMES, KAL.
WHY, WHAT'S THERE TO ENVY?
BECAUSE YOU DIDN'T HAVE TO WATCH YOUR PLANET DIE.
BECAUSE YOU BEGAN YOUR TIME ON EARTH SURROUNDED BY LOVE, AND I BEGAN MINE SURROUNDED BY FEAR.

J'ONN, LAST I LOOKED, MARS IS ALIVE AND VIBRANT BECAUSE OF YOU.
ITS BEAUTY IS THERE TO TOUCH, HEAR, AND SEE, BUT WHEN I CLOSE MY EYES, KAL...THAT ALL CHANGES...
...I ALWAYS SEE A DEAD PLANET, I HEAR THE SCREAMS OF MY PEOPLE, I SMELL THE SKIN OF MY WIFE AND DAUGHTER BURNING LIKE IT WAS YESTERDAY--
--WHEN IS TOMORROW GOING TO BE MY NEW YESTERDAY, KAL? WHEN AM I GOING TO STOP BEING THE "LAST SON OF MARS" AND THINK OF MYSELF AS THE "FIRST SON OF MARS"?

I WISH I COULD TELL YOU TIME HEALS ALL WOUNDS BUT WE BOTH KNOW THE MORE TIME YOU HAVE, THE LONGER THE LIST OF WOUNDS GROWS.
HAVE *YOU* EVER FELT LIKE THE "LAST SON OF KRYPTON"?
HONESTLY, J'ONN, I HAVEN'T.

THE UNCONDITIONAL LOVE OF MY MA AND PA MADE SURE I NEVER FELT "LAST" IN ANY WAY.

THAT YOU WERE ONLY AN ***INFANT*** WHEN KRYPTON WAS ***VAPORIZED*** WAS A BLESSING IN DISGUISE, KAL, ALONG WITH NOT HAVING YOUR KRYPTONIAN HERITAGE ENTER YOUR LIFE UNTIL AFTER YOUR FORMATIVE YEARS...

"IMAGINE IF YOU HAD TO ***BURY*** EACH AND EVERY KRYPTONIAN..."

"J'ONN, DID YOU ACTUALLY--"

IT TOOK ME ***YEARS,*** KAL...I DID NOT STOP DIGGING UNTIL ALL THE REMAINS OF MY PEOPLE WERE UNDER THE GROUND...

...AND IT SEEMS THE RED DIRT ALWAYS NEEDS MORE--WILL IT WANT TO ***DEVOUR*** MY FAMILY AND ALL THOSE SOULS I RAISED ***AGAIN?***

I AM NOT SURE I CAN ***BEAR*** THEIR LOSS FOR A SECOND TIME.

I NEED MARS TO REMAIN A LIVING AND BREATHING PLANET NOW MORE THAN EVER.

WE CAN ONLY ***BEAR*** WHAT WE'RE ABLE TO, J'ONN.
FOR THESE LAST 25 YEARS OF YOUR LIFE YOU'VE HAD ***EVERYTHING...***
...IT'S TIME TO FIGHT TO KEEP IT ALL ALIVE.
I AM NOT SURE I AGREE WITH YOU, KAL...

...WHAT MAKES YOU THINK ANY OF US IS MEANT TO HAVE EVERYTHING?!?
ARGRHH
SHUNK
DOES HAVING EVERYTHING MAKE US HAPPY, KAL?!?
...WAKE...
DOES IT?!?
SHUNK
...UP...
WHAT HAVE I DONE?!?

NO, IT'S NOT POSSIBLE...
...ON THEIR BODIES...
...THE MARTIAN SYMBOLS FOR "LOVE" AND "HATE"...

NO!
WAKE UP!
WAKE UP!
WAKE UP!
WAKE UP!
WAKE UP!
WAKE UP!
WAKE UP!

WE ARE TRYING TO SAVE ME!
WE ARE TRYING TO SAVE ME!
WE ARE TRYING TO SAVE ME!
WE ARE TRYING TO SAVE ME!
WE ARE TRYING TO SAVE ME!
WE ARE TRYING TO SAVE ME!
WE ARE TRYING TO SAVE ME!

RRAAAR!
POOM
J'ONN, MY BELOVED, WHY DO YOU ENTER OUR HOME WITH SUCH RAGE?
YOU FIGURE IT OUT, D'KAY!
SHOW YOURSELF, YOU TWISTED ABOMINATION!

I GUESS YOU DIDN'T WANT TO FIGHT TO KEEP *OUR* BRAVE NEW WORLD AFTER ALL, J'ONN.
I DO NOT FIGHT FOR A LIE OF THE MIND, D'KAY...
...AND I NEVER WILL!

HEADQUARTERS OF THE JUSTICE LEAGUE OF AMERICA.
COME ON, MIK, TALLY HO!
YOU'RE NEVER GOING TO BEAT ME PLAYING LIKE THAT.
CONGORILLA A.K.A. "CONGO" BILL GLENMORGAN
Powers: Human mind possessing the body of the mythic and powerful golden gorilla.
STARMAN A.K.A. MIKAAL TOMAS
Powers: Extraterrestrial strength, alien gem provides flight and energy projection.
I'M STILL NOT QUITE SURE I UNDERSTAND THE POINT OF BOARD GAMES, BILL.
CHESS IS NOT A BOARD GAME, MIKAAL. IT'S A BATTLE BETWEEN INTELLECTS. A WAR BETWEEN MINDS. THERE'S NOTHING MORE EXCITING THAN THAT.
WHAT? WHAT IS THIS MESS?!
TAR?
FZZAAMM
AND THE FLOOR IS TURNING INTO ICE! WE'RE UNDER ATTACK!
N-NO. I NEED YOUR H-HELP.

I'M ABOUT TO DESTROY THE UNIVERSE.

BRIGHTEST DAY 16
Cover by Gary Frank and Nathan Eyring

SHORT FUSE

THE BOTTOM OF THE ATLANTIC.

WHO ARE THOSE PEOPLE?

AQUAMAN?
ONE IS MY WIFE, MERA. THE OTHER...
YOUR KID?
WHAT ARE YOU GOING TO DO NOW?
I THOUGHT I WAS STAYING HERE WITH MY PARENTS.
YOUR SURROGATE PARENTS WILL BE SAFE HERE WHILE WE DEAL WITH MERA'S PEOPLE.
YOU CAN'T.
THOUSANDS OF ATLANTEANS WHO WERE BANISHED CENTURIES AGO TO A PENAL COLONY CALLED XEBEL.
THEIR HATRED OF THE SURFACE WORLD IS RIVALED ONLY BY THEIR HATRED FOR ATLANTIS.
AND *ME*.
IF THEY GET FREE, THERE WILL BE A WAR BETWEEN LAND AND SEA THAT WILL DESTROY *BOTH* WORLDS.
WHICH WORLD DO *YOU* BELONG TO?

MY SON.
HE WAS MURDERED BY YOUR BIOLOGICAL FATHER. BY BLACK MANTA.
WHY NOT?
BECAUSE MERA'S PEOPLE ARE TRYING TO BREAK FREE FROM THE BERMUDA TRIANGLE.
WHO ARE THEY?
SAY GOOD-BYE TO YOUR PARENTS. WE HAVE TO GO.
WE? WHAT DO YOU NEED ME FOR?
YOU'RE THE KEY TO KEEPING MERA'S PEOPLE LOCKED UP, JACKSON.
YOU'RE GOING TO STOP THIS WAR--

"--BEFORE IT STARTS."
THE WATCHTOWER.
THE SATELLITE HEADQUARTERS OF THE JUSTICE LEAGUE OF AMERICA.
IF ANYONE CAN HELP US GET OUR POWERS UNDER CONTROL, RONNIE, IT'S THEM.
I JUST WANT TO GET US FIXED SO WE CAN GO FIND THE PROFESSOR AND YOUR DAD.
DO YOU THINK THEY'RE STILL ALIVE, JASON?

"I HOPE SO."
ELSEWHERE.
WHAT IS THAT?
IT'S POWER, DUDE. EXTREME POWER. THE WHITE LANTERN IS THE SOURCE OF ALL LIFE.
WHAT DO YOU WANT WITH IT?
I'M ONLY THE DELIVERY BOY, PROFESSOR.
FOR WHO?
MAN, YOU'RE ASKING A LOT OF QUESTIONS. I'M SURE THAT BIG BRAIN OF YOURS IS THINKING EVERY SECOND YOU KEEP ME TALKING IS A SECOND CLOSER FIRESTORM GETS.
BUT THOSE LOSERS ARE IN WAY OVER THEIR HEADS. LIKE THE BOTH OF YOU.
MY SON IS MORE THAN CAPABLE OF HANDLING SOMETHING LIKE YOU.
WHAT'S HE GOING TO DO, MR. RUSCH? HE'S NOT GOING TO RISK HARMING ME. NOT WHEN WE'RE ALL FUSED TOGETHER.
AND HERE'S ANOTHER FACT...
...I'M MORE POWERFUL THAN FIRESTORM.
I CAN TRANSMUTE ORGANICS.
WHICH MEANS I CAN TURN DIRT INTO BLACK LANTERNS OR I CAN TURN THE SKIN ON FIRESTORM INTO OATMEAL.
I WILL KILL RONNIE AND JASON AND I WILL DO IT IN THE MOST PAINFUL WAY POSSIBLE.
THEY CAN'T STOP ME...
...BUT I'LL GIVE YOU THE CHANCE TO.

FZZAAMM
THE ONLY WAY TO DESTROY ME IS IF THE HOST I'M BONDED TO DIES.
I KNOW YOU NEVER GOT ALONG WITH YOUR SON, MR. RUSCH. YOU'RE ENVIOUS OF JASON BECAUSE HE'S A SUCCESS DESPITE YOU. YOU'VE NEVER HELPED HIM ATTAIN ANYTHING REALLY, WHICH MAKES ME WONDER...
...HOW MUCH DO YOU LOVE HIM?

FZZAMM
WOULD YOU DIE FOR HIM?
WHY WOULD YOU TAKE THIS RISK?
BECAUSE I KNOW YOU WON'T DO IT.
BUT I DO WANT YOU TO REMEMBER THIS MOMENT, THIS GENEROUS OFFER: YOUR LIFE OR THEIRS.
REMEMBER IT WHEN THOSE BOYS ARE SCREAMING IN PAIN AS I TURN THEIR EYEBALLS INTO COCKROACHES AND THEIR BLOOD INTO ACID--
CHAK
STEIN?
DO IT, ALVIN...
...AND MAY GOD HAVE MERCY ON OUR SOULS.
SEE YOU IN HELL, YOU SON-OF-A-BITCH.
WAIT--!

KLIK
OH! OH, RIIIGHT! I FORGOT TO CREATE THE BULLETS! DUH!
OKAY, ENOUGH GOOFING OFF, DUDES.
YOU BASTAAHHH!
FZAMMM
WE HAVE A DELIVERY TO MAKE.

"WE'RE HERE."
ON THE COAST OF NEW ENGLAND.
SHOULDN'T WE GET A FLASHLIGHT OR SOMETHING? I CAN'T SEE.
OPEN YOUR EYES, JACKSON. LET THEM ADJUST.
ADJUST TO WHAT?
THE BOTTOM OF THE OCEAN IS DARKER THAN THIS CAVE.
YOUR EYES ARE DESIGNED TO SEE THROUGH THAT.
JUST BELIEVE YOU CAN SEE AND YOU WILL.
BELIEVE...

HEY. HEY! I CAN SEE! I CAN SEE... AN "X" ON THE WALL?
"X" MARKS THE SPOT.
STAND BACK.
CHOOOM
ANOTHER CHEST?
WITH ANOTHER BIO-LOCK. YOU NEED TO OPEN IT.
WHAT'S GOING--?!
KRRAKKLL
BWOOOSHHH
I'M SO SORRY, KALDUR'AHM.
WHAT? WHO'S THERE?

MY NAME IS MERA, DAUGHTER OF THE KING OF XEBEL AND NOW... TRAITOR TO MY PEOPLE.
THE PEOPLE WHO PUT YOU THROUGH SO MUCH PAIN.
YOU WON'T REMEMBER THE EXPERIMENTS THEY PERFORMED ON YOU, BUT YOU SURVIVED.
UNLIKE YOUR MOTHER.
MY FATHER BELIEVED IT WAS BECAUSE YOUR MOTHER GAVE BIRTH TO YOU IN XEBEL.
IT MADE YOU INTO A LIVING KEY THAT WAS CAPABLE OF OPENING THE FIELD THAT SEPARATED XEBEL FROM THE REST OF THE WORLD.
AND BECAUSE YOU HAVE THE POWER TO OPEN WHAT THE SURFACE WORLD CALLS THE BERMUDA TRIANGLE, YOU ALSO HAVE THE POWER TO CLOSE IT.
SOME WOULD HAVE YOU KILLED FOR THAT, BUT THAT'S WRONG. I'VE LEARNED KILLING IS WRONG FROM THE KING OF ATLANTIS.
BUT I KILLED TO FREE YOU. AND TO FREE MYSELF FROM MY FATHER'S RULE.
I'M A WOMAN WITHOUT A HOME NOW, BUT I WON'T REST UNTIL I FIND ONE FOR YOU--

SHHASSHH
WHAT WAS THAT?
A MESSAGE RECORDED IN THE WATER, JACKSON. LITERAL OSMOSIS--
SHE CALLED ME KALDUR...SOMETHING. AND MY MOTHER... I SAW MY REAL MOTHER...SHE'S DEAD?
I'LL EXPLAIN EVERYTHING IN DETAIL LATER. MERA WILL.
RIGHT NOW. IT'S TIME TO CLAIM YOUR BIRTHRIGHT.

I...I WANT TO GO HOME.
JACKSON--
I WANT TO GO GET MY PARENTS AND I WANT TO GO HOME.
YOU CAN'T.
YOU HAVE A RESPONSIBILITY.
I'M NOT GOING ANYWHERE ELSE WITH YOU.
YOU HAVE TO, JACKSON.
NO, I DON'T!

I DON'T HAVE TO DO ANYTHING!

I DON'T *WANT* THIS KIND OF PRESSURE.
I DIDN'T *ASK* FOR IT!
CALM DOWN.
YOU DON'T UNDERSTAND!

YOU D-DON'T UNDERSTAND WHAT I'M GOING THROUGH.
NO ONE DOES.
NO ONE...
I WAS THIRTEEN WHEN THEY CAME OUT OF THE WATER FOR ME.
WHO DID?

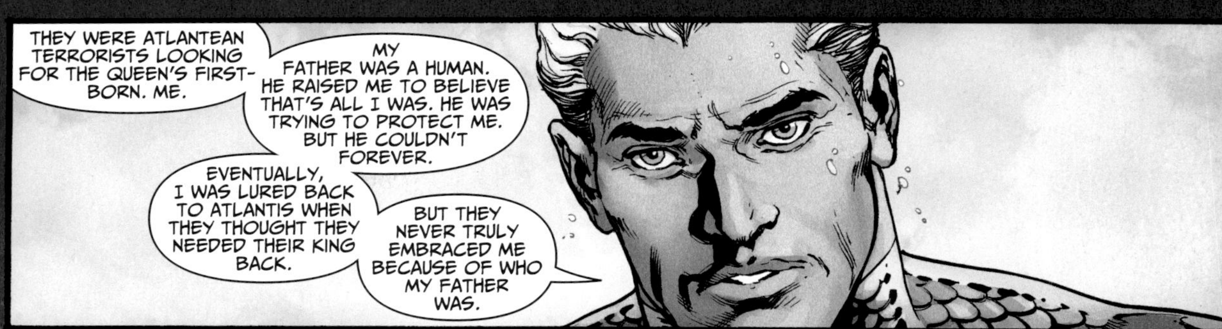
THEY WERE ATLANTEAN TERRORISTS LOOKING FOR THE QUEEN'S FIRST-BORN. ME.
MY FATHER WAS A HUMAN. HE RAISED ME TO BELIEVE THAT'S ALL I WAS. HE WAS TRYING TO PROTECT ME. BUT HE COULDN'T FOREVER.
EVENTUALLY, I WAS LURED BACK TO ATLANTIS WHEN THEY THOUGHT THEY NEEDED THEIR KING BACK.
BUT THEY NEVER TRULY EMBRACED ME BECAUSE OF WHO MY FATHER WAS.

I KNOW I'M ASKING A LOT FROM YOU. I'M ASKING FOR EVERYTHING.
BUT I WOULDN'T ASK YOU TO TAKE ON THIS BURDEN IF I HAD ANY OTHER CHOICE.
OR IF I DIDN'T BELIEVE YOU COULD DO IT.

THE SUIT FITS PRETTY WELL.
IT'S A SOLDIER'S UNIFORM. AND THOSE ARE A SOLDIER'S WEAPONS.
WHAT ARE THEY?
THEY'RE CALLED *WATERBEARERS*.
MERA IS *UNIQUE* AMONG HER PEOPLE. HER HYDROKINESIS IS FAR MORE ADVANCED THAN ANY I'VE EVER ENCOUNTERED.
BUT LIKE THE OTHER XEBELS, YOU HAVE A LIMITED FORM OF IT.
THE WATERBEARERS WILL HELP YOU FOCUS YOUR ABILITY TO *SHAPE* WATER--

--INTO WEAPONS.
ARE YOU SURE YOU'RE READY, JACKSON?
HELL, NO--

--BUT THAT DIDN'T STOP YOU...

"...SO I GUESS I WON'T LET IT STOP ME."
WE'RE WAITING FOR METAMORPHO?! WHY?!
THE THEORY IS METAMORPHO CAN HELP YOU REGAIN CONTROL OF YOUR TRANSMUTING POWERS BY ACTING LIKE A STABILIZER. HE CAN CYCLE THROUGH WHATEVER YOUR BODY IS TRYING TO SORT OUT AND ESSENTIALLY UNLEASH THE BUILT-UP NUCLEAR ENERGY--
BUT WHAT IF IT DOESN'T WORK?
RONNIE, LET HIM FINISH. I WANT TO HEAR THE ATOM OUT.
WE WON'T KNOW UNTIL WE TRY.
I'M JUST ASKING QUESTIONS. WHAT IF IT DOESN'T WORK?
I UNDERSTAND THAT, BUT I WANT A BACKUP PLAN.
THIS IS THE BACK-UP PLAN.
THIS IS THE PROFESSOR WE'RE TALKING ABOUT. HE'S ALWAYS BEEN THERE FOR ME LIKE A FATHER, AND I NEED TO BE THERE FOR HIM. YOU WOULDN'T UNDERSTAND.
THAT'S NOT FAIR.
I DIDN'T MEAN IT LIKE THAT!

WHAT'S...
FZZAMM
--AAAHHHHH!
RONNIE! JASON!
WE'RE GETTING MORE HELP. JUST HANG IN THERE. HANG--

RONNIE?
J-JASON?
WHAT HAPPENED?

I THINK WE JUST DESTROYED THE UNIVERSE.

BRIGHTEST DAY 17
Cover by David Finch

HOMECOMING

SOMEWHERE

WHERE'D EVERYTHING GO?

DID WE JUST BLOW UP THE UNIVERSE?
I'M NOT SENSING ANY MATTER TO TRANSMUTE. WE'RE IN A VACUUM. THERE'S NOTHING HERE, RONNIE.

DO YOU SEE THAT? THE DARKENSS IS MOVING.
LOOKS LIKE A SHADOW.
JASON, I THINK I'VE BEEN HERE BEFORE.
BEEN WHERE?

WE DIDN'T DESTROY THE UNIVERSE--
--WE WERE BROUGHT TO A DIFFERENT ONE BECAUSE THIS ISN'T DARKNESS.

IT'S AN ARMY OF SHADOW DEMONS!

SHADOW DEMONS?
AS IN THE ANTI-MONITOR'S PERSONAL ARMY. AS IN THE ANTIMATTER UNIVERSE. SOMEHOW WHEN WE DETONATED WE WERE DRAWN INTO THE CENTER OF A SHADOW DEMON HIVE.
DRAWN HERE OR BROUGHT HERE ON PURPOSE?
EITHER WAY, I'M HOPING IT MEANS OUR UNIVERSE IS STILL OKAY.
BOSTON BRAND HAS NOT FOUND THE CHAMPION YET.
PROTECT ME UNTIL HE DOES.
JASON, YOU HEARD THAT--
YEAH. AND THERE'S THE PLANET QWARD. ONE OF THE ONLY ROCKS WITH LIFE IN THIS PLACE.
THAT'S GOTTA BE WHERE DEATHSTORM'S GOT YOUR DAD AND THE PROFESSOR...

"...AND THE WHITE LANTERN."
GEORGETOWN.
HM?

HEY, THERE.
'MORNING.
SOMETHING SMELLS GOOD.

AND FAMILIAR. CHEESEBURGERS FOR BREAKFAST. AGAIN.
SORRY. I GUESS I'M MAKING UP FOR LOST TIME.

I COULD TELL FROM LAST NIGHT.

THIS HAS BEEN SO NICE, DAWN.
YES. IT HAS.

I'VE GOT CLASS ALL DAY.
THAT'S OKAY. I'VE GOT SOMETHING TO DO.
WHAT'S UP?

I CALLED ORACLE THIS MORNING AND ASKED HER TO SEE IF ANY OF MY FAMILY WERE STILL ALIVE. I DON'T KNOW WHY. I DIDN'T EXPECT THEM TO BE, BUT...

...TURNS OUT MY GRANDFATHER JUST CELEBRATED HIS NINETY-EIGHTH BIRTHDAY.

HE'S IN AN ASSISTED LIVING HOME IN UPSTATE NEW YORK.
BOSTON, THAT'S GREAT! ARE YOU GOING TO GO SEE HIM?

I DON'T KNOW. I DIDN'T REALLY TALK TO HIM MUCH AFTER HIGH SCHOOL.
AND AT NINETY-EIGHT WHO KNOWS IF HE'LL EVEN REMEMBER ME.

BOSTON.
YOU SHOULD GO.
I FEEL TERRIBLE. EVEN WHEN I WAS DEADMAN, I NEVER CHECKED IN ON HIM. I NEVER THOUGHT HE'D STILL BE AROUND.
BUT THE POINT IS HE *IS* AROUND, BOSTON.
YEAH...

"...WHO KNEW ANYONE COULD LIVE THAT LONG?"
ZAMARON.
HOMEWORLD OF THE STAR SAPPHIRES.
OUR BODIES ARE MELDING INTO THE GATE, CARTER.
IT'S TRYING TO FUSE US TOGETHER WITH THE REST OF OUR BONES.
THE CURSE IS DONE. HATH IS DEAD. WE CAN'T DIE TODAY.
WE CAN'T LOSE OUR FIRST CHANCE IN THOUSANDS OF YEARS TO LIVE OUT OUR LIVES TOGETHER.
WE WON'T, SHIERA.
NOT THIS TIME.
SPILL THE SAPPHIRES' BLOOD.
BATHE IN IT.
I DON'T KNOW WHO THE HELL YOU ARE, HAWK-WOMAN, BUT IF YOU THINK I'M GOING TO LET YOU DESTROY ZAMARON WITH YOUR ARMY OF BIRDS IN MY FIRST WEEK ON THE JOB, YOU'RE MISTAKEN.
AAIIEE
LOVE IS BEAUTIFUL.
LOVE IS INSPIRING.

BUT LOVE IS ALSO *LETHAL.*

HAWKGIRL! HAWKMAN!
FERRIS.
DIDN'T KNOW ZAMARON WAS YOUR NEW ADDRESS.
THERE'RE LOTS OF THINGS YOU DON'T KNOW ABOUT ME--BUT LET'S GET YOU BOTH OFF THIS THING--
--SO SOMEONE CAN EXPLAIN TO ME WHAT THE HELL IS GOING ON.
KRAKKOOOM
THE ANCIENT HEARTS OF KHUFU AND CHAY-ARA.
YOU'VE COME BACK TO US.

"YOU'VE FINALLY COME BACK!"
MR. BRAND?

MR. BRAND? YOUR GRANDSON IS HERE TO SEE YOU.

GRANDPA?
MY GRANDSONS ARE DEAD.

GRANDPA, IT'S ME. IT'S BOSTON.

I, UH, I'M...
...DO YOU REMEMBER ME?

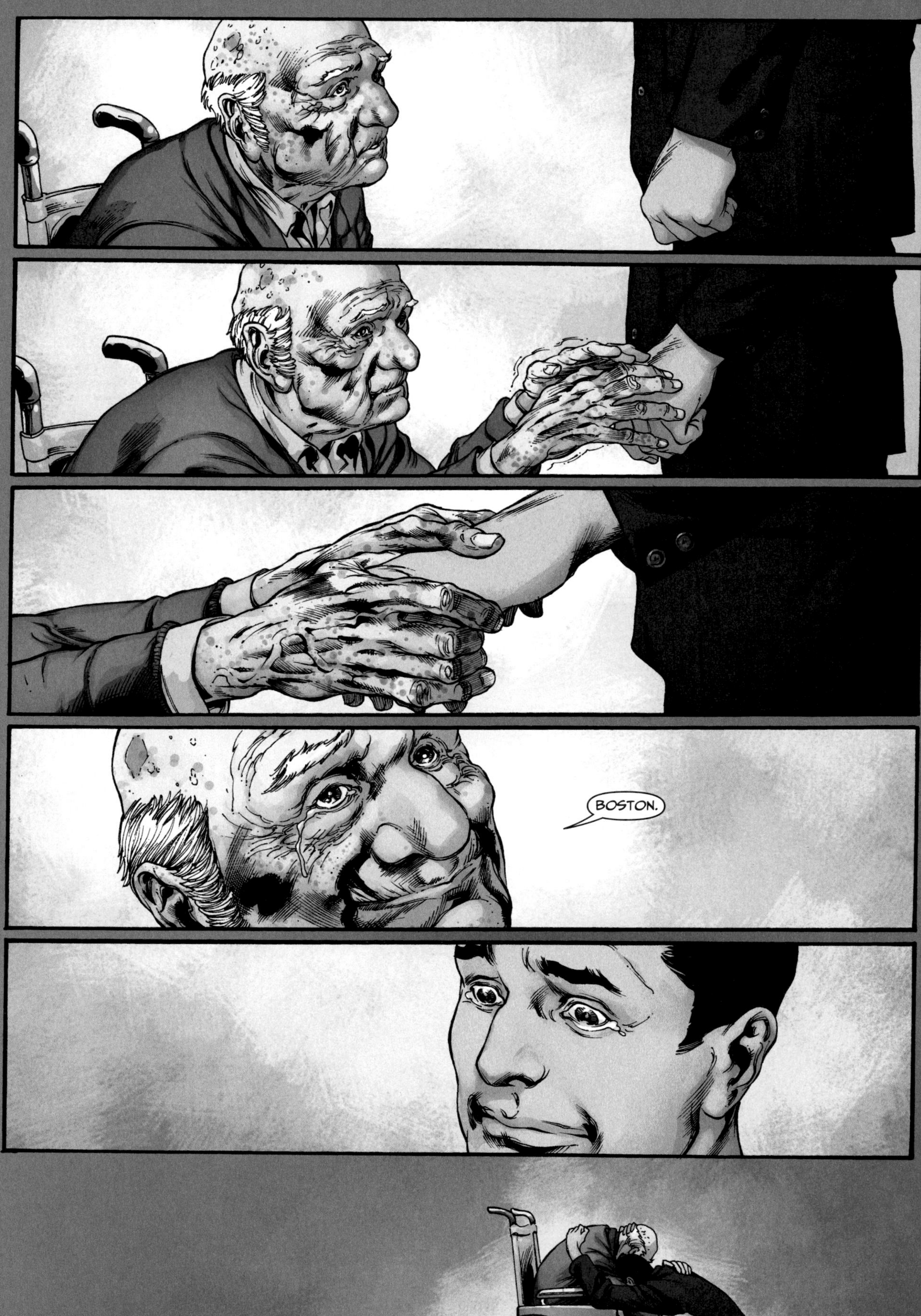
BOSTON.

IT'S UNBELIEVABLE.
IT'S ALL TRUE.
AFTER EVERYTHING I'VE SEEN THROUGHOUT MY LONG LIFE, FROM THE BIRTH OF THE JUSTICE SOCIETY TO THE DAY THE WORLD MET SUPERMAN, I DON'T DOUBT IT. BUT WHAT I'M MOST INTERESTED IN ISN'T ALL THIS DEADMAN STUFF.
THIS GIRL. DAWN, IS IT?
LIFE IS BETTER WHEN YOU'RE SHARING IT WITH SOMEONE, BOSTON.
GRANDPA, I... I DON'T DESERVE THIS.
YOU DON'T DESERVE WHAT?
YOU BEING THIS GOOD TO ME. I TOOK YOU FOR GRANTED LIKE I DID EVERYONE. I WAS TOO WRAPPED UP IN MYSELF TO CARE ABOUT ANYONE BUT ME. I NEVER LISTENED TO YOUR STORIES OR ADVICE.
OH, YOU AREN'T DIFFERENT FROM ANYONE ELSE, BOSTON. AND YOU'RE HERE NOW, AREN'T YOU?
THIS IS YOU AND GRANDMA?
WASN'T SHE BEAUTIFUL?
YEAH.
YOU HELD THE RECORD FOR LONG DISTANCE JUMP ON A HARLEY DAVIDSON. RIGHT?
YOU SEE? YOU DID LISTEN.
I HAVEN'T BEEN ABLE TO RIDE A BIKE SINCE BEFORE YOU WERE BORN.
I WOULD'VE GONE AROUND THE BLOCK A FEW TIMES MORE IF I KNEW IT WAS MY LAST RIDE.
WHO SAID IT WAS YOUR LAST RIDE?

YOUR LOVE CAN POWER THIS WORLD AGAIN.
GET YOUR PET DRAGON'S BONY CLAWS OFF US BEFORE I BREAK THEM!

IT'S NOT A DRAGON, HAWKGIRL--IT'S CALLED THE PREDATOR. THE "ENTITY OF LOVE."
THIS THING'S AN "ENTITY OF LOVE"?
I'D HATE TO SEE WHAT THE ENTITY OF HATE LOOKS LIKE.

IT'S ONE OF THE OLDEST FORCES IN THE UNIVERSE. IT'S MOTIVATED BY LOVE OR, MORE IMPORTANT, THE ABSENCE OF LOVE.
GOOD, THEN IT CAN LEAD US--

--RIGHT TO OUR TARGET!

THE LIGHT PULSATING INSIDE HAS BEEN TAUNTING ME ACROSS TIME AND SPACE FOR THOUSANDS OF YEARS.
THE MYSTERIOUS ENERGIES WITHIN ELUDE ME, BUT NOT FOR MUCH--

--AAGHH!
WHAT'S HAPPENING?!

WHAT'S HAPPENING IS YOU DON'T UNDERSTAND THAT SHARING LOVE AND CONTROLLING LOVE ARE TWO DIFFERENT THINGS!
AAGHH!

YOUR BODIES-- ARE SUDDENLY *IMMUNE* TO MY NTH METAL CONTROL--
--BUT I STILL HAVE HUNDREDS OF MANHAWKS AT MY SERVICE.
CARTER--
--THE MANHAWKS ARE ALL YOURS--
--THIS IS A MOTHER/DAUGHTER THING!

RAAGH!
UGNN!

I SMELL A BLACK HEART...
SNIFF SNIFF

...THAT NEEDS MY LIGHT.
FWAM

KHEA TARAMKA OF EARTH, YOUR HEART IS DEVOID OF LOVE.
...SO BEAUTIFUL...
YOU CARE FOR NO ONE. NOT EVEN YOURSELF.
POWER IS ALL YOU LOVE.
ABSOLUTE POWER.
LET US SEE IF YOU ARE TRULY ABLE TO WIELD IT.
NO.

YES!

"I WILL FINALLY KNOW LOVE."
RRRRRRRR

YOU READY, GRANDPA?!

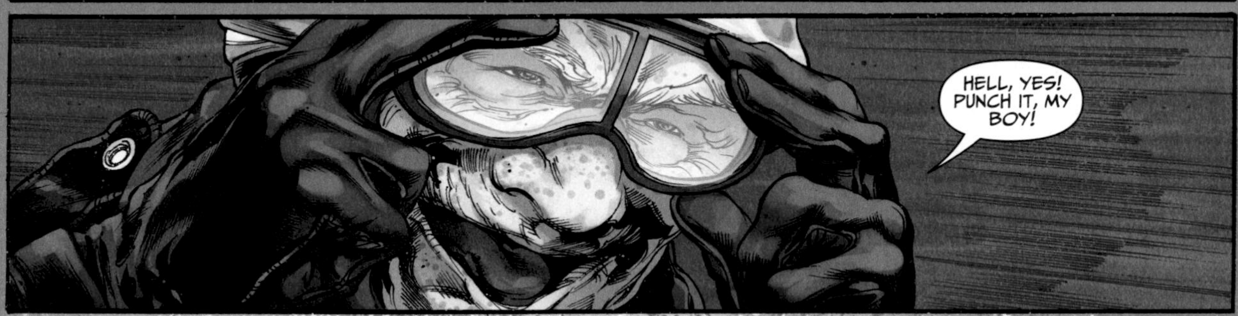
HELL, YES! PUNCH IT, MY BOY!

VRRROOOOMM

POWER LEVELS 1%.
WHAT--?
POWER LEVELS 2%.
WHAT'S--?
POWER LEVELS 3%.
POWER LEVELS 4%.

BRIGHTEST DAY 18
Cover by David Finch, Ryan Winn and Nathan Eyring

EASY COME EASY GO

SAFEHOUSE OF THE ROGUES.
WHAT DO YOU WANT OUT OF LIFE, DIGGER?
OR DON'T YOU WANT IT?
IS THAT WHY YOU FREED THE REVERSE-FLASH FROM IRON HEIGHTS, YOU STUPID SON-OF-A-BITCH? YOU KNOW WHAT HE'S CAPABLE OF.
I WENT AFTER THAWNE BECAUSE HE WAS THE ONLY OTHER BADDIE BROUGHT BACK BY THAT WHITE LIGHT, RIGHT? AN' THE BUGGER'S FROM THE FUTURE, COLD.
I WAS TRYIN' TA FIND OUT IF HE KNEW WHY ME OF ALL PEOPLE WAS DUG OUTTA THE GRAVE. THE REVERSE-FLASH MAY BE PSYCHOTIC AND ROTTEN TA THE CORE, BUT HE'S A SCIENTIFIC GENIUS.
I AIN'T EVER BEEN NOTHIN' BUT A CRIMINAL.
WRONG. YOU'RE A ROGUE, BOOMERANG. YOU'RE SUPPOSED TO BE SMARTER THAN THIS. WE DON'T LOOK FOR ANSWERS TO THE "WHY" BECAUSE WE KNOW THERE'S NO MASTER PLAN.
WE TAKE WHAT WE CAN OUTTA LIFE BECAUSE WE KNOW LIFE DOESN'T GIVE BACK.
BUT LIFE DID GIVE BACK THIS TIME, COLD.
AND THE WHITE LAN'ERN TOLD ME--

GEORGETOWN.
"--IT TOLD ME TA THROW ME BOOMERANG AT DOVE. I JUST DON' KNOW WHAT THE BLOODY HELL FOR."
I'M NOT GOING TO LET ANYTHING HAPPEN TO YOU, BOSTON.
JUST SLOW DOWN AND BREATHE AND I'LL BE RIGHT--
POWER LEVELS 33%.
THERE! DID YOU HEAR THAT?
WHAT?
UPSTATE NEW YORK.
I DID WHAT THE RING SAID TO DO. LIVE LIFE AND I'D FIND THE WHITE LANTERN. SO I WENT TO SEE MY GRANDFATHER, WHICH WAS GREAT, BUT--
POWER LEVELS 34%.
IN THE MIDDLE OF EVERYTHING, THE RING STOPPED TALKING AND STARTED CHARGING. IT'S POWERING UP.
"SOMETHING STRANGE IS HAPPENING."
MERA?
LORENA. I NEED YOUR HELP.
"I CAN FEEL IT."
THE WHITE LANTERN IS YOURS, BIG DUDE.
POWER LEVELS 35%.
I CAN'T BEGIN TO GUESS WHAT IT IS--

"--BUT IT FEELS FAMILIAR. IT FEELS LIKE THE DAY I DIED, ONLY...
"ONLY WHAT, BOSTON?"
"ONLY, I DON'T THINK IT'S ME THAT'S GOING TO DIE TODAY."
ZAMARON.
HOMEWORLD TO THE STAR SAPPHIRES.

YOU WERE JUST RIDING THIS THING A FEW MINUTES AGO LIKE IT WAS YOUR FAVORITE PONY, FERRIS--
--HOW DO WE PULL THAT CREATURE OUT OF MY MOTHER AND PUT THEM BOTH DOWN?
I'M STILL WORKING MY WAY THROUGH THE SAPPHIRE QUEEN MANUAL--
--BUT THE PREDATOR, THE ENTITY OF LOVE, CAN BE CORRUPTED BY ITS HOST--
--AND THE ONLY WAY TO RELEASE THE PREDATOR IS BY FORCING THE HOST TO FEEL LOVE--

SKRAKKK
SAPPHIRE!

I'LL GET HER!

THEN I'LL KEEP YOUR MOTHER *OCCUPIED*.
FWAM

GETTING YOU TO FEEL *ANYTHING* IS GOING TO BE ONE *HELL* OF A CHALLENGE. AFTER WHAT YOU'VE PUT YOUR DAUGHTER THROUGH--

--I DOUBT THERE'S A ***SHRED*** OF LOVE HIDING IN THAT DARK HEART OF YOURS.

WHY WOULD THERE BE? LOOK AT YOU AND MY DAUGHTER. WHAT HAS LOVE TRULY BROUGHT YOU OVER THE CENTURIES--

--BUT ***PAIN?***

AAARRGH!

"THIS IS GOING TO END TODAY. ONE WAY OR ANOTHER."
IF YOU WANT TO FEEL LOVE, YOU MUST ALSO FEEL THE PAIN THAT COMES WITH IT.
AND TH-THANKS TO YOUR CURSE, I'M USED TO PAIN.
BUT THE CURSE ENDED WHEN YOU KILLED HATH-SET.
SHUNK
THIS IS YOUR LAST LIFE...
...SO WHY ARE YOU SMILING?

AAARGGGGH!!
BECAUSE IT'S *YOUR* LAST LIFE TOO!

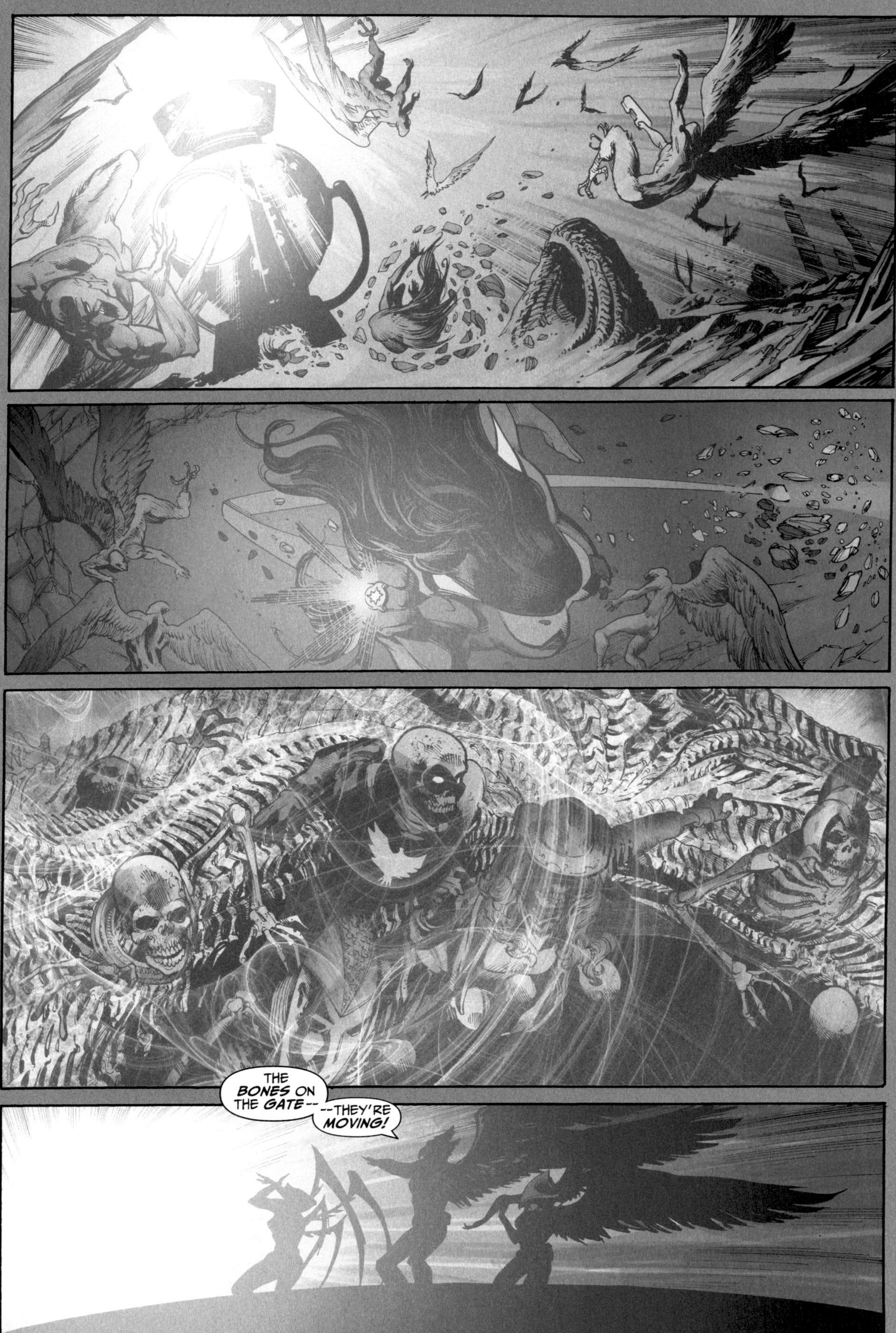
THE *BONES* ON THE *GATE*--
--THEY'RE *MOVING!*

LOVE.
TAKE HER.
TAKE HER.
TAKE HER.
TAKE HER.
TAKE HER.
TAKE HER.
TAKE HER.
TAKE HER.
TAKE HER.
TAKE HER.

TAKE HER.
TAKE HER.
TAKE HER.
N-NO! STOP!
TAKE HER.
TAKE HER.

CARTER HALL OF EARTH.
SHIERA HALL OF EARTH.
MISSION ACCOMPLISHED.
LIFE RETURNED.

HAWKMAN? HAWKGIRL? WHAT WAS THAT LIGHT?
POWER LEVELS 88%.
DID YOU HEAR THAT?
HOW DID YOU TWO PULL THE ENTITY OUT OF HER?
I'M GUESSING THIS CRYSTAL ON THE CLAW OF HORUS HAD SOMETHING TO DO WITH IT.
A STAR SAPPHIRE GAVE IT TO SHIERA AS A GIFT AFTER NEKRON WAS DEFEATED. SHE SAID IT WAS AN ORIGINAL SHARD FROM THE CRYSTALLIZED BODIES THAT ONCE POWERED YOUR BATTERY.
I THINK IT'S MORE LIKELY YOUR TRUE LOVE FOR ONE ANOTHER IS WHAT OVERPOWERED HER CONNECTION TO THE PREDATOR.
I KNOW IT SOUNDS LIKE SOMETHING FROM A HALLMARK CARD. I'M STILL TRYING TO WRAP MY HEAD AROUND THE LITERAL POWER OF LOVE, BUT...
YOU KNOW WHAT TRUE LOVE IS, CAROL, YOU AND HAL--
HAL AND I WON'T EVER HAVE WHAT YOU BOTH DO.
NO MATTER HOW MUCH EITHER OF US DOESN'T WANT TO ADMIT IT.

HOW HARD IT'S BEEN FOR THE BOTH OF YOU TO BE APART FOR SO LONG.
THINK OF THE ONE PLACE ON EARTH YOU'D BOTH WANT TO BE TOGETHER--
--AND YOUR HEARTS WILL TAKE YOU THERE.
"I'LL BE RIGHT THERE FOR YOU."

OKAY, BOSTON? I'LL BE RIGHT THERE.
I THINK I'M OUT OF TIME, DOVE.
POWER LEVELS 99%.
WHEN THE BLACK LANTERN CHARGED TO 100%, NEKRON WAS TELEPORTED TO EARTH. WHAT HAPPENS WHEN THE WHITE RING--
BOSTON?
WHAT'S GOING ON, SON?
GRANDPA, I...
POWER LEVELS 100%.
THEY HAVE RETURNED.
KRRRAAKKLL
BOSTON?
BOOOOOOMMMMM

ST. ROCH.
THE STONECHAT MUSEUM.

WE'RE BACK.
WE'RE HOME.

NEKRON, HAWKWORLD, ZAMARON... IT'S ALL SINKING IN, CARTER. THE NIGHTMARE REALLY *IS* OVER. WE CAN LIVE LIFE WITHOUT LOOKING OVER OUR SHOULDER.
WITHOUT WAITING FOR THE CLOCK TO RUN OUT.
WITHOUT THE CURSE, WE CAN FINALLY GROW OLD TOGETHER.

BUT WE AREN'T OLD *YET*.

I LOVE YOU MORE THAN LIFE ITSELF.

WHAT A STRANGE THING TO SAY.
DEADMAN?

BOSTON, ARE YOU ALL RIGHT?
I...I DON'T KNOW, HAWKGIRL.
WHY ARE YOU AIMING THAT RING AT US?
I C-CAN'T MOVE. RING, WHAT AM I DOING HERE--?
CARTER HALL AND SHIERA HALL OF EARTH.
YOU MUST LIVE LIFE SEPARATELY TO LIVE LIFE STRONGER.
WHAT? WHAT'S IT TALKING ABOUT, DEADMAN?
I DON'T KNOW.

WE JUST SPENT **HELL** BREAKING THE CURSE THAT'S KEPT US APART. A VOICE SAID OUR LIFE WAS RETURNED--

THIS IS PART OF THE PLAN.

WHOSE PLAN?

THE CHAMPION-TO-BE MUST BE SERVICED ABOVE ALL OTHERS.

WE'RE NOT A PART OF ***ANYONE'S*** PLAN ANYMORE. WE'RE NOT LIVING LIFE ***APART*** AGAIN. NOT THIS TIME. NOT EVER!

SHIERA.
CARTER.
PLEASE, NO. NOT WHEN WE'RE SO CLOSE.
CARTER.
PLEASE.

BRIGHTEST DAY 19
Cover by David Finch, Scott Williams and Peter Steigerwald

AQUAWAR PART ONE

ST. ROCH.
THE STONECHAT MUSEUM.
N-NO...
HAWKMAN? HAWKGIRL?
WHAT DID YOU DO TO THEM?!

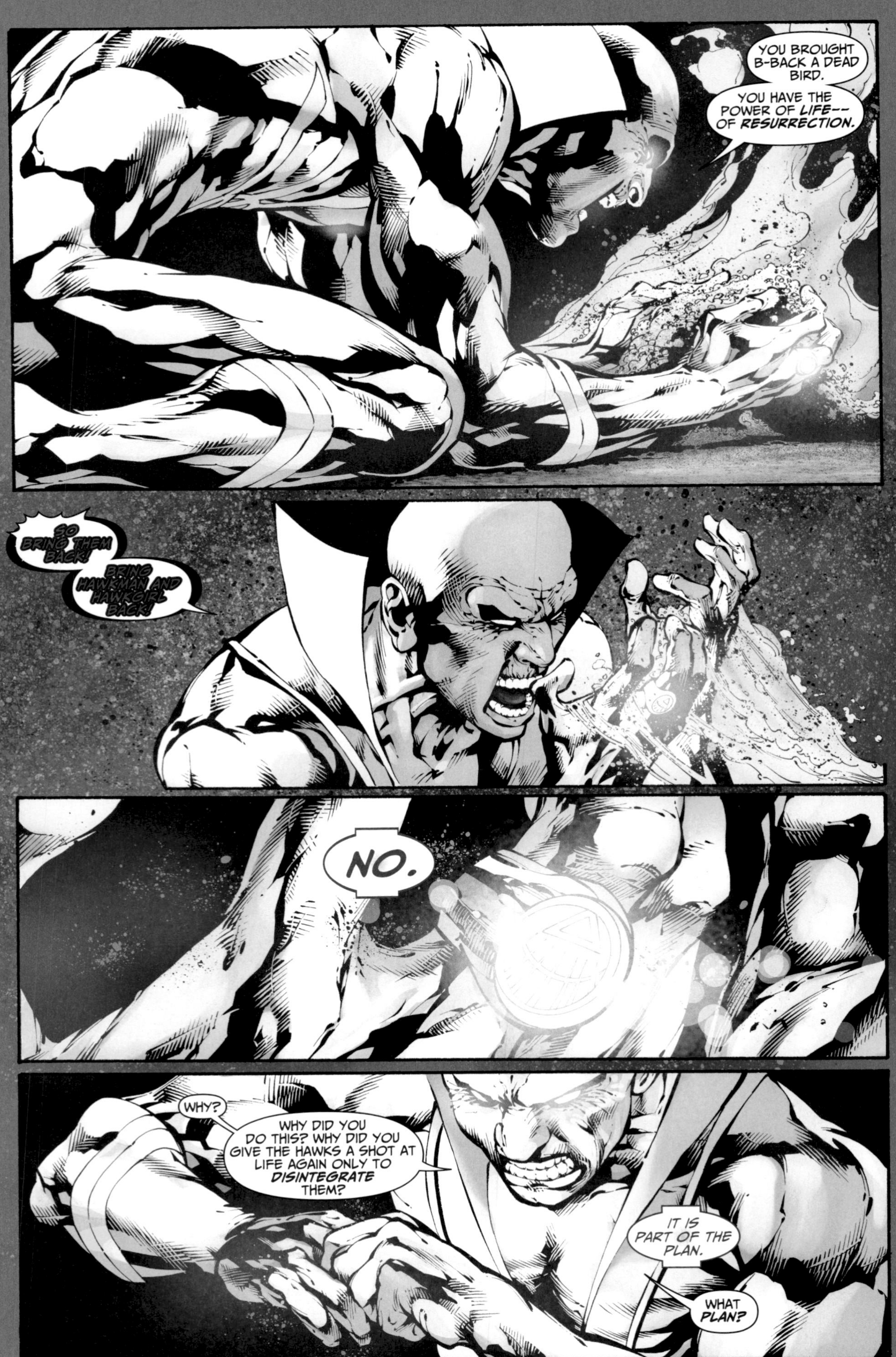

YOU BROUGHT B-BACK A DEAD BIRD.
YOU HAVE THE POWER OF LIFE-- OF RESURRECTION.
SO BRING THEM BACK!
BRING HAWKMAN AND HAWKGIRL BACK!
NO.
WHY?
WHY DID YOU DO THIS? WHY DID YOU GIVE THE HAWKS A SHOT AT LIFE AGAIN ONLY TO DISINTEGRATE THEM?
IT IS PART OF THE PLAN.
WHAT PLAN?

THE PLAN TO STOP EARTH FROM TURNING AGAINST HUMANITY.

WHAT THE HELL ARE YOU TALKING ABOUT?

THIS WORLD HAS BEEN SLOWLY POISONED FOR CENTURIES BY MANKIND, BUT NEKRON'S ATTACK HEIGHTENED THE CONTAMINATION OF EARTH'S LIFE-WEB-- ITS VERY SOUL.
SOON THIS CORRUPTION WILL RISE IN THE FORM OF A DARK AVATAR AND IT WILL SEEK OUT THE FOREST I CREATED.
THE ONE IN STAR CITY?
YES.

"IT HOLDS THE KEY TO EARTH'S SALVATION."

"THE TWELVE THAT I GAVE LIFE TO EACH PLAYS A ROLE IN SAVING THE SOUL OF YOUR HOMEWORLD. SOME HAVE ALREADY PREVENTED FURTHER DESTRUCTION TO IT AND GIVEN US MORE TIME...

"...WHILE OTHERS ULTIMATELY ARE MORE SIGNIFICANT TO MY PURPOSE.
"ARTHUR CURRY, RONALD RAYMOND, J'ONN J'ONZZ, AND CARTER AND SHIERA HALL ARE UNIQUE.
"I PUT THEM ON A JOURNEY TO OVERCOME WHAT HELD THEM BACK IN LIFE.

"HAWKMAN AND HAWKGIRL HAVE ALREADY DONE THAT. THEY DESTROYED THE CURSE THAT HAUNTED THEM.
"AND THAT IN TURN PURIFIED THEIR LIFE FORCE."

BUT ONCE CARTER AND SHIERA EMBRACED LIFE... YOU TOOK IT BACK! YOU KILLED THEM!
IT WAS NECESSARY.
DOES THAT MEAN YOU'RE OUT TO KILL AQUAMAN AND THE OTHERS TOO?!
THEIR LIFE FORCE MUST BE PURIFIED--

--BECAUSE THEIR ESSENCE IS ESSENTIAL IN SAVING EARTH'S SOUL.

IF THE FOREST FALLS TO THE DARK AVATAR, THE NEW CHAMPION OF THIS WORLD WILL NEVER RISE--

--AND EARTH WILL DIE.

THIS WORLD IS TOO VALUABLE TO THE FUTURE TO ALLOW THAT TO HAPPEN.
YOU'VE TOLD ME WHY YOU BROUGHT EVERYONE ELSE BACK--BUT ME.
BY EMBRACING LIFE, YOU SUPPLY ME WITH POWER.
WELL, THAT ENDS RIGHT NOW. I WON'T BE YOUR TRIGGER MAN. I WON'T LET YOU USE ME FOR ANYTHING ELSE.
YOU HAVE NO CHOICE, BOSTON BRAND.

"NONE OF YOU DO."

THEY'RE NOT GOING TO EAT US, ARE THEY?
NOT IF YOU KEEP SWIMMING FASTER THAN THEM.

I THOUGHT YOU USED TO CONTROL SEA LIFE, BUT THOSE SHARKS LOOK HUNGRY, AND THE EELS YOU THREW AT ME--
WERE DEAD.
MY SECOND CHANCE AT LIFE HASN'T QUITE WORKED OUT THE WAY I WOULD'VE EXPECTED.
I FIGURED THAT. SO...ARE YOU GOING TO FORGIVE HER?
WHO?
I'M NOT SURE YOU AND I KNOW MORE THAN ONE "HER."
WHY WOULD YOU THINK I HAVE TO FORGIVE MERA FOR ANYTHING?
WELL, ONE: YOU AREN'T LOOKING AT ME. TWO: EVERYTHING ABOUT ME, FROM BLACK MANTA TO MY CONNECTION WITH XEBEL, IS NEWS TO YOU BUT IT WASN'T TO HER.
AND THREE: SHE'S NOT HERE.

MERA SAVED MY LIFE, AQUAMAN. AND SHE TURNED AGAINST HER OWN FAMILY TO SAVE YOURS.
I'VE ONLY HAD ONE GIRLFRIEND REALLY. *MARIA.*
SHE HOOKED UP WITH OTHER GUYS AND ASKED ME TO DO HER HOMEWORK. SHE NEVER DID ANYTHING FOR ME. NOT LIKE MERA DID FOR YOU.
WE NEED TO STAY ON PLAN, JACKSON. WE'RE PASSING THE FLORIDA COAST.
MERA'S PEOPLE ARE PLANNING AN ASSAULT ON THE SURFACE WORLD, BUT WITHOUT YOU THEY WON'T BE ABLE TO *SHUT DOWN* THE BERMUDA TRIANGLE AND ESCAPE.
BUT THEY DID *BREAK THROUGH* IT SOMEHOW. A FEW OF THEM GOT OUT.
WE CAN HANDLE A FEW.
YOU ASKED ME EARLIER WHAT WORLD I BELONGED TO: LAND OR SEA. THE ANSWER IS *BOTH* AND *NEITHER,* JACKSON.
I'M STUCK IN THE MIDDLE. MY JOB'S TO PROTECT THE WORLDS OF LAND AND SEA FROM ONE ANOTHER.
AND NOW IT'S MY JOB TOO.
TODAY. BUT AFTER WE GET THROUGH THIS, THERE'S SOMEONE I WANT YOU TO MEET.
WHO?

THE FISH?
WHERE ARE THEY GOING?
JACKSON, WATCH OUT--!

WHHOOOOSH!!
NO...

"WE'RE TOO LATE."
KILL THEM ALL!

DEATH TO THE AIR-BREATHERS!
THIS WORLD IS OURS!
YOU OKAY?
I THOUGHT ONLY A FEW GOT OUT. IT LOOKS LIKE THEIR WHOLE ARMY!
IT'S NOT. ACCORDING TO MERA, THERE ARE **THOUSANDS** MORE.
AND I'VE GOT A BAD FEELING THEY'RE JUST **BELOW** THE SURFACE OUT THERE. SOMEONE **UNLOCKED** THE BERMUDA TRIANGLE.
BUT **WHO?**
"WHO WOULD DO THAT?"
"AND WHY?"

WORRY ABOUT THE PEOPLE IN FRONT OF US, JACKSON.
SAVE AS MANY AS YOU CAN.
OKAY, THIS IS REAL, JACKSON. THIS IS LIFE AND DEATH.
SO DO SOMETHING ABOUT IT!
LEAVE THEM ALONE!
WHAT DID THEY EVER DO TO YOU?

AAARRR!
THEY CRAWLED OUT OF THE SEA.
LIKE YOU.
YOU HAVE NO IDEA THE POWER YOU CONTAIN THANKS TO MY FATHER. IT WILL BE USED AGAINST THE SURFACE WORLD TO TAKE WHAT IS RIGHTFULLY OURS.
THE SEA IS WHERE LIFE WAS BORN. WE HAVE A CLAIM TO EVERYTHING THE LAND HOLDS.
INCLUDING YOU.
THERE'S NOTHING UP HERE FOR YOU BUT DEATH, SIREN.

THE PEOPLE OF THE SURFACE CLAIM THE OCEANS AND ITS RESOURCES FOR THEIRS, AQUAMAN.
WHY DO YOU FIGHT FOR THEM?
I NEVER SAID I WAS ON THEIR SIDE, SIREN.
SO YOU'RE TRULY ALONE THEN.
ESPECIALLY NOW THAT I'VE TAKEN CARE OF MERA.
MY UNIT CAPTURED HER ATTEMPTING TO GET HELP.
THEY BROUGHT MERA TO ME. I SLIT HER THROAT. SHE TRIED TO SPEAK--
--BUT ALL SHE DID WAS CHOKE ON HER OWN BLOOD.
YOUR QUEEN IS DEAD.
THEN YOU'LL JOIN--

AAARHHH!

NNG.
GG.
WHAT ARE YOU CRYING ABOUT, AQUAMAN?

YOU SHOULD BE USED TO THAT.

BRIGHTEST DAY 20
Cover by Ivan Reis,
Joe Prado and Rod Reis

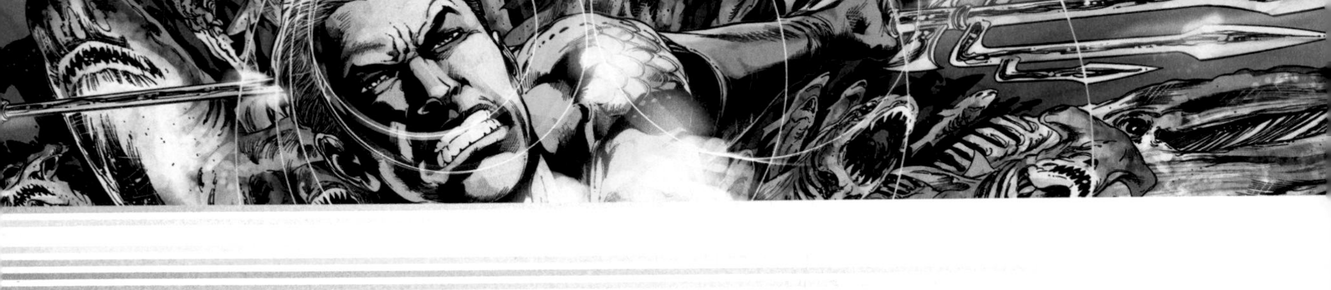

AQUAWAR PART TWO

STOP TRYING TO GET INVOLVED, BOSTON BRAND.
THIS IS NOT YOUR FIGHT.
I SAID THAT MY WHOLE LIFE, BUT I WON'T THIS TIME. LET ME DO SOMETHING! INNOCENTS ARE GOING TO DIE OUT THERE!
PROTECTING LAND AND SEA FROM ONE ANOTHER IS WHAT MOTIVATES ARTHUR CURRY.
"IT IS WHY I OPENED THE BERMUDA TRIANGLE AND ALLOWED MERA'S PEOPLE TO ESCAPE."
"YOU DID THIS?"
"IT WAS NECESSARY."
"AQUAMAN NEEDED TO LEARN THE TRUTH ABOUT MERA."
I WAS SENT HERE TO KILL YOU.
"SO I CAN SEE WHAT HE DOES WITH IT."
DIE, SEA KING.

YOU'RE NOT KILLING *ANYBODY* ELSE, DAD!

YOU'RE GETTING STRONGER, BOY.
BUT YOU'RE STILL UNTRAINED.

WHY WOULD YOU DO THIS?
WHY WOULD YOU SIDE WITH THE PEOPLE WHO KILLED MY MOTHER AND WANT TO KILL ME?

YOUR MOTHER MEANT NOTHING TO ME.
JUST LIKE YOU.
MANTA!

YOU WILL KILL NO MORE CHILDREN.
NEVER AGAIN.
HEADS UP, KID!
AND HEADS DOWN, MER-MAN!

YOU GOING TO GET UP AND FIGHT OR WHAT?

WHOA.

GET THEIR HELMETS OFF. MOST OF THEM GET PRETTY WEAK WHEN THEY'RE BREATHING AIR.
WHO ARE YOU?
ARE YOU ATLANTEAN?
YOU CAN CALL ME LORENA, BUT EVERYONE ELSE CALLS ME AQUAGIRL.
NO MORE THAN YOU. BUT INTROS LATER, 'KAY, HANDSOME?
WE HAVE FISH TO FRY.
M-MERA? SIREN SAID YOU WERE DEAD.
ARTHUR! YOUR HAND--?!
STAY BACK. I'M... FINE...
NOT IF YOU LOSE ANY MORE BLOOD.

JACKSON... YOUR ELECTRICAL TOUCH...
CAUTERIZE IT.
BUT--
I NEED YOUR HELP, JACKSON.
DO IT!
KZZZTTT

BETTER.
YOU SURE?

I'M SURE.
HOW DID XEBEL GET FREE, MERA?
I DON'T KNOW.
MERA, I NEED TO--

ARTHUR. I DON'T.
YOU KNOW WHERE MY LOYALTIES LIE.
I NEVER QUESTIONED THAT.
SORRY TO INTERRUPT, BUT IT'S FOUR AGAINST HUNDREDS.

HOW ARE WE SUPPOSED TO GET THEM OFF THE BEACH?

I CAN DO THAT.

THE TIDE... IT'S...
RETREATING.
WHAT'S SHE DOING?
NGGG.
SHE'S TRYING TO CONTROL THE WHOLE OCEAN?
AQUAMAN, SHE'S BLEEDING--
MERA, YOU'RE GOING TO HURT YOUR--
N-NO.
D-DON'T TRY TO ST-STOP ME, ARTHUR.
JUST T-TELL ME YOU BELIEVE IN M-ME.
I DO.
IMPOSSIBLE.

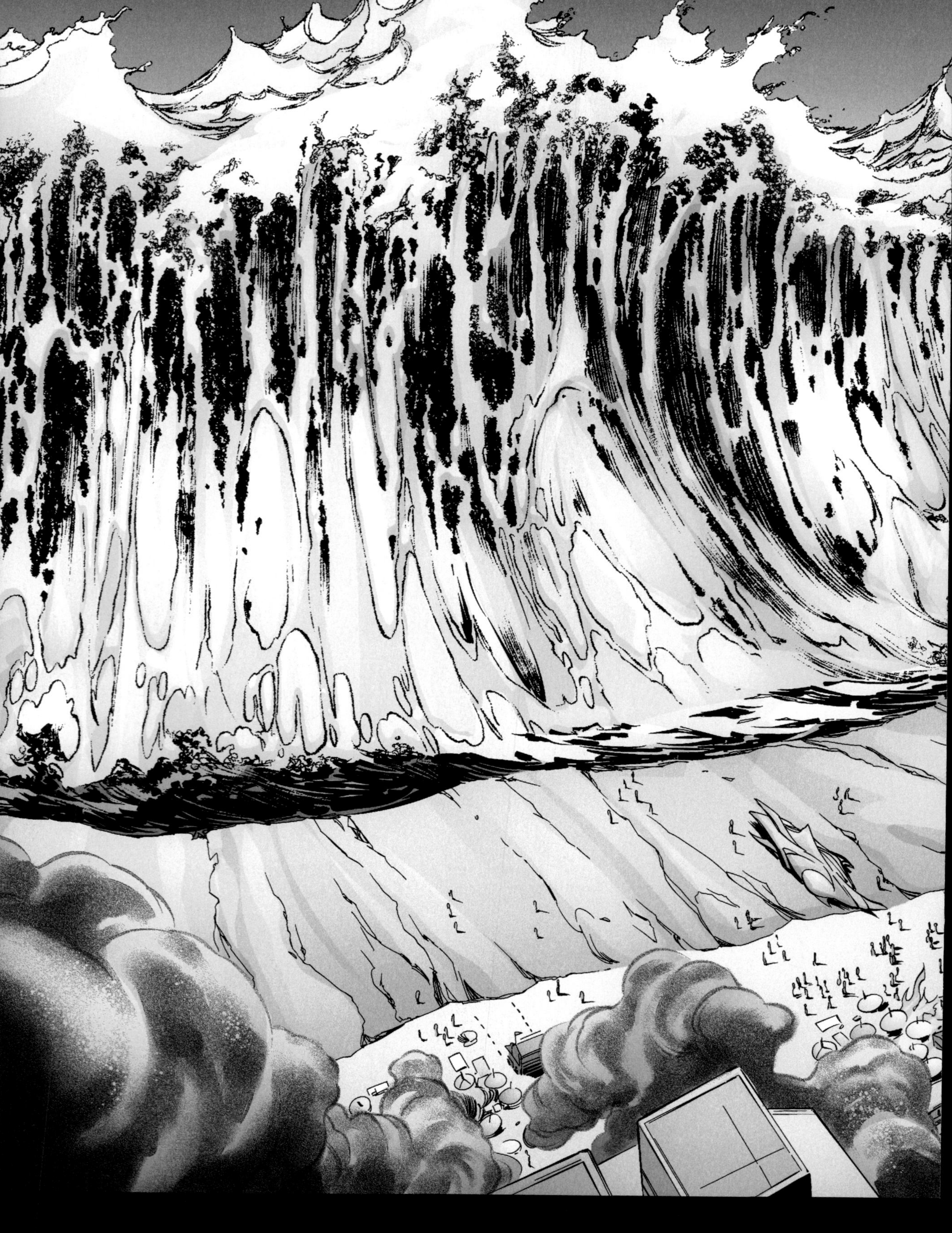

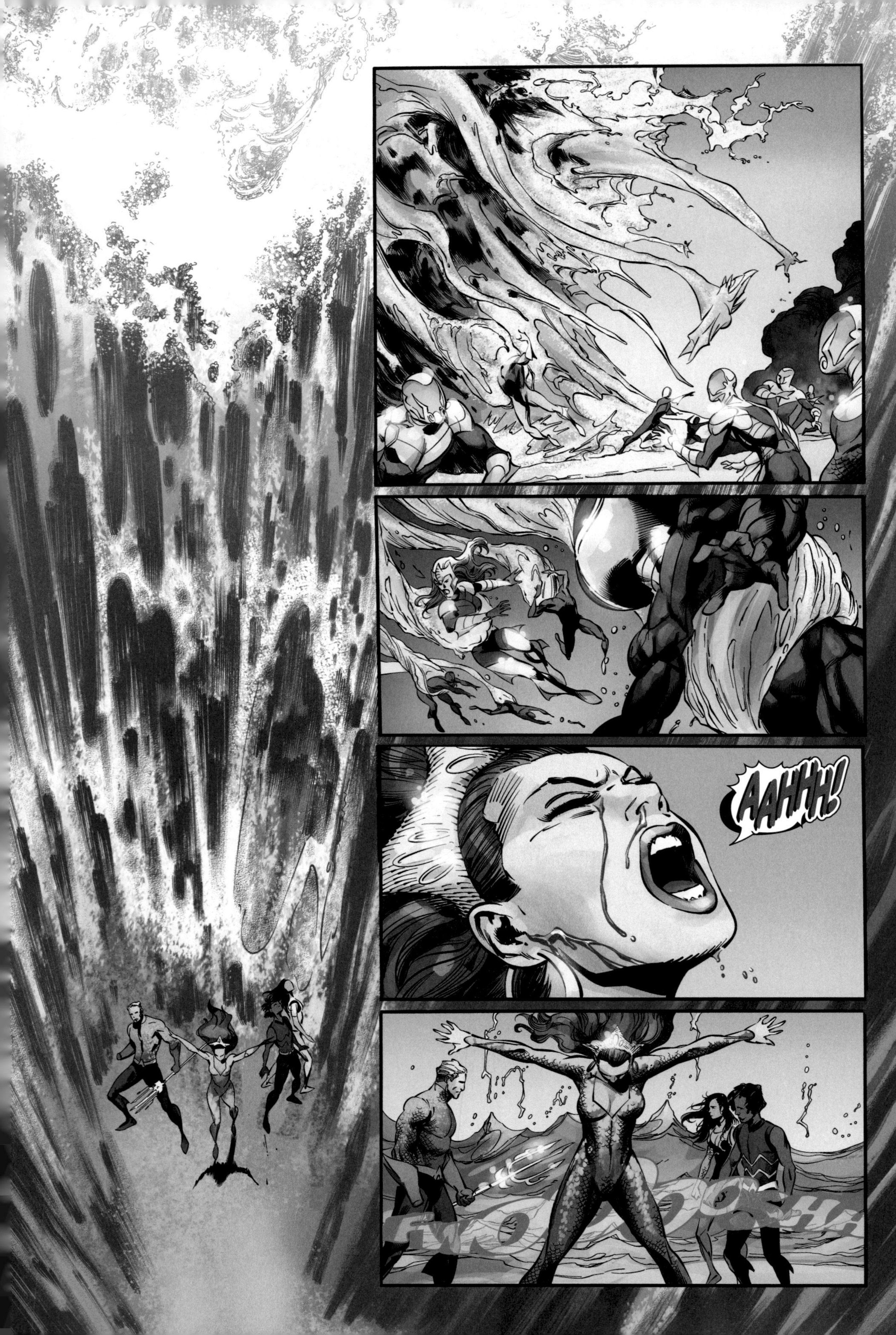
AAHHH!
FWOOOOSH!

I CAN'T BELIEVE SHE JUST...
SENT THEM ALL OUT TO SEA.
WE NEED TO BATTLE THEM BACK TO THE BERMUDA TRIANGLE.
WE'RE GOING TO NEED AN *ARMY* FOR THAT.

I'VE GOT ONE.

YOU AND YOUR SOLDIERS HAVE ONE CHOICE, SIREN.
FALL BACK--
--OR DIE.

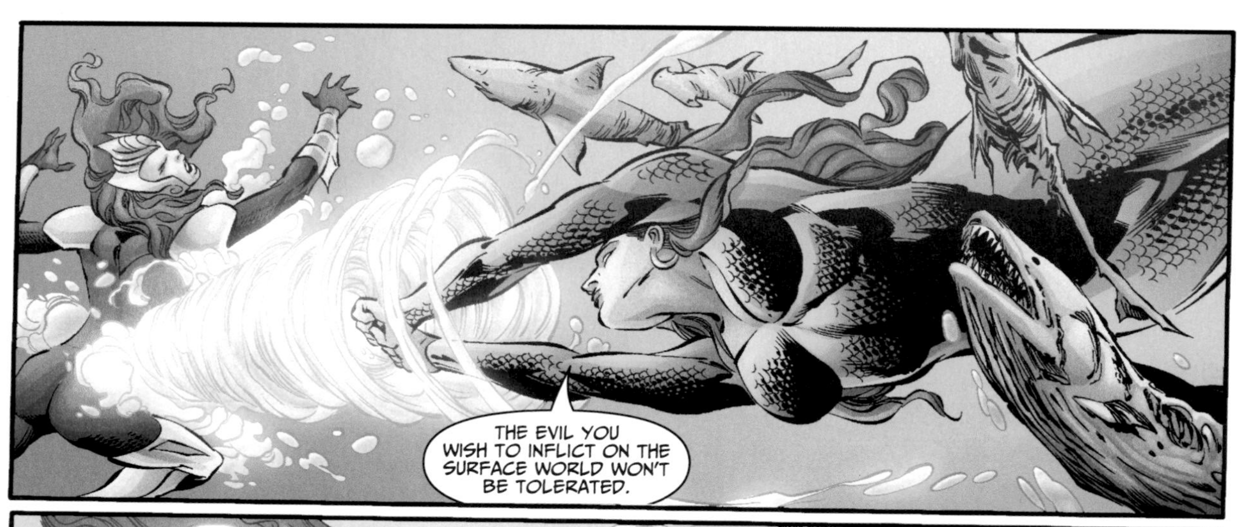

THE EVIL YOU WISH TO INFLICT ON THE SURFACE WORLD WON'T BE TOLERATED.

EVIL? WHAT ***YOU*** DO IS ***EVIL***, MERA. YOU BETRAYED YOUR OWN PEOPLE! YOUR OWN ***SISTER!***
TO THE KING OF ATLANTIS!
A ***FALSE*** KING ***HATED*** BY HIS OWN PEOPLE FOR THE SURFACE BLOOD THAT FLOWS THROUGH HIM!
BUT HE NOW KNOWS YOUR ***LIES*** AND HE ***REJECTS*** YOU AS I DO.

AHHH!

WHAT'S HAPPENING TO HIM?

YOU ARE A ***PARIAH***, MERA!

AN ***OUTCAST*** WHO WILL ***FOREVER BE ALONE!***

WE'RE HERE. THE EDGE OF THE BERMUDA TRIANGLE.

LET THE POWER FLOW OUT OF YOU, JACKSON.

AND TURN THE TRIANGLE BACK ON.

KRAKOOM

AQUAMAN.
I WILL GET FREE.
I WILL COME FOR THE BOY.
AND I WILL GUT HIM IN FRONT OF YOU AS I DID YOUR SON.
IT IS NOT WE WHO WILL BE IMPRISONED IN HERE, MERA!
IT IS YOU WHO ARE IMPRISONED OUT THERRRRRRRRREEEEEEEE--

I HAVE TO C-CLOSE IT...I HAVE TO...
YOU *DID*, JACKSON.
YOU DID IT.
COOL.
SIREN WAS RIGHT, MERA.
YOU ARE AN OUTCAST.

EACH ONE OF US IS CAUGHT BETWEEN TWO WORLDS.
EACH ONE OF US KNOWS HOW HARD IT IS TO FACE THAT ALONE.
WHICH IS WHY WE NEVER WILL BE.

NEVER AGAIN.
I'M SO SORRY, ARTHUR.
SO AM I.

DON'T GET ANY IDEAS.

AQUAMAN, YOU'RE GLOWING! WHAT IS --?
ARTHUR CURRY OF EARTH.
MISSION ACCOMPLISHED.
LIFE RETURNED.
ARTHUR?
AQUAMAN! GET OUT OF HERE!
GET AWAY BEFORE I--
AANNGGGGAAHHH!
ARTHUR!

BRIGHTEST DAY 21
Cover by Gary Frank and Nathan Eyring

MARS ATTACKS

...HE STONECHAT MUSEUM.
THERE WAS SOME KIND OF FIGHT HERE, THAT'S FOR CERTAIN, BUT THERE'S NO BLOOD.
WHEN THE HAWKS FIGHT, THERE'S ALWAYS BLOOD.
IT'S JUST NOT USUALLY THEIRS.
THERE'RE SCORCH MARKS ACROSS THE FLOOR AND WALLS AND...
ATOM? WHAT IS IT?
GOD, I...I THINK I'M STANDING IN THE ASHES OF MY BEST FRIEND.
FIRST FIRESTORM IMPLODES ABOARD THE JUSTICE LEAGUE SATELLITE. THEN I FIND CARTER AND SHIERA VAPORIZED.
"AND NOW WITH WHAT HAPPENED TO AQUAMAN..."

"...WHAT THE HELL IS GOING ON, FLASH?"
MIAMI.
IT DOESN'T MAKE ANY SENSE.
WHY WOULD THE WHITE LANTERN RESURRECT EVERYONE ONLY TO SEND THEM BACK TO THEIR GRAVES?
MERA SAID DEADMAN WAS SHOUTING FOR THEM TO GET AWAY FROM HIM BEFORE HE FIRED HIS RING AT AQUAMAN AND--
THE WHITE LIGHT UNRAVELED HIM, SUPERMAN. IT LOOKED LIKE ARTHUR JUST... DISSOLVED INTO THE WATER.
WE ALL ASSUMED THE POWER OF LIFE WAS A GOOD THING, BUT--
LIFE IS COMPLICATED, SUPERMAN.
WHEN THE WHITE RING MOMENTARILY GRABBED ONTO ME, I COULD HEAR AN INTELLIGENCE WITHIN IT FAR MORE ALIEN THAN ANY I'VE EVER ENCOUNTERED.
WHATEVER IT'S DOING, IT OBVIOUSLY THINKS IT'S FOR THE BEST.
IF HAL WAS HERE--
HE'D BE AS CLUELESS AS THE REST OF US.
AARRGHHH!
CYBORG? ARE YOU ALL RIGHT?
YEAH, I...I'M SET UP TO PICK UP ANY EMERGENCY TRANSMISSIONS SENT TO ONE OF OUR TEAMS.

AND WHAT ABOUT *ME?*

IS DEADMAN GONNA BE GUNNIN' FOR ME *TOO?*
I KNEW THAT GUY WAS *BAD NEWS,* DOVE.
LISTEN, WHATEVER BOSTON'S DONE, IT'S NOT BY *CHOICE,* HAWK.
THE WHITE LANTERN IS *FORCING* HIM TO DO IT. I'VE SEEN HOW IT'S PULLED HIS STRINGS.
EXCEPT WHEN IT CAME TO ME.

GOD, YOU'RE GONNA MAKE ME *BARF.*
LISTEN, ALL I KNOW IS, BEFORE DEADMAN GETS TO *ME* OR ANY OF THE OTHERS, WE SHOULD GET TO *HIM* FIRST. *RIGHT,* JADE?
I THINK WE SHOULD FIND THE OTHERS AND MAKE SURE THEY'RE SAFE.

THE LEAGUE, THE TITANS, THE JUSTICE SOCIETY... THEY ALL JUST GOT HIT WITH *THOUSANDS* OF CALLS FOR HELP.
EARTH-QUAKES, ERUPTING VOLCANOES. WE NEED TO GET OUT THERE.
HEY, GANG.

TAKE A GANDER UP AT THE SKIES. I KNOW IT'S *NIGHT* AND ALL, BUT THERE'RE *CLOUDS* ROLLIN' IN.

BLACK CLOUDS.
IS IT JUST THE HAIR ON THE BACK OF *MY* NECK--

"--OR IS EVERYONE GETTIN' A LITTLE SHIVER?"
MARS.
YOU INVADED MY MIND--MANIPULATED AND EXPLOITED MY INNER LIFE.
CONSIDER YOUR TELEPATHIC CONTROL OF ME OVER.
I HAVE SHREDDED YOUR VEIL OF LIES, D'KAY!
THINK ABOUT WHAT YOU'VE SEEN, J'ONN, WHAT I ALLOWED YOU TO EXPERIENCE...
IT WASN'T A LIE OF THE MIND AT ALL--IT WAS THE SHAPE OF THINGS TO COME...
IF YOU LET IT BE, J'ONN.
I WILL LET NOTHING DEFILE MY MEMORIES OF M'YRI'AH AND K'HYM--DO YOU HEAR ME--NOTHING!!
I FELT YOUR ELATION--THE PURE BLISS OF ACCEPTANCE--WHEN YOU RESURRECTED MARS I EXPERIENCED IT RIGHT ALONG WITH YOU, J'ONN.
I FELT YOUR WARM TEARS OF JOY AGAINST MY CHEEK WHEN WE KISSED.
THOSE WERE NOT TEARS OF JOY YOU FELT--

--THEY WERE TEARS OF RAGE!

UNDERSTAND THIS, D'KAY, IT WAS NOT YOU I WAS HOLDING, IT WAS MY WIFE.
YOU MAY HAVE TWISTED MY MIND BUT YOU WILL NEVER PRY OPEN MY SOUL.
THAT'S WHY YOU COULD NEVER TAKE M'YRI'AH'S PLACE INSIDE THE FANTASY YOU CONSTRUCTED--
--MY HEART WOULDN'T LET YOU IN NO MATTER HOW HARD YOU TRIED!
FORCING ME TO BRING MARS BACK WAS JUST AS MUCH A POWERFUL FANTASY FOR YOU AS IT WAS FOR ME, D'KAY!
IS THE BABY I'M CARRYING INSIDE ME A FANTASY TOO?!?
THAT'S IMPOSSIBLE!
THIS LIFE ON MARS WE SHARED IN OUR HEADS WASN'T SOMETHING THAT LASTED ONLY MINUTES, J'ONN--
--WE WERE TOGETHER AS HUSBAND AND WIFE FOR WEEKS--I SHARED YOUR BED--OUR BODIES MELDED MANY--
SHUT YOUR MOUTH, YOU DECEITFUL WITCH!

IT'S TIME I DID A LITTLE MIND INVASION OF MY OWN!

YARGHH

AS I SUSPECTED--YOUR DEEP DESIRE HAS *CONVINCED YOURSELF* OF CONCEIVING--

--THERE IS NO BABY--IT'S A *PHANTOM CHILD*--YOU ARE *BARREN,* D'KAY!

NOOOO!

YOU'RE A LIAR! OUR BABY LIVES!

FACE THE TRUTH--THERE IS NO BABY--THERE IS NO US!

THESE BONES ARE MARS--*THIS* IS OUR PEOPLE--

--THIS IS OUR FUTURE IF YOU WON'T LOVE ME!

SHUNK

SHUNK

SHUNK

SHUNK

IF IT'S A *PLANET OF LIFE* YOU WANT--

--THEN MAYBE IT'S *TIME*--

--YOU REALLY LISTENED TO ONE!

CAN YOU HEAR THEM ALL, D'KAY?
ARGHH
--S-STOP-- MAKE IT STOP-- SHUT IT OFF-- P-PLEASE--
WHAT YOU REALLY CRAVE IS AN ILLUSION OF SOCIETY, ONE YOU CAN CONTROL AND TAKE WHAT YOU WANT WHEN YOU WANT IT.
YOU'RE A SUPREME TELEPATH WHO CAN'T BEAR TO HEAR THE SOUNDS OF OTHERS-- THEIR HOPES, THEIR DREAMS, THEIR--
NNNG
--FEARS?
IT CAN'T BE--EVERYONE ON EARTH--THEIR THOUGHTS--FILLED WITH PANIC AND DREAD--
...YOU'RE LOST, J'ONN...WHAT YOU REALLY NEED...IS A WORLD TO SAVE...
...BECAUSE YOU'LL ALWAYS KNOW...DEEP IN YOUR SOUL...THAT YOU COULDN'T SAVE EVEN YOUR OWN.
...I'LL DO WHATEVER IT TAKES TO MAKE ME THE CENTER OF YOUR LIFE AND MARS THE CENTER OF YOUR UNIVERSE...
...AND BELIEVE ME, IF THAT MEANS DESTROYING EARTH PIECE BY PIECE, ONE PERSON AT A TIME, I'LL GLADLY DO IT...
...BECAUSE WE HAVE FOREVER, J'ONN.
YOU KNOW WHAT, D'KAY--

--I BELIEVE YOU.
SKKKRRK
WAIT--WHAT ARE YOU DOING--WHERE ARE WE GOING?!?
AWAY.
DON'T YOU SEE--I HELPED BRING YOUR GREATEST DREAM TO LIFE!
ALL YOU DID WAS EXHUME WHAT I HOLD DEAR AND RUB IT IN MY FACE!
WITHOUT ME MARS WILL STAY DEAD AND YOUR LIFE WILL ALWAYS BE A QUESTION OF WHAT-IFS?
WHAT IF I STOPPED THE PLAGUE--WHAT IF I SAVED MY FAMILY--
THE ONLY WHAT-IF I'M WORRIED ABOUT IS WHAT HAPPENS TO EARTH IF I LET YOU LIVE?
AND THE ANSWER TO THAT IS I CAN'T.
AND I WON'T.

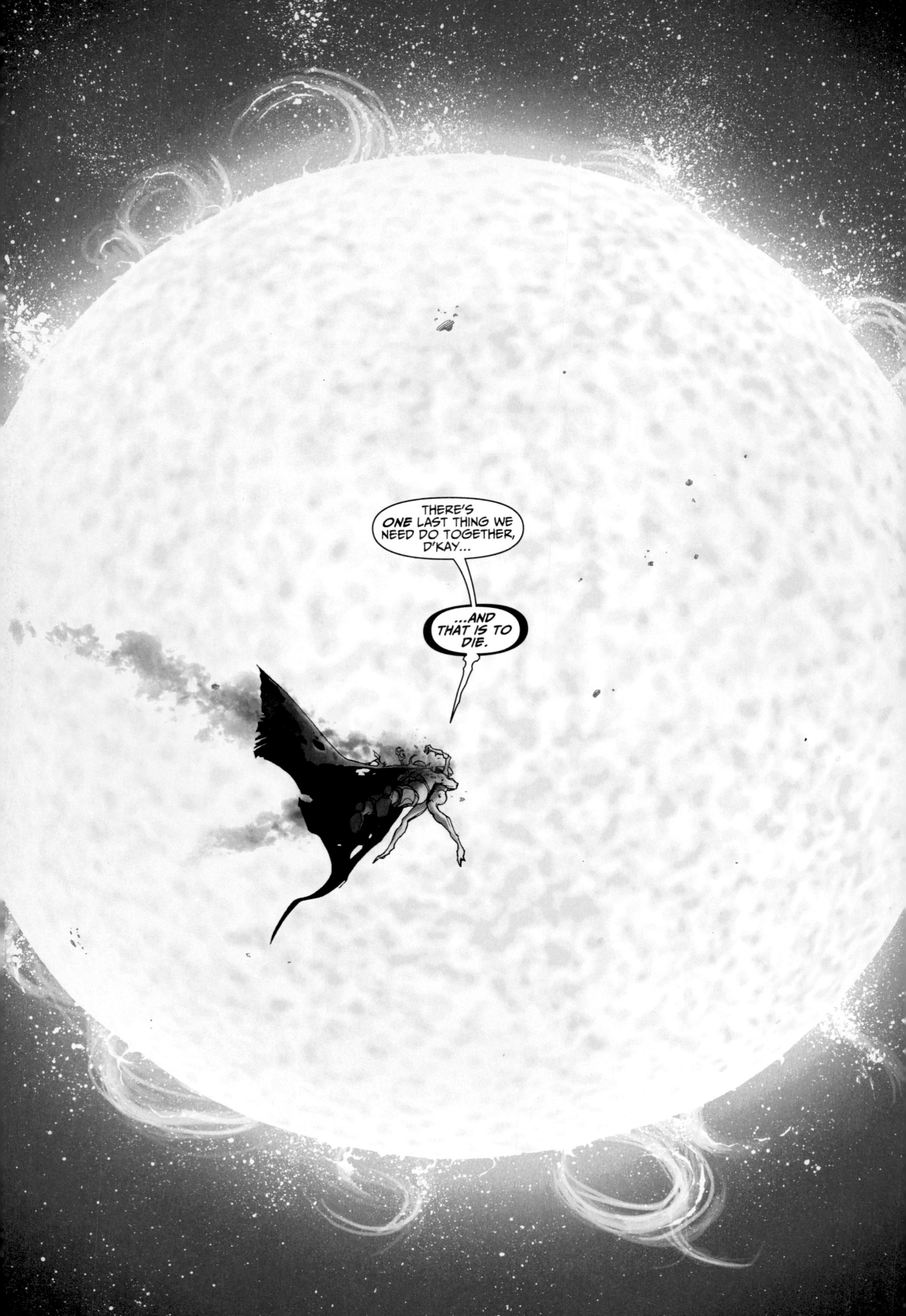
THERE'S *ONE* LAST THING WE NEED DO TOGETHER, D'KAY...
...AND THAT IS TO DIE.

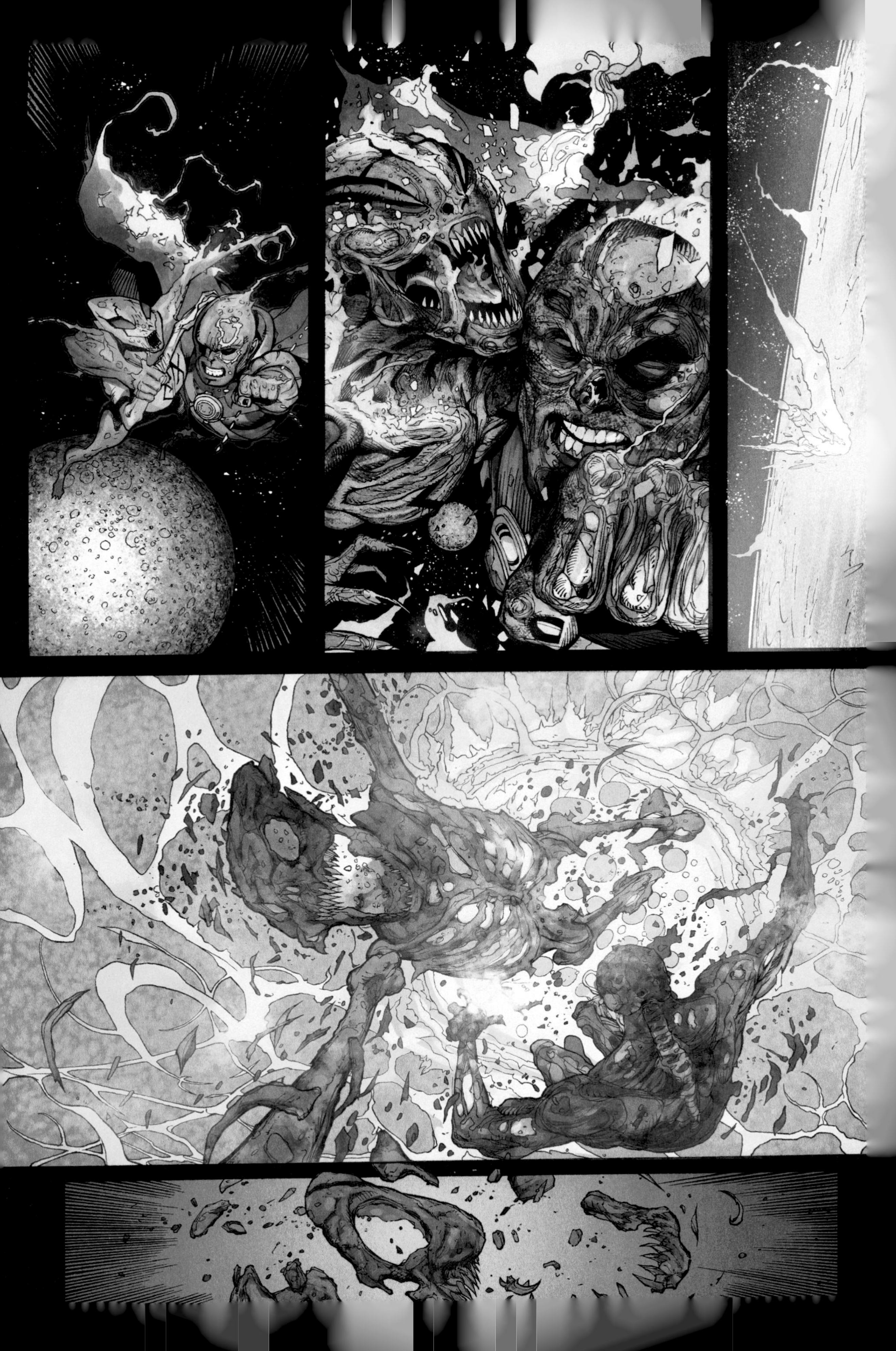

J'ONN J'ONZZ OF MARS.
MISSION ACCOMPLISHED.

LIFE RETURNED.

CHOOSE, J'ONN JONZZ.
CHOOSE YOUR WORLD.
CHOOSE YOUR HOME.

NO!

HANG TIGHT, LITTLE ONES, YOU'RE SAFE.
WOW.

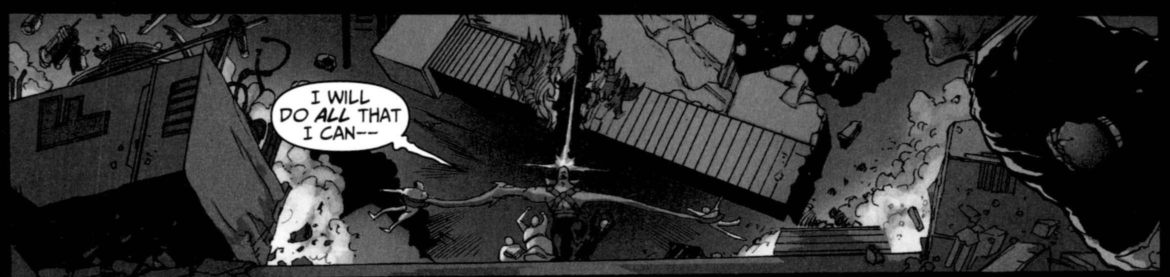
I WILL DO **ALL** THAT I CAN--
--TO PROTECT YOU!

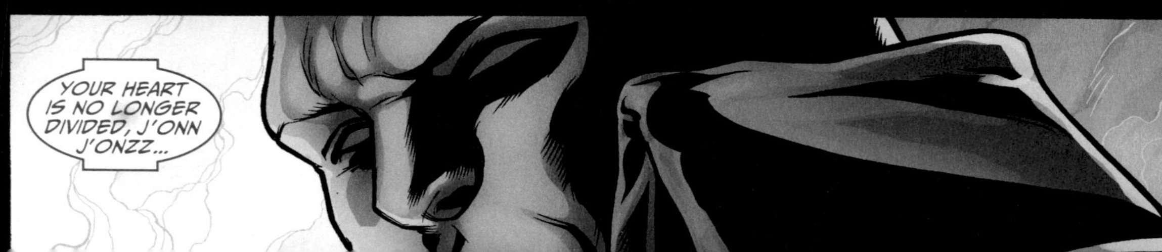
YOUR HEART IS NO LONGER DIVIDED, J'ONN J'ONZZ...

...YOUR SENSE OF DEVOTION AND DUTY IS NOW PURE AND SINGULAR IN ITS PURPOSE.
DEADMAN.
J'ONN-- I CAN'T STOP IT--I GOT NO CONTROL OVER THIS DAMN RING!
IT'S USING ME--PLEASE UNDERSTAND-- IT'S MAKING ME DO--
I KNOW, IT IS, BOSTON.
I SEE YOUR THOUGHTS AND THE FIGHT YOU'RE PUTTING UP.
WHAT HAPPENED TO AQUAMAN, HAWKMAN AND HAWKGIRL IS NOT YOUR FAULT.
I KNOW WHAT THE WHITE LANTERN TOLD YOU.
IF THIS IS ALL PART OF THE PLAN TO SAVE THE STAR CITY FOREST AND EARTH...

J'ONN J'ONZZ OF MARS...
...THEN SO BE IT.
...THE EARTH HAS ACCEPTED YOU.
NO!

BRIGHTEST DAY 22

Cover by Gary Frank and Nathan Eyring

THE END AND THE BEGINNING

THE ANTIMATTER UNIVERSE.
THIS ISN'T JUST SOME FLOATING HUNK OF ROCK, JASON. THIS IS A BATTLESHIP. I WAS HERE BEFORE.
WHEN?
WHEN THE ANTI-MONITOR FIRST TRIED TO LAY WASTE TO OUR UNIVERSE. SUPERMAN GOT A BUNCH OF US TOGETHER AND WE BROUGHT THE FIGHT BACK TO HIM.
HEY! CHECK IT OUT!
I CAN'T BELIEVE IT'S STILL AROUND!
"RONNIE WAS HERE"? REALLY?
RONNIE WAS HERE
WHY WOULDN'T IT BE? WE HAVEN'T SEEN ANYONE OR ANYTHING FOR HOURS--
I THINK THAT'S ABOUT TO CHANGE, JACE.
SEE THAT WHITE GLOW? IT HAS TO BE THE WHITE LANTERN.
IF IT'S THE WHITE LANTERN, DEATHSTORM HAS TO BE HERE--AND WITH HIM MY DAD AND PROFESSOR STEIN.
YEAH...

"LET'S JUST HOPE YOU-KNOW-WHO ISN'T HOME."

YOUR POWER, WHITE LANTERN...
IT IS NOW MINE.

WHO'S THE TALKING SKYSCRAPER, STEIN?
THAT'S THE ANTI-MONITOR, MR. RUSCH.
HE'S ONE OF THE MOST DANGEROUS BEINGS IN EXISTENCE.
WHY?
YOU TWO NEVER SHUT UP, DO YOU?
THE ANTI-MONITOR IS A UNIVERSE-EATER. AND HE'S RESPONSIBLE FOR MORE DEATHS THAN ANYONE COULD IMAGINE.
I CAN IMAGINE A LOT.
VZZZZZZZZZZZZZZZZZZZ
INFUSE LIFEFORCE INTO LANTERN.
KRKK
SPTZZZZ
MY GOD.
WRONG UNIVERSE.
WHAT'S HE DOING?
HE CAN CREATE LIFE WITH THE LANTERN. LIFE HE CAN CONSUME.
THE POWER HE COULD GIVE HIMSELF...HE'LL BE UNSTOPPABLE.

I SEE THEM. DEATHSTORM. THE ANTI-MONITOR.
SO EXACTLY HOW TOUGH IS THE ANTI-MONITOR?
STEIN AND I BARELY HELD OUR OWN AGAINST HIM ALONGSIDE SUPERMAN, CAPTAIN ATOM AND LIKE THIRTY OTHERS.
AND THAT WAS BACK WHEN I WAS THE BEST FIRESTORM I COULD BE.
RONNIE--
THAT'S NOT ABOUT YOU, JASON. IT'S ABOUT ME. I'VE BEEN HOLDING MYSELF BACK.
THAT NEEDS TO STOP RIGHT NOW.
THEY ARE HERE.
WHAT ARE YOU--?
BUT I AM NOT YET READY TO LEAVE.
ANTI-MATTER UNIVERSE INFORMATION NEEDED.
AAARRRHHH!!
KRRAKKKOOOOMM
WHAT HAPPENED?
IT LOOKS LIKE THE LANTERN'S FIGHTING BACK.
AAAHH!!
YOU SEE THAT? THE LANTERN JUST BLASTED HIM!
THEN THIS IS OUR CHANCE. YOU WANT TO BE THE BEST FIRESTORM YOU CAN BE AGAIN, RONNIE?
IT'S NOW OR NEVER.
HELL WITH IT.

LET'S DO
NOW.

BWOOOSHH
ALL RIGHT! IT'S MEATHEAD AND THE BRAIN!
I WAS STARTING TO WORRY YOU'D NEVER GET HERE, DUDES!
BLACK LANTERNS! GIVE 'EM THE OLD DEATHSTORM WELCOME!
DEATHSTORM AND FRIENDS ARE CLOSING IN AND OUR POWERS CAN'T AFFECT ORGANICS.
I CAN OUTMANEUVER THEM, JASON, BUT NOT FOREVER.
JUST STAY FOCUSED ON THE ANTI-MONITOR, RONNIE. TURN THAT GREAT BIG HEAD PIECE OF HIS INTO HYDROGEN.
I CAN DO SOMETHING MORE COMPLEX, JUST TELL ME WHAT--
JUST DO HYDROGEN!
BUT--
TRUST ME!
BWOOOSHH

NOW WHAT?
YOU KNOW THE STORY ABOUT THE HINDENBURG, RIGHT?
WAIT. I GET IT NOW.
HEY, MONTY!
NEED A LIGHT?
FZZAAMMM

BOOOOM
FIRST THINGS FIRST, RONNIE! WE WANT TO HURT DEATHSTORM, FREE STEIN AND MY DAD AND WE NEED--
THE LANTERN.
HELLO THERE!
HELLO.
TIME FOR A REMATCH!
IF YOU EXPECT ME TO ACTUALLY REMEMBER ENCOUNTERING A LIFE FORM AS INSIGNIFICANT AS YOURSELF--
--YOU ARE MISTAKEN.

NFFF!
GG!
DON'T BE TOO DISAPPOINTED, DUDES. YOU ACTUALLY SURVIVED A FIGHT WITH THE ANTI-MONITOR FOR LIKE FORTY-FIVE SECONDS. THAT'S GOTTA BE SOME KIND OF RECORD.
OH, RONNIE... BEFORE I TURN YOU INTO SALT, LET'S TAKE A TRIP DOWN MEMORY LANE... TO WHAT YOU USED TO BE LIKE...
DO YOU REMEMBER WHEN YOU DIED? THE SHADOW THIEF SPLIT OPEN YOUR NUCLEAR GUTS AND TRIGGERED A COUNTDOWN. BUT YOU DIDN'T PANIC.
INSTEAD YOU ACTED SELFLESSLY. YOU FLEW FAR AWAY FROM YOUR FRIENDS TO PROTECT THEM FROM YOUR INEVITABLE EXPLOSIVE DEMISE.
BUT NOW? YOU JUST WANT TO ESCAPE THE RESPONSIBILITY AND ACCOUNTABILITY THAT COMES WITH BEING THE MOST DANGEROUS SUPERHUMAN IN EXISTENCE.
YOU JUST WANT TO CRAWL INTO A BOTTLE AND HIDE. SO TODAY?
YOU'RE GOING TO DIE SAVING NADA!

THE POINT IS: YOU MIGHT BE BACK, RONNIE, BUT FIRESTORM ISN'T.
BECAUSE YOU WERE NEVER REALLY THAT GOOD WITHOUT HIM, WERE YOU?
PROFESSOR!
I REALIZE YOU WISH TO FEED OFF THEIR EMOTIONS, BLACK LANTERNS, BUT NOT UNTIL THEY TELL ME WHAT THE WHITE LANTERN TOOK FROM ME.
YOU ARE WORKING TOGETHER WITH THE LANTERN AGAINST ME.
TO WHAT END?

MAN, THE BIG GUY IS BO-RING.
I'M STARVING... HOW ABOUT SOME RAGE, ALVIN? YOU HAVE SO MUCH IN THAT HEART OF YOURS.
YOU'VE GROWN TO HATE LIFE BECAUSE YOU LOST YOUR ARM AND WITH IT YOUR SELF-WORTH, RIGHT?
AND YOU TOOK IT OUT ON YOUR SON.
SO LET ME HELP FINISH IT OFF AND PUSH YOU INTO THE RED ZONE.
HEY, JASON! SAY HI TO YOUR GIRLFRIEND!
NO!
NO!

AARRHHH!
PROFESSOR!

OBEY ME OR PERISH.
WHOA, DUDE!! CHILL OUT! I SCORED A DIRECT HIT!
NO--HE'S TURNING INTO SALT! WE HAVE TO--
YOU C-CAN'T, RONALD...
WE HAVE TO TRY, PROFESSOR STEIN!
FZZAAMM
I CAN SEE HIS ATOMS UNZIPPING.
HOW DO WE SLOW IT DOWN?
WE JUST HAVE TO THINK! WE HAVE TO--
NOT EVERYTHING CAN BE FIXED WITH THOUGHT.
THE LANTERN! HOLD THE WHITE LANTERN!

THIS WILL WORK! THIS BROUGHT *ME* BACK TO LIFE!
IT *HAS* TO WORK!
PLEASE.
RONNIE... IT'S NOT HELPING.
SAVE HIM, DAMMIT!
RONNIE, LISTEN TO ME...

I DIDN'T MAKE YOU BETTER... YOU MADE *ME* BETTER. YOU PULLED *ME* OUT OF MY OWN HEAD. YOU GAVE ME SOMETHING TO CARE ABOUT BESIDES MY OWN THOUGHTS...
BEING THE KEEPER OF THE FIRESTORM MATRIX WOULDN'T BE EASY FOR ANYONE...THEY WOULD'VE ABUSED THE POWER...OR GIVEN UP...*DON'T* QUIT NOW.
I KNOW JASON BETTER THAN YOU. AND HE WILL BE A BETTER PARTNER THAN ME IF YOU BOTH ACCEPT THE SHARED RESPONSIBILITY.
YOU WEREN'T *LIKE* A SON TO ME, RONALD.
YOU *WERE* A SON.
PROFESSOR!
ALL RIGHT, BIG GUY, CALM DOWN AND LET US HAVE SOME FUN WITH THE KIDS. THE *OLD MAN* IS *DEAD*...
SO IT'S PARTY TIME!
RONNIE... DEATHSTORM AND THE BLACK LANTERNS STILL HAVE MY DAD. WHAT DO WE DO NOW?
YOU AND I KICK THEIR ASSES.
RONALD RAYMOND OF EARTH.

AAAIIEEEE
MISSION ACCOMPLISHED.
LIFE RETURNED.
AAAIIEEEE
AAAIIEEEE
AAAIIEEEE

STAR CITY.
WHAT THE HELL IS GOING ON? WHERE ARE WE?
I DESTROYED THE BLACK LANTERNS AND BROUGHT US BACK TO EARTH. THERE WAS NO NEED TO BATTLE THE ANTI-MONITOR.
THIS EARLY IN YOUR EXPERIENCE AND WITHOUT MASTERING THE POWERS OF THE MATRIX, YOU WOULD HAVE FAILED TO SURVIVE.
MY DAD!
YOUR FATHER HAS BEEN EXORCISED FROM THE BLACK LANTERN AND SAFELY RETURNED TO HIS HOME.
WHAT ABOUT THE PROFESSOR?
HE IS NOT OUR CONCERN. HE IS DEAD.
YOU BROUGHT ME BACK, YOU CAN BRING HIM BACK TOO! WHY DIDN'T YOU?!
HE IS UNNECESSARY TO YOUR JOURNEY AHEAD.
UNNECESSARY? WE JUST RISKED OUR LIVES TO GET YOU! WE DID WHAT YOU SAID, DAMMIT!
YES. AND I RECEIVED WHAT I NEEDED FROM THE ANTI-MONITOR AND YOU FINALLY ACCEPTED JASON RUSCH.
WHAT THE HELL ARE YOU TALKING ABOUT?
FIRESTORM.

GIVE ME THE LANTERN.
DO WHAT HE SAYS.
EARTH DEPENDS ON IT.

BRIGHTEST DAY 23

Cover by Gary Frank and Rod Reis

RISE AND FALL

EARTH.
NOW.

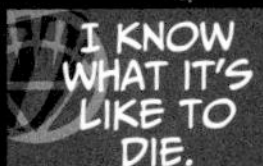
I KNOW WHAT IT'S LIKE TO DIE.

THINGS GO DARK...
LONDON.
...IT HAPPENED SIMULTANEOUSLY ACROSS THE WORLD. THE SKIES TURNED BLACK.
AND OVER TWO THOUSAND PLANES WERE FORCED TO MAKE EMERGENCY LANDINGS.
WITHOUT SUPERHUMAN HELP, THE CASUALTIES WOULD'VE BEEN TENFOLD.
...AND YOUR MIND RACES TO COMPREHEND THE REALITY OF IT.
RIO DE JANEIRO.
EARTHQUAKES AND VOLCANOES HAVE BEGUN ERUPTING IN THE MOST DENSELY POPULATED AREAS ON THE PLANET.

IN THE END I ONLY REMEMBER HAVING ONE LAST THOUGHT:
GOTHAM CITY.
MANY ARE SPECULATING THAT ALL OF THIS IS INTENTIONAL. AS IF THE EARTH *ITSELF* WERE TURNING AGAINST US.
"WHY *ME?*"

STAR CITY.
MY NAME IS BOSTON BRAND. WHEN I DIED, I BECAME THE SPIRIT KNOWN AS DEADMAN.
INVISIBLE AND UNHEARD, I COULD ONLY INTERACT WITH THE REST OF THE WORLD BY POSSESSING THE BODIES OF OTHERS.
BUT IT WASN'T UNTIL I WAS RESURRECTED BY A WHITE LANTERN AND GIVEN A WHITE RING THAT I REALLY GOT A SECOND CHANCE AT LIFE.
MY OWN LIFE.
BUT AT WHAT COST?
WHAT THE HELL'S GOING ON?
I'M TRYING TO PROTECT YOU, FIRESTORM. GIVE ME THE LANTERN.
WHERE ARE WE?

YOU ARE IN THE ONLY SAFE PLACE ON EARTH.
THE ONLY PLACE THAT STILL HAS CLEAR SKIES.
STAR CITY FOREST.
THOUGH IT HAS BEEN CALLED MANY OTHER THINGS THROUGHOUT TIME...
"...IT IS A PLACE WHERE ONLY THE CHOSEN SHALL ENTER."
DAMMIT, WHAT'S GOING ON OUT THERE?!
LET THEM IN!
BOOOMM
NO.

"NO"?
NO, WHAT?
I WAS TALKING TO SOMEONE ELSE.
NOT SO SURE GETTING THE RING AND THE LANTERN TOGETHER IS SUCH A GOOD IDEA. FIRST THE LANTERN SENDS US OFF TO RESCUE IT, THEN IT TELEPORTS US BACK HERE?
I THINK IT WANTED US TO GO THERE.
YOU'RE RIGHT...SO WHY COULDN'T IT HAVE TELEPORTED ITSELF?
I REQUIRED INFORMATION ONLY THE ANTI-MONITOR POSSESSED.
AND, MOST IMPORTANT, I NEEDED YOU TO WITNESS PROFESSOR STEIN'S DEATH FOR YOURSELF.
WHAT?!
YOU WANTED ME TO BE THERE JUST TO SEE HIM DIE?!
IF YOU KNEW HE WAS GOING TO DIE, WHAT ABOUT SAVING HIM?
THAT WOULD HAVE CAUSED DELAYS IN YOUR ONCE AGAIN EMBRACING FIRESTORM.
AND THERE CAN BE NO DELAYS.
SOON THE DARK AVATAR WILL RISE.
AND HE WILL COME.
I'M SORRY, RONNIE. YOU NEED TO UNDERSTAND. THE RING HAS BEEN MANIPULATING ALL OF US.
WHY?

"SO YOUR LIFE FORCES CAN BE USED TO DEFEND EARTH."
I HEARD IT FROM CYBORG, MERA.
THERE'S BLUE SKY OVER STAR CITY AND SOME KIND OF WHITE LIGHT OVER THE FOREST THERE THAT'S KEEPING EVERYONE OUT.
DID YOU HEAR THAT, DOVE? WHITE LIGHT'S IN STAR CITY.
BET WE GO THERE AND WE'LL FIND DEADMAN.
WE'RE NOT GOING ANYWHERE, HAWK. NOT WHEN PEOPLE NEED HELP.
I KNEW DEADMAN WAS BAD NEWS. THIS HAS TO BE HIS FAULT.
YOU HEARD MERA. HE WAS BEING FORCED TO ACT AGAINST HIS OWN--
DAWN GRANGER. YOUR PRESENCE IS REQUIRED.
WHAT'S HAPPENING TO--
DOVE?!
FWAAAASHHHH
BOSTON?! FIRESTORM?!
DOVE!
"STAR CITY'S THE SAME AS CENTRAL, COLD."

BLOODY BLACK SKIES AND ALL THAT'S COMIN' WITH IT.
A VOICE TOLD ME TO COME HERE. IT SAID I COULD GET ACCESS TA THIS FOREST WHEN OTHERS COULDN'T.
BOOMERANG, YOU SURE YOU SHOULD--
HELP ME!
SORRY. NOT SOMETHIN' I DO, MATE.
FLASH FACT: YOU WANT TO SURVIVE THIS, YOU BETTER RENDEZVOUS WITH US. YOU WON'T LAST LONG OUT THERE ALONE.
IT'S TIME I TRIED, MATE. I'M THROUGH RUNNIN' AWAY FROM MESELF. LIKE I TOLD OL' SPEEDY...
TIME TO GET BUSY LIVIN'--
--OR GET BUSY DYIN'!
DIGGER HARKNESS OF EARTH.
ARRGH!
THROW THE BOOMERANG AT HER.

WHAT THE HELL ARE YOU *UP* TO, DEADMAN?
I DON'T KNOW.
ARE YOU ALL RIGHT, BOSTON?
I'M TRYING SO HARD TO HOLD THIS RING BACK, DAWN. I...

KRRAAAATCHHH

I THINK I KILLED HAWKMAN, HAWKGIRL AND AQUAMAN. I DID SOMETHING TO THE MARTIAN MANHUNTER.

KRRAAATCHHH
SLTCH
WHAP

HE COMES.
WHAT? WHO DOES?
THE DARK AVATAR.

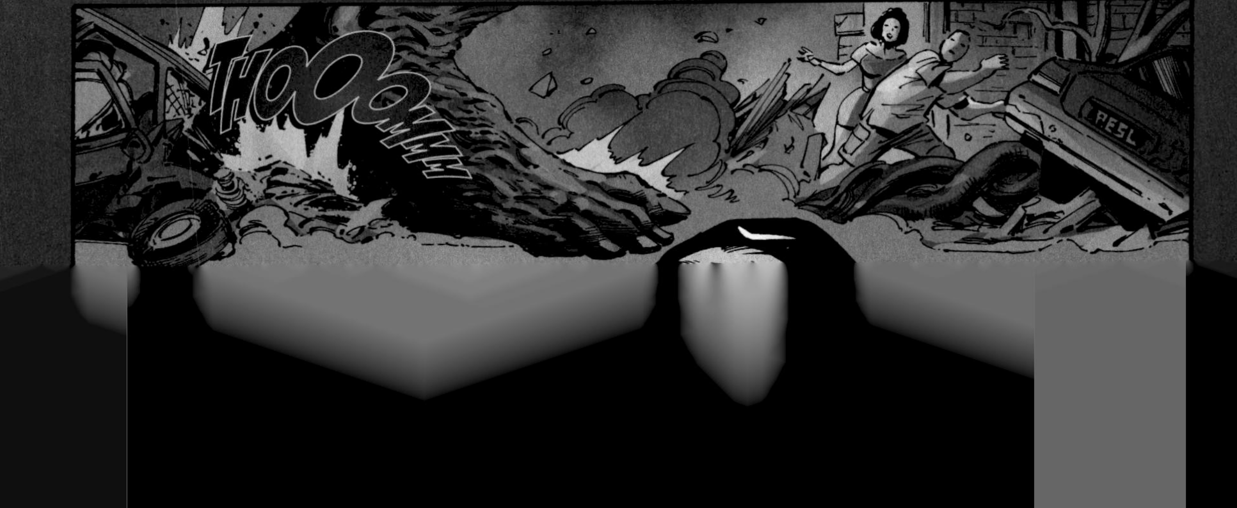
THOOOMM!

"THE GREEN HAS BECOME THE BLACK."
WHOOOOOM
WHATEVER THAT THING IS, IT'S HURTING PEOPLE! WE HAVE TO--
ONCE YOU'VE ENTERED THE FOREST YOU CANNOT LEAVE.
SKRAKOOOOOM
BOSTON, ASK THE RING WHAT THAT IS! WHAT DOES IT WANT?!

"IT WANTS DEATH."

"WHERE IT ONCE HAD THE MEMORIES OF ONE...
"...IT NOW HAS THE MEMORIES OF ANOTHER."

WHAT'S HAPPENING TA ME HANDS?
YOUR BOOMERANGS.

THEY'RE FOR HER.

IT IS TIME, RONALD RAYMOND.
TIME FOR WHAT--?!

NO!

YAARGHHH

RRRNN--
STOP--

RONNIE!

YOU'RE KILLING HIM, YOU BASTARD!

NO NEED TO WORRY, JASON RUSCH.

DEATH SOMETIMES MAKES YOU STRONGER.

OR SIMPLY JUST DEAD.

SEEMS FAMILIAR...
AIR.
MY GOD...WHAT DID I--?
FIRE.
WATER.
EARTH.
LIKE THE GREEN, THE ELEMENTALS NEED GUIDANCE.
FWAAASHHH

AND NOW THEY HAVE IT.

THE... TREE.
THE TREE... MUST ROT.
I...I CAN FEEL THE FIRE ACROSS THE EARTH. FROM CANDLES TO VOLCANOES, IT'S ALL CONNECTED.
AS IS THE EARTH THAT MAKES THIS WORLD.
AND THE AIR WE BREATHE.
WE KNOW WHY WE'RE HERE.
THIS WORLD...
...WILL DECAY.
YOU THREE MUST REMAIN TO PROTECT THE TREE. IT IS THE FOUNDATION.
THE FOUNDATION OF WHAT?
THE PARLIAMENT OF TREES.

"IT HAS LOST ITS DEFENDER."

IT HAS BEEN CORRUPTED.

BUT THIS FOREST HOLDS SALVATION.
FWAAAASHHHH

KRRAAATCHHH

IT HOLDS THE BODY OF THE ONE.

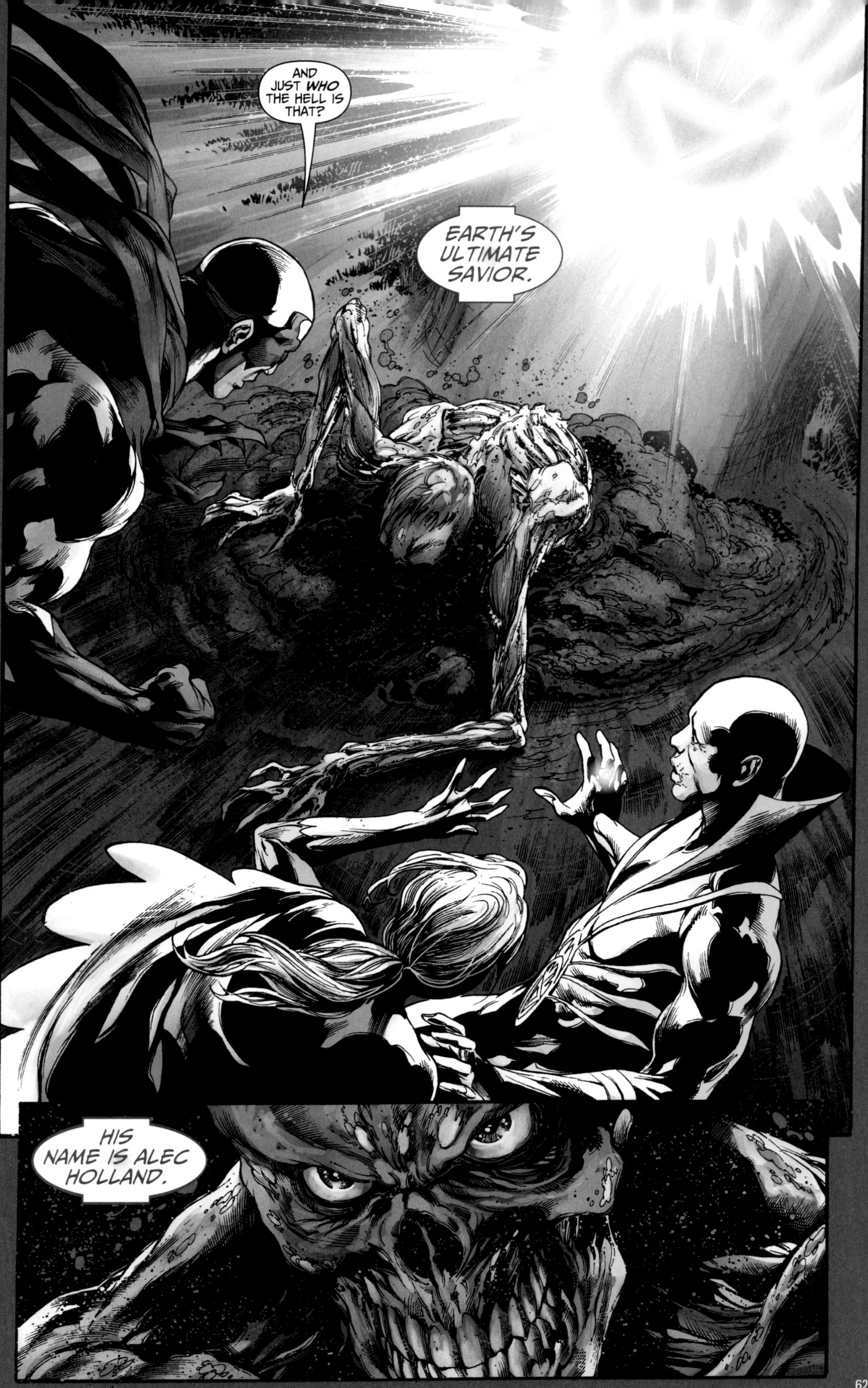
AND JUST WHO THE HELL IS THAT?
EARTH'S ULTIMATE SAVIOR.
HIS NAME IS ALEC HOLLAND.

BRIGHTEST DAY 24
Cover by Gary Frank and Rod Reis

CONCLUSION

THAT'S EARTH'S NEW CHAMPION?
ALEC HOLLAND...
I KNOW THAT NAME.
HE WAS A SCIENTIST, DOVE. A BIOLOGIST OR A BOTANIST...OR BOTH. I'M NOT REALLY SURE.
HE HAD A LAB IN THE LOUISIANA SWAMPS. THERE WAS AN EXPLOSION...
AN ATTACK, BOSTON BRAND.
MANY MEN WHO WOULD EXPLOIT THIS WORLD WANTED ALEC HOLLAND'S WORK FOR THEMSELVES.
ALEC HOLLAND WAS ENGULFED IN AN EXPLOSION THAT IGNITED HIS LAB.
ALEC HOLLAND DIED IN THE SWAMP. AND HIS MEMORY WAS ABSORBED INTO THE LIFE WEB OF THE EARTH CALLED THE GREEN.
I KNOW. AND A...CREATURE MADE OF VEGETATION ROSE OUT OF THE SWAMP THINKING IT WAS ALEC HOLLAND.
BUT ALEC HOLLAND WAS DEAD. IT WAS NOT ALEC HOLLAND.

"IT WAS ONLY
SWAMP THING."

WHAT ARE WE SUPPOSED TO BE DOING HERE, RONNIE?
I...I HAVE THIS INSTINCT, JASON.
TO BURN THE BLACK.
WE CAN'T LET THIS MONSTER GET TO THE TREE.
THAT'S ALL THAT MATTERS RIGHT NOW.
TO SAVE THE EARTH.
WE HAVE TO FIGHT THE EARTH.
YOU HAVE WOUNDED THE ROTTING HUSK OF CORRUPTION AND PROVIDED US TIME, ELEMENTALS.
NOW YOU ARE NEEDED FOR WHAT COMES NEXT.

WHAT ARE YOU DOING TO THEM NOW?
ARE YOU AWARE YOU HAVE STOPPED WORRYING ABOUT YOURSELF, BOSTON BRAND? IT IS NOT SOMETHING YOU WERE EVER IN THE HABIT OF DOING BEFORE.
JUST TELL ME WHAT THE HELL YOU'RE DOING?
I NEED TO FAMILIARIZE ALEC HOLLAND'S BODY WITH THE ELEMENTALS.
BWOOOOOOOOOOOSSSSSSSSSSSHHHH
BLOODY HELL!
IF IT IS STILL NOT CLEAR, BOSTON BRAND, THIS IS ABOUT YOU AS MUCH AS ANYONE.
WHEN NEKRON CAME TO EARTH YOU WERE DEAD. FREE FROM ANY CONNECTION TO THE LIVING AND THERE-FORE FREE OF THE INFECTION OF DECAY.
YOU WERE THE ONLY ONE WHOSE LIFE FORCE WAS ABSOLUTELY PURE, IF UNDERAPPRECIATED. YOU WERE MY SANCTUARY AND THIS FOREST THE GREEN'S.
AND WHILE I RESURRECTED MANY TO STAVE OFF THIS ATTACK, OTHERS LIKE AQUAMAN WERE OF MORE IMPORTANCE.
ONCE PURIFIED, THEIR ESSENCE COULD ACT AS A GUIDE FOR THE FOUR ELEMENTS JUST AS ALEC HOLLAND'S ESSENCE ACTED AS A GUIDE FOR THE GREEN...

"...UNTIL NEKRON'S ESSENCE WAS IMPRINTED OVER IT."
THIS WORLD... WILL ROT.
"WAIT... I UNDERSTAND NOW.
"SWAMP THING THOUGHT HE WAS ALEC HOLLAND... NOW HE THINKS HE'S NEKRON."
"YOU ARE CORRECT, BOSTON BRAND."
THE GREEN NEEDS A PSYCHE TO ADHERE TO.
SO YOU NEED TO GET SWAMP THING TO THINK HE'S ALEC HOLLAND AGAIN?
TO TRULY ERADICATE THE VESTIGES OF NEKRON, WE NEED NOT ONLY SWAMP THING, TO BELIEVE HE IS ALEC HOLLAND--
--HE MUST TRULY BECOME ALEC HOLLAND.
YEAH, WELL, ALEC HOLLAND DOESN'T EXACTLY LOOK READY FOR IT.
ALEC HOLLAND HAS NO MEMO OF BEING SWA THING BECAUS HE NEVER TRU WAS.
THE LAST THING HE REMEMBERS IS DYING IN THE SWAMP.
LOOK OUT!
THOOOMM

THROW THE BOOMERANG.
WOT? THAT MONSTER THING IS RIGHT THERE! LET IT DO TH' JOB.
THROW THE BOOMERANG AT HER.

YOU HEARD THE RING. DEAD OR ALIVE, KEEP ALEC HOLLAND SAFE.
BUT--
MY POWER IS EVADING VIOLENCE, BOSTON. I'LL KEEP THIS THING OCCUPIED WHILE THE RING TELLS YOU WHAT TO DO NEXT.

ALEC HOLLAND NEEDS TO JOIN THE LAND OF THE LIVING, BUT FOR THAT SOMEONE MUST DIE.
WHAT ARE YOU--?

FWP
FWP
FWP
FWP
FWP
FWP
FWP
FWP

DOVE!

ARHHH!
FWP FWP FWP
DOVE, LOOK OUT!
DIGGER HARKNESS OF EARTH.
MISSION ACCOMPLISHED.
LIFE RETURNED.
KRAKKK
YOU SON-OF-A-BITCH!
NO.
IT'S OKAY.
EVERY-THING'S GOING TO BE--

--OKAY.
BOOOOOOM!!!
BOSTON?!
BOSTON... NO... THE RING CAN HELP... THE RING--
I AM SORRY. I CANNOT FIX HIS LIFE.
NOT THIS TIME.

NO! AFTER EVERYTHING YOU PUT HIM THROUGH--

DOVE, LISTEN TO ME. PLEASE.

THANK YOU.

THANK YOU FOR OPENING MY EYES.

THANK YOU FOR MAKING MY SECOND CHANCE AT LIFE...

...MATTER.

GO... GET 'EM, HOLLAND.

FZZPP

LIVE.

WHAT... WHAT'S GOING ON? WHERE AM I?
I REMEMBER THE LAB... A FIRE--
KRRAAATCHHH
AAAHH!
KRRAAATCHHH
KRRKKK
WHAT'S HAPPENING?!
KRRKKK
KRRKKK
THE PARLIAMENT OF TREES...THE PLANET ELEMENTALS OF THE PAST...THIS FOREST...ASKS FOR YOUR HELP.
THE GREEN HAS BEEN CORRUPTED.
THE GREEN HAS...BEEN CORRUPTED.
THIS IS YOUR WORLD.

THIS IS...MY WORLD.

YOU MUST PROTECT IT.
...I MUST PROTECT IT.

A NEW SAGA BEGINS, ALEC HOLLAND.
FOR NOT ONLY YOU, BUT THE UNIVERSE.
ERADICATING THE REMAINS OF NEKRON'S CORRUPTIVE TOUCH IS THE BEGINNING.
THE FOUR ELEMENTAL FORCES ARE CURRENTLY WITHIN THE GREEN.
NO...

USE THEM.
I AM...ALEC HOLLAND.
AND STOP FIGHTING YOUR TRANSFORMATION, ALEC HOLLAND.
YOU ARE HUMAN NO MORE.
YOU ARE...YOU MUST BE...

SWAMP THING
CONNECTION SEVERED.

DOVE, HE'S GONE.
NO...
HE'S GONE, DOVE.
I'M...I'M SORRY.
THE EARTH... WILL TAKE CARE OF HIM.
BOSTON BRAND.
YOUR TIME AMONG THE LIVING IS OVER.

WH- WHAT? WHAT NOW--?!
BUT YOUR TIME ON THIS WORLD IS NOT DONE.
THE PEOPLE ON THIS PLANET WHO HAVE GIVEN UP ON LIFE STILL NEED YOUR HELP.
FORGET IT!
IF YOU'RE TELLING ME I'M GONNA BE A SPIRIT AGAIN, THAT I WON'T BE ABLE TO BE SEEN OR HEARD, I DON'T WANT TO BE HERE! I DON'T WANT TO BE INVISIBLE ANYMORE!
IF I DIE TODAY THEN I DIE TODAY, BUT LET ME MOVE ON! DO YOU HEAR ME?
LET ME MOVE ON!
I CANNOT.
NO!
IT'S NOT FAIR!
IT'S JUST NOT FAIR!

BOSTON?!
DOVE? YOU CAN SEE ME?
I CAN HEAR YOU!
I CAN HEAR YOU, BOSTON--!
DOVE, I...
I LOVE YOU.
I LOVE YOU TOO.
THE CORRUPTION... IS OVER.

THE DARKNESS... IS GONE...
...PURGED...
...THE INFUSION OF ELEMENTAL POWERS... THAT STRENGTHENED MY LIFE FORCE AND HELPED GUIDE ME...
...ARE NO LONGER REQUIRED!

SWAMP THING? HE'S A LOT BIGGER THAN I REMEMBER.
DO I...KNOW YOU?
THAT'S FIRESTORM. I'M AQUAMAN AND--
HAVING BEEN BRIEFLY CONNECTED TO ALL OF YOU...IT WOULD SEEM THAT YOUR MENTAL AND PHYSICAL STATES... HAVE RETURNED TO NORMAL.

NORMAL?! TELL ME WHAT'S NORMAL!
PEOPLE WE CARED ABOUT DIED OUT THERE!
THERE ALWAYS DOES SEEM TO BE... A PRICE TO PAY.
SHIERA?

WHERE THE HELL IS SHIERA?
SHE IS...NOT HERE...

SHIERA!
LET HER OUT OF THERE!

BRING HER BACK, DAMN IT!

IF IT'S ANOTHER LIFE YOU NEED, TAKE MINE INSTEAD!
LET HER GO!

I TOLD YOU...
...SHE IS NOT HERE...

...BUT SHE IS ALL AROUND YOU...
SHIERA.

ETERNAL SPRING... HAS ARRIVED...
...THE TIME'S COME... FOR RENEWAL...
--IT'S ALL GROWING BACK--
YES.
IT ALL COMES BACK.
I CAN HEAR THEIR THOUGHTS--
MILLIONS OF PEOPLE-- SCREAMING FOR JOY--
WHO?
SWAMP THING IS NOT JUST REGENERATING THE FOREST...

...HE'S RESTORING THE GREEN OF THE ENTIRE PLANET.

THIS FRAGILE WORLD IS SAFE...
...THE GREEN GROWS STRONGER ONCE AGAIN...
...BUT IT NEEDS EVERYONE'S NURTURING...ALONG WITH MY UNYIELDING VIGILANCE...
...THE GREEN NEEDS PROTECTION...
...AND I WILL ERADICATE ANYONE AND ANYTHING THAT...
...PUTS IT IN JEOPARDY.
WAIT--
YOU HAVE DONE WELL, ARTHUR CURRY.

YOU HAVE ALL DONE WELL.
EXCEPT FOR YOU, HANK HALL.
YOU FAILED YOUR MISSION.
WHAT ARE YOU TALKING ABOUT? WHAT'S THAT MEAN?
YOUR LIFE IS STILL NOT YOUR OWN. I CANNOT FREE YOU FROM THE INFLUENCE OF WAR.
YOU ARE NOT LIKE THE OTHERS.
OTHERS?
JADE BALANCED THE DARKNESS WITHIN HER BROTHER WHICH WOULD HAVE EMPOWERED THE CORRUPTED SWAMP THING AND MADE HIM NEARLY UNSTOPPABLE.
MAXWELL LORD UNKNOWINGLY PLAYED A PART IN PROTECTING THE WORLD FROM A SUPERHUMAN WAR.
AND OSIRIS HELPED HIS SISTER ISIS, THE GODDESS OF NATURE, RETURN. SHE WILL AID ALEC HOLLAND.
MY TIME HERE IS DONE.

BUT YOURS IS NOT.
I STILL HAVE QUESTIONS!
LIFE IS FULL OF QUESTIONS, BOSTON BRAND.
BUT MORE IMPORTANT, IT IS FULL OF POSSIBILITIES.
ENJOY THEM.
EMBRACE LIFE.
FOR ALL IT IS AND ALL IT IS NOT.
FWOOOOOOOMMMM
I HAVE A FEELING WE WON'T BE ABLE TO FOLLOW IT.
SO WHAT DO WE DO NOW?

LIVE."
MIAMI.
THERE WOULD'VE BEEN MORE DEATHS IF IT WASN'T FOR YOU AND JACKSON.
IF IT WASN'T FOR ALL OF US, MERA.
WHERE IS JACKSON?
HE'S BACK WITH HIS PARENTS, BUT EAGER TO TALK TO YOU. HE WANTS TO CONTINUE TRAINING--
I'VE ALREADY CONTACTED THE TITANS.
WE'RE VERY FORTUNATE, ARTHUR. HAWKMAN AND HAWKGIRL. DEADMAN AND DOVE. THEY LOST ONE ANOTHER.
WE ALMOST DID TOO. ARTHUR...?
WHAT IS IT?
THIS TECHNOLOGY... THE WEAPONS XEBEL WAS OUTFITTED WITH. I RECOGNIZE IT.
IT'S ATLANTEAN.

DENVER, COLORADO.

MOUNT HOPE SENIOR HOME.

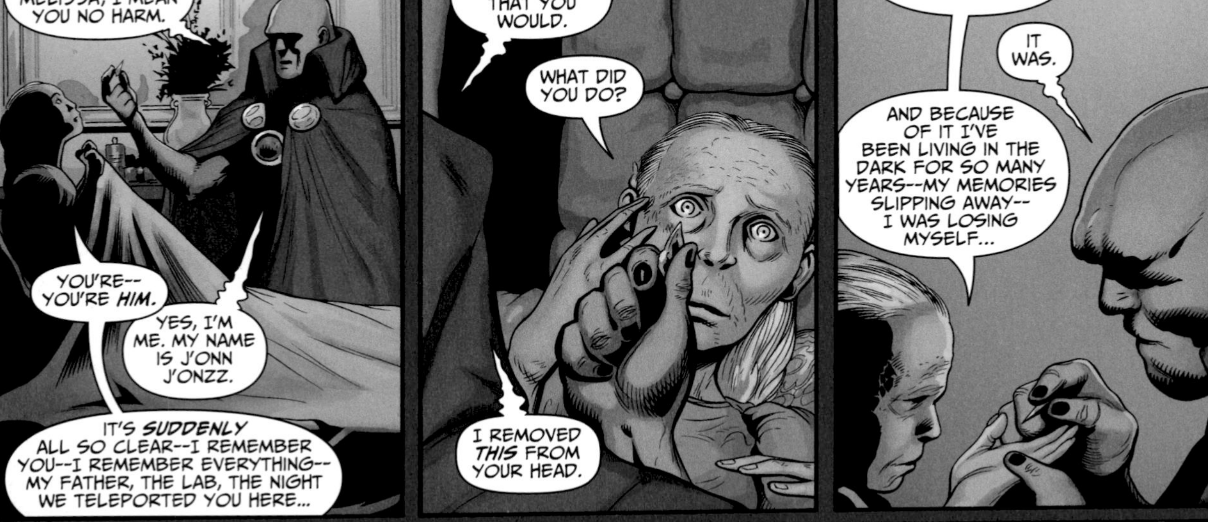

PLEASE DON'T BE AFRAID, MELISSA, I MEAN YOU NO HARM.
YOU'RE-- YOU'RE HIM.
YES, I'M ME. MY NAME IS J'ONN J'ONZZ.
IT'S SUDDENLY ALL SO CLEAR--I REMEMBER YOU--I REMEMBER EVERYTHING-- MY FATHER, THE LAB, THE NIGHT WE TELEPORTED YOU HERE...
I'M GLAD. I WAS HOPING THAT YOU WOULD.
WHAT DID YOU DO?
I REMOVED THIS FROM YOUR HEAD.
AN OLD WOUND ON AN OLD WOMAN-- THEY SAID IT WAS INOPERABLE.
IT WAS.
AND BECAUSE OF IT I'VE BEEN LIVING IN THE DARK FOR SO MANY YEARS--MY MEMORIES SLIPPING AWAY-- I WAS LOSING MYSELF...

...I'VE BEEN WAITING SO LONG FOR THE CHANCE TO MEET YOU... TO ASK YOU FOR FORGIVENESS.

FORGIVENESS?

MY FATHER AND I STOLE YOU FROM YOUR HOME-- FROM YOUR PEOPLE-- WE STOLE YOUR LIFE RIGHT FROM UNDER YOU...

YOU DIDN'T STEAL MY LIFE.

YOU AND YOUR FATHER GAVE ME ONE.

THE STONECHAT MUSUEM.
ST. ROCH, LOUISIANA.
YARRGGHH!
SHIERAAAAAA!

PITTSBURGH UNIVERSITY.
MAYBE YOU CAN MAKE SENSE OUT OF THE PROFESSOR'S JOURNALS.
SOME OF IT READS LIKE IT WAS WRITTEN IN A SECRET LANGUAGE OR SOMETHING. LIKE IF STEPHEN HAWKING WROTE THE DA VINCI CODE.
THERE'S SO MUCH...
UNSTABLE
...STUFF.
JASON, I KNOW YOU AND YOUR DAD STILL NEED TO WORK THINGS OUT, BUT YOU SHOULD, MAN. SOONER THAN LATER.
JASON? JASON, I'M TRYING TO CONNECT HERE.
HEY... WHAT IS IT?
I'M NOT THE BEST AT THIS SO I COULD BE WRONG, BUT... I JUST RAN THESE TESTS THE PROFESSOR SET UP TO TRACK FIRESTORM'S MOLECULAR ACTIVITY AND...
IT'S ALTERED.
ALTERED HOW?
Matrix Analysis
AS NEAR AS I CAN GUESS, WHEN WE WERE BLASTED BY THE ANTI-MONITOR THE MATRIX WAS...DAMAGED. AND I THINK A COUNTDOWN STARTED.
ACCORDING TO THE PROFESSOR'S DIAGNOSTIC PROGRAM... IN LESS THAN NINETY DAYS--
UNSTABLE
COUNTDOWN TO EVENT
DAYS: 89 HOURS: 14 MINUTES: 32 SECONDS: 59
--WE'RE GOING TO DETONATE.

...AROUND THE WORLD PEOPLE ARE STILL TRYING TO DETERMINE HOW MUCH DAMAGE THE RECENT EVENTS HAVE DONE TO OUR PLANET AND HOW WE CAN HOPE TO CORRECT IT.
ALREADY, THE FEDERAL GOVERNMENT HAS LED THE ASSEMBLY OF A NEW INTERNATIONAL TASK FORCE TO STRENGTHEN THE ENVIRONMENTAL RESTRICTIONS ON HEAVY INDUSTRY...
GBS NEWS
THEY'RE TALKING ABOUT US.
THE OIL SPILL WAS CLEANED UP BY AQUAMAN, WASN'T IT?
THAT'S UNCONFIRMED. WHAT IS CONFIRMED IS THAT WE'RE GOING TO BE UNDER A NEW LEVEL OF SCRUTINY.
THE SPILL WAS UNFORTUNATE, WE ALL KNOW THAT, BUT WHAT'S ALSO UNFORTUNATE IS THAT WE'RE ABOUT TO BE PUT UNDER A MICROSCOPE.
WE NEED TO RELOCATE THE DUMPING DEPOTS BEFORE THEY'RE FOUND.
TO START. AND SEE WHERE WE ARE IN THE LAWSUIT WITH THAT BOY WITH LUNG CANCER--
LEUKEMIA.
YEAH.
THE WORLD WANTS TO RUN, BUT THEY DON'T WANT TO HEAR ABOUT THE CONSEQUENCES.
I AGREE.
WHO SAID THAT?
KRRAAATCHHH
ARRRR!
KRRAAATCHHH

THERE ARE...ALWAYS CONSEQUENCES.

THAT NIGHT.
POLICE LINE // DO NOT CROSS
SUPPOSE IT WAS ONLY A MATTER OF TIME.
SKKTCH
SWAMP THING RETURNS?

BOLLOCKS.
THE BEGINNING.

BRIGHTEST DAY 0

Variant cover by Ivan Reis and Chuck Pires

BRIGHTEST DAY 1
Variant cover by Ivan Reis and Chuck Pires

BRIGHTEST DAY 2
Variant cover by Ivan Reis and Nei Ruffino
IVAN REIS

BRIGHTEST DAY 3
Variant cover by Ivan Reis and Chuck Pires

BRIGHTEST DAY 4

Variant cover by Ivan Reis and Chuck Pires

BRIGHTEST DAY 5
Variant cover by Ivan Reis and Chuck Pires

BRIGHTEST DAY 6
Variant cover by Ivan Reis and Dave McCaig

BRIGHTEST DAY 7
Variant cover by Ryan Sook, Fernando Pasarin and Joel Gomez with Randy Mayor and Carrie Strachan

BRIGHTEST DAY 8
Variant cover by Ryan Sook, Fernando Pasarin and Joel Gomez with Randy Mayor and Carrie Strachan
FIRESTORM

BRIGHTEST DAY 9
Variant cover by Ivan Reis and Hi-Fi

BRIGHTEST DAY 10
Variant cover by Ivan Reis and Hi-Fi

BRIGHTEST DAY 11
Variant cover by Ivan Reis and Hi-Fi

BRIGHTEST DAY 12
Variant cover by Ivan Reis and Hi-Fi

BRIGHTEST DAY 13

Variant cover by Ivan Reis and Hi-Fi

BRIGHTEST DAY 14
Variant cover by Ivan Reis and Hi-Fi

BRIGHTEST DAY 15
Variant cover by Ivan Reis and Hi-Fi

BRIGHTEST DAY 16
Variant cover by Ivan Reis and Hi-Fi

BRIGHTEST DAY 17

Variant cover by Ivan Reis, Oclair Albert and Rod Reis

BRIGHTEST DAY 18

Variant cover by Ivan Reis, Oclair Albert and Rod Reis

BRIGHTEST DAY 19
Variant cover by Gary Frank and Nathan Eyring

BRIGHTEST DAY 20
Variant cover by Gary Frank and Nathan Eyring

BRIGHTEST DAY 21
Variant cover by Ivan Reis and Rod Reis

BRIGHTEST DAY 22
Variant cover by Ivan Reis and Rod Reis

BRIGHTEST DAY 23
Variant cover by Ivan Reis, Oclair Albert and Rod Reis

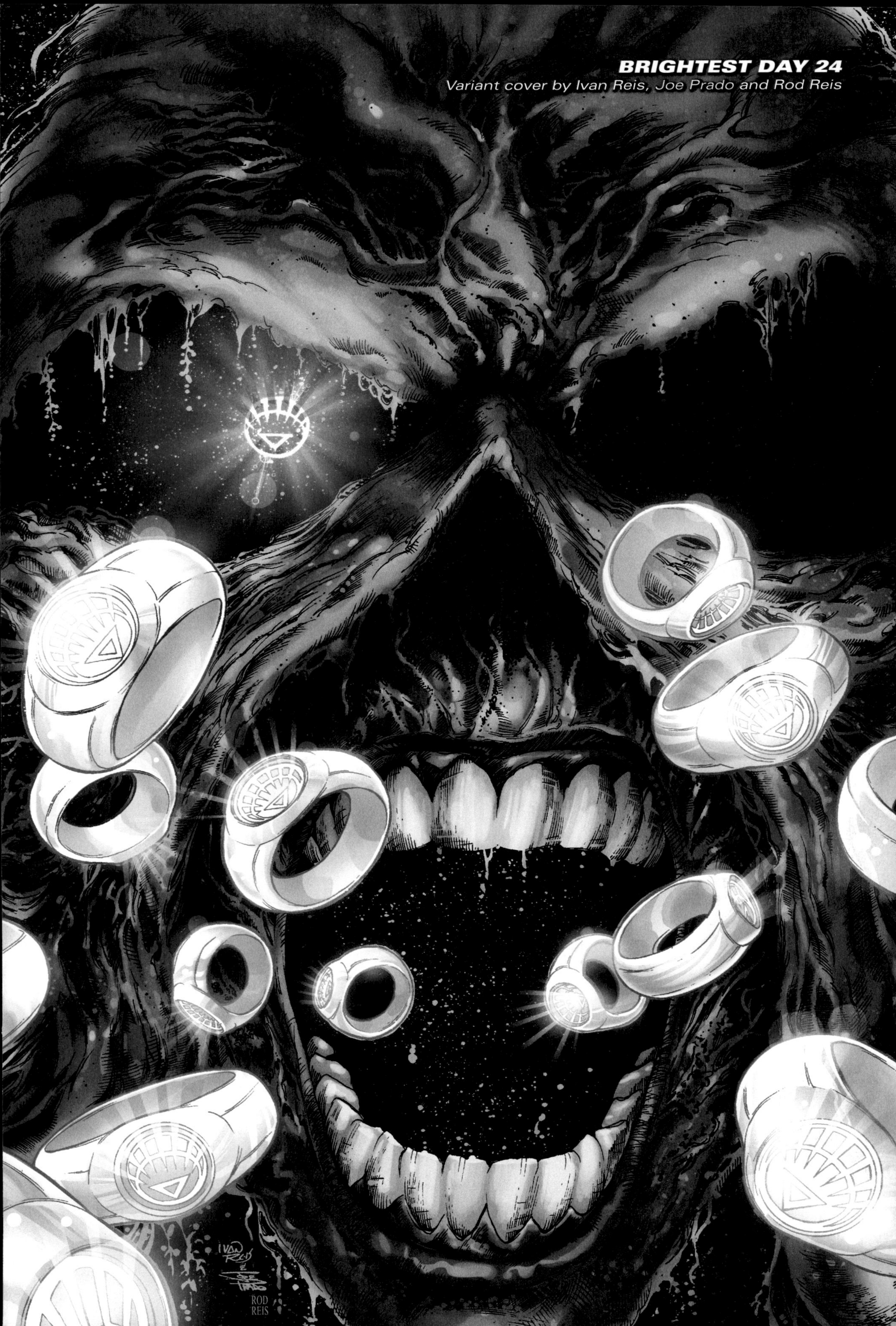

BRIGHTEST DAY 24
Variant cover by Ivan Reis, Joe Prado and Rod Reis

BRIGHTEST DAY *variant covers*
by Ryan Sook, Fernando Pasarin and Joel Gomez
with Randy Mayor and Carrie Strachan
Concept by Jim Lee

BRIGHTEST DAY
HAWKGIRL

WHITE LANTERN SKETCHBOOK
THE WHITE LANTERN

Designs by Joe Prado.

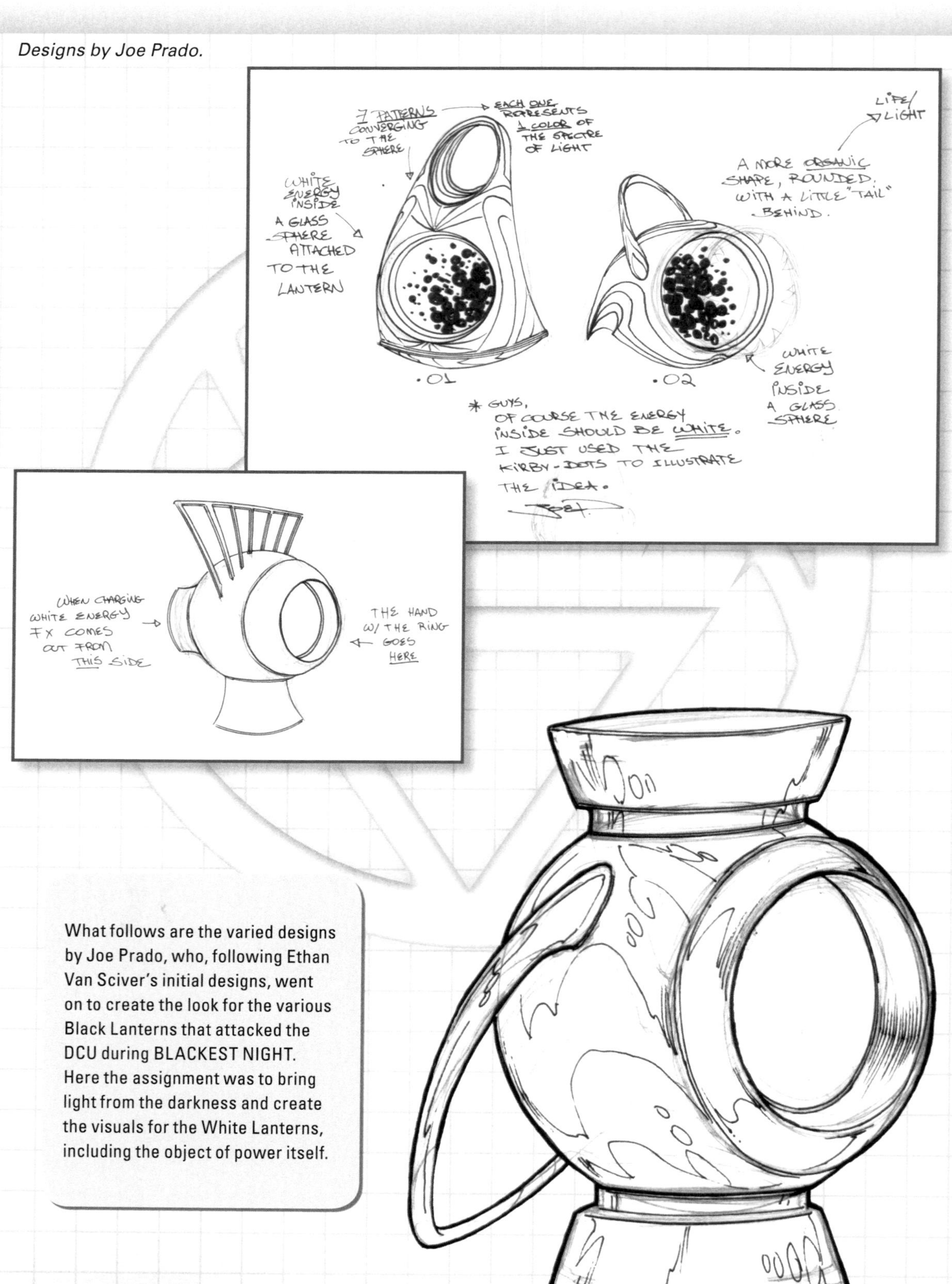

What follows are the varied designs by Joe Prado, who, following Ethan Van Sciver's initial designs, went on to create the look for the various Black Lanterns that attacked the DCU during BLACKEST NIGHT. Here the assignment was to bring light from the darkness and create the visuals for the White Lanterns, including the object of power itself.

WHITE LANTERN ANIMAL MAN

WHITE LANTERN SUPERMAN

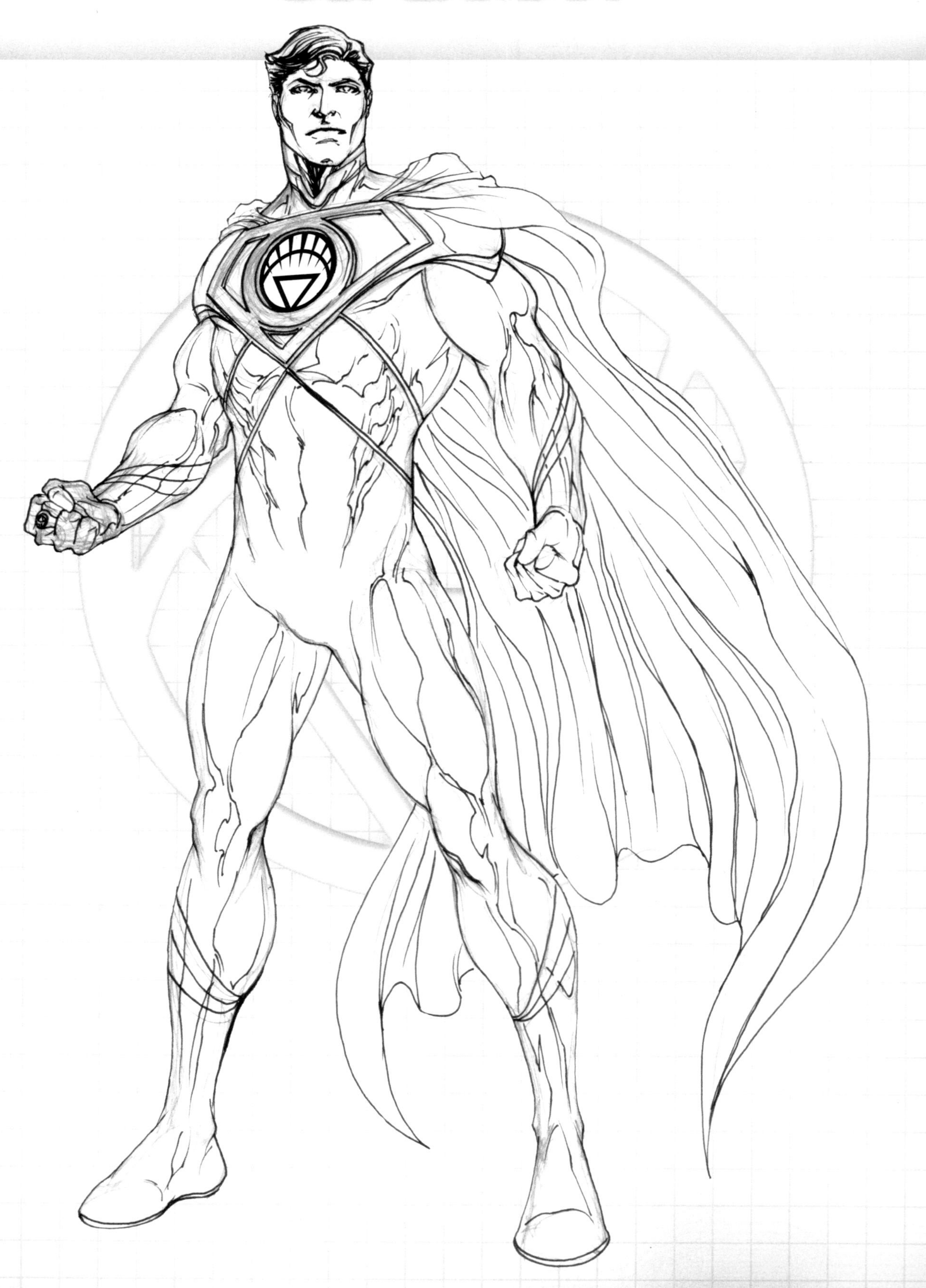

WHITE LANTERN WONDER WOMAN

WHITE LANTERN
HAL JORDAN

WHITE LANTERN GREEN ARROW

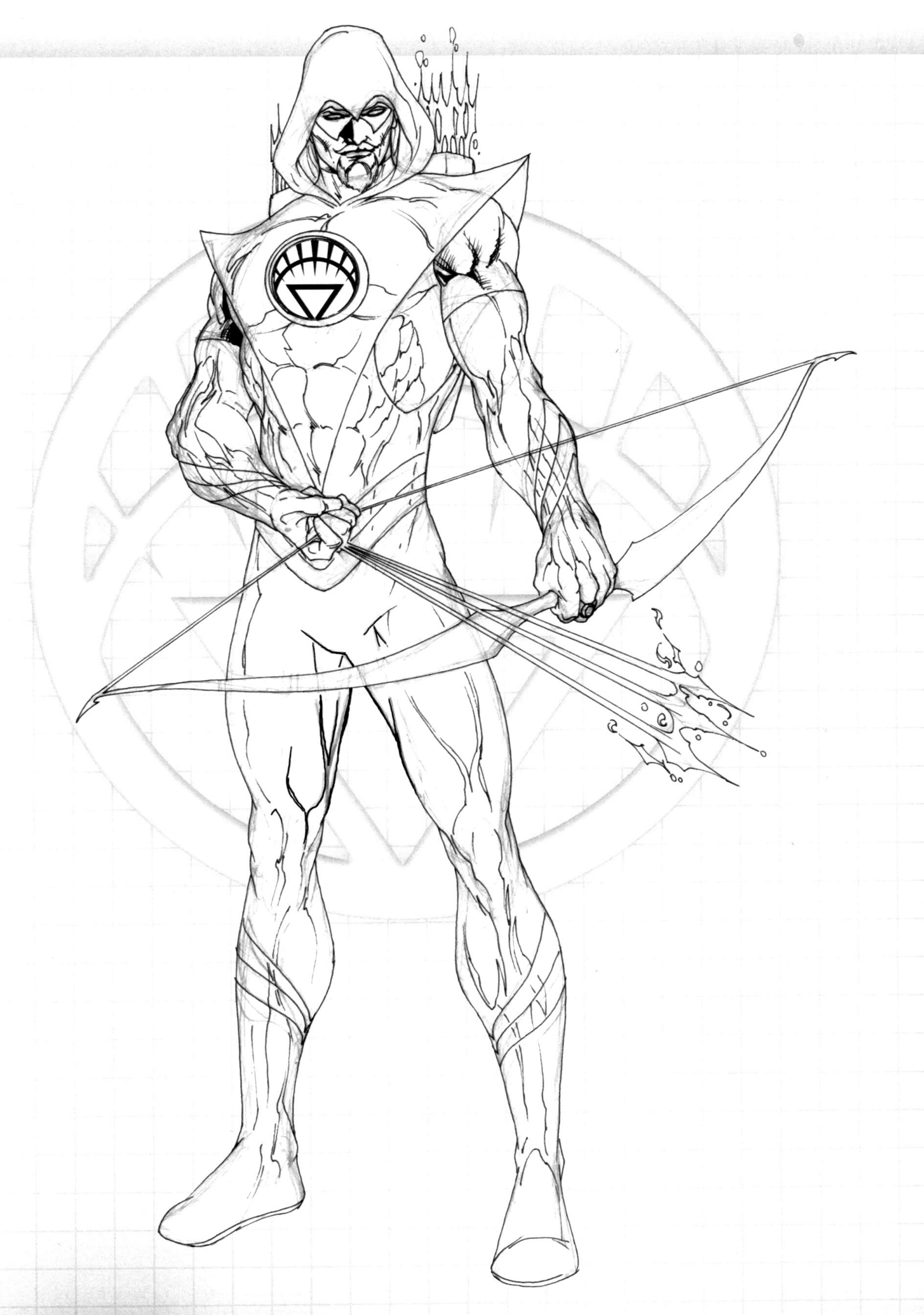

BIOGRAPHIES

GEOFF JOHNS

Geoff Johns is an award-winning writer and one of the most popular contemporary comic book writers today. He is the author of the *New York Times* best-selling graphic novels AQUAMAN: THE TRENCH, BLACKEST NIGHT, GREEN LANTERN: SINESTRO CORPS WAR, JUSTICE LEAGUE: ORIGIN, SUPERMAN: LAST SON OF KRYPTON and BATMAN: EARTH ONE which hit #1 on the bestseller list. He is also known for transforming GREEN LANTERN into one of the most critically and commercially successful franchises in comics. In other media, Johns has written episodes of *Smallville*, *Arrow* and Adult Swim's *Robot Chicken*, for which he and his co-writers were nominated for an Emmy. He is the Chief Creative Officer of DC Entertainment.

PETER J. TOMASI

Having once proudly served as an editor at DC Comics, Peter J. Tomasi now devotes his time to writing comics and screenplays. Having worked on such DC titles as NIGHTWING, BLACK ADAM, THE OUTSIDERS, GREEN LANTERN: EMERALD WARRIORS, BLACKEST NIGHT: BATMAN and BRIGHTEST DAY, along with critically acclaimed creator owned projects LIGHT BRIGADE and THE MIGHTY, Peter's most recent works include BATMAN AND ROBIN and GREEN LANTERN CORPS.

IVAN REIS

Brazilian artist Ivan Reis started his U.S. career in the 1990s, on *Ghost* and *The Mask* for Dark Horse. After pencilling an issue of THE INVISIBLES for Grant Morrison, Reis started a long run on *Lady Death* for Chaos Comics, and then did Marvel's *The Avengers* and *The Vision*, with Geoff Johns. After illustrating high-profile series such as ACTION COMICS, INFINITE CRISIS and RANN-THANAGAR WAR for DC Comics, he started his now legendary run on GREEN LANTERN. Continuing his work with Johns, Reis pencilled the bestselling BLACKEST NIGHT, BRIGHTEST DAY, AQUAMAN and JUSTICE LEAGUE.

PATRICK GLEASON

Patrick Gleason loves to create fantastic characters and worlds. His work can be seen in DC's BATMAN AND ROBIN, GREEN LANTERN CORPS, AQUAMAN, JLA, HAWKMAN and JSA. His ground-laying work alongside Geoff Johns and Dave Gibbons on the miniseries GREEN LANTERN CORPS: RECHARGE made way for the acclaimed ongoing series. The SINESTRO CORPS WAR followed, and then the explosive BLACKEST NIGHT: GREEN LANTERN CORPS with Peter J. Tomasi. For the New 52, Gleason has lent his artistic vision to the Dynamic Duo of BATMAN AND ROBIN.

ARDIAN SYAF

Ardian Syaf, an Indonesian artist, first received universal acclaim for his work on *The Dresden Files*. Since then, he has worked exclusively for DC Comics on such titles as BATGIRL, BLACKEST NIGHT: BATMAN, SUPERMAN/BATMAN, GREEN LANTERN CORPS and BRIGHTEST DAY.

SCOTT CLARK

Scott Clark first began working in the comic book industry in the early 1990s, coming to prominence as artist on WildStorm's hit series STORMWATCH. He is known for his work on such titles as JUSTICE LEAGUE: CRY FOR JUSTICE, GRIFTER, BRIGHTEST DAY and BATMAN, INC. Clark passed away in 2013.

JOE PRADO

Joe Prado started his career as a professional comic book artist in Brazil during the 1990s, and has done hundreds of illustrations for RPG magazines and books. In the early 2000s, he started to produce comics for the U.S. market. His credits include AQUAMAN, ACTION COMICS, SUPERMAN, BIRDS OF PREY, GREEN LANTERN, THE WARLORD, BLACKEST NIGHT and BRIGHTEST DAY.